Writing Britain's Ruins

Writing Britain's Ruins

Edited by Michael Carter,
Peter N. Lindfield and Dale Townshend

First published in 2017 by
The British Library
96 Euston Road
London NW1 2DB

Cataloguing in Publication Data
A catalogue record for this publication is available from
The British Library

ISBN 978 0 7123 0978 3

Text copyright © the contributors 2017
Illustrations copyright © The British Library Board
and other named sources 2017

Designed and typeset by Goldust Design
Cover design by Maggi Smith, Sixism
Printed in the Czech Republic by PB Tisk

Frontispiece: Peter Van Lerberghe, *An Internal View of Tintern Abbey Seen by Moonlight*. Watercolour, 1772 or 1773.

Contents

Acknowledgements 7
Notes on Editors and Contributors 8

Introduction: The Making of Britain's Ruins: Monasteries and Castles, 1536–1650, Michael Carter 12
Ruins in Focus:
Caernarfon Castle, David Punter 40

Chapter 1: Antiquaries and Ruins, Rosemary Sweet 43
Ruins in Focus:
Croyland Abbey, Rosemary Sweet 72
The Antiquities at Stonehenge, Kelsey Jackson Williams 76
Glastonbury Abbey, Nick Groom 79

Chapter 2: The Aesthetics of Ruin, Dale Townshend 83
Ruins in Focus:
Byron and the 'Ruins' of Newstead Abbey, Holly Hirst 116
The Gothic Folly at Wimpole, Cambridgeshire, Peter N. Lindfield 125
Cardiff Castle, David Punter 128

Chapter 3: Exploring Britain's Ruins, Emma McEvoy 131
Ruins in Focus:
Icolmkill: The Ruins of Iona, Sally Foster 158
Dryburgh Abbey, James A. McKean 162
Rhuddlan Castle, David Punter 165

Chapter 4: Writing the Ruined Abbeys of Netley, Tintern and Melrose, James Watt, Dale Townshend and Nicola J. Watson   167
Ruins in Focus:
Tintagel Castle, Nick Groom   204
Harlech Castle, David Punter   207

Chapter 5: The Haunting of Britain's Ruins, Hamish Mathison and Angela Wright   210
Ruins in Focus:
The Haunting of Minster Lovell Hall, Alicia Edwards   229
Conwy Castle, David Punter   233
Rosslyn Chapel, James A. McKean   236
Berry Pomeroy Castle, Nick Groom   240

Chapter 6: The Politics of Ruin, James Kelly   243
Ruins in Focus:
Beaumaris Castle, David Punter   270
Shobdon's Folly, Peter N. Lindfield   273

Conclusion: Conserving Britain's Ruins, 1700 to the Present Day, Marion Harney   275

Picture Credits   297
Index   298

Acknowledgements

The editors would like to thank the Arts and Humanities Research Council (AHRC) for generously funding 'Writing Britain's Ruins, 1700–1850: The Architectural Imagination', an AHRC Leadership Fellowship from which the title and subject-matter of this book derives. Based at the University of Stirling, and running from June 2015 to November 2016, this research project was led by Dale Townshend (Principal Investigator) and supported by Peter Lindfield (Research Assistant). AHRC funding made possible the hosting of two symposia at Stirling over the course of the Fellowship's duration, occasions on which the volume's contributors and other participants enthusiastically engaged one another in stimulating interdisciplinary exchange on the topics explored in this book. Over a six-week period in the spring of 2016, earlier versions of some of the chapters in this volume were presented as public lectures at Strawberry Hill House, Twickenham. We would like to thank all of those involved for having made 'Writing Britain's Ruins' such an intellectually rewarding project, singling out for particular mention Fiona Robertson and David Punter who, in their capacity as academic advisers, offered shrewd advice, encouragement and support throughout. Thanks, too, to our editor Robert Davies at British Library Publishing for having responded so warmly to our initial proposal, as well as to Carolyn Jones, our copy editor, Sally Nicholls, our picture researcher, and Pauline Hubner, our indexer.

Notes on Editors and Contributors

Editors

Michael Carter is Senior Property Historian at English Heritage with a special focus on monasteries, a subject on which he has published widely. He has a doctorate from the Courtauld Institute of Art, London, and is a Fellow of the Society of Antiquaries of London.

Peter N. Lindfield is a Leverhulme-funded Early Career Research Fellow at Manchester Metropolitan University, working on antiquarian forgery in Georgian Britain, and in 2016 was elected a Fellow of the Society of Antiquaries of London. His doctorate was on the Gothic aesthetic in Georgian Britain and the intersection between architectural theory and practice, antiquarianism, and fashionable and antiquarian architecture, interior design and applied arts. He has published widely on the Gothic Revival, heraldry, antiquarian arts and the relationship between architecture and literature, including *Georgian Gothic* (Boydell & Brewer, 2016). Peter has held four fellowships at Yale University and in 2013 was the inaugural Dunscombe Colt Research Fellow in Georgian architecture at the University of Oxford.

Dale Townshend is Professor of Gothic Literature in the Centre for Gothic Studies at Manchester Metropolitan University. He has published widely in the fields of eighteenth- and nineteenth-century Gothic literature. The recipient of an AHRC Leadership Fellowship for a project entitled 'Writing Britain's Ruins, 1700–1850: The Architectural Imagination', he is currently completing a monograph entitled *Gothic Antiquity: History, Romance, and the Architectural Imagination, 1760–1840*, and editing, with Angela Wright and Catherine Spooner, the three-volume *Cambridge History of the Gothic*.

Contributors

Alicia Edwards is a PhD candidate in the Department of English at Manchester Metropolitan University, examining Gothic and Dark tourism practices in London from the nineteenth century to the present. Her wider research interests include the supernatural in popular culture, representations of the city, the serial killer in popular culture and broader topics in Gothic and cultural studies.

Sally Foster is a medieval archaeologist by training, and worked in cultural heritage management for around twenty years. Returning to academia in 2010, she joined the University of Stirling as Lecturer in Heritage and Conservation in 2014. Her research is interdisciplinary in nature, cutting across cultural heritage management, archaeology, history, art history and museology.

Nick Groom is Professor in English at the University of Exeter. He has published widely on literature, art and music, and is the author of several books, including *The Gothic: A Very Short Introduction* (Oxford University Press, 2012), as well as editing *The Castle of Otranto*, *The Monk*, *The Italian* and *Frankenstein* (all Oxford University Press). He is currently researching vampires.

Marion Harney is Senior Lecturer in Conservation, Department of Architecture and Civil Engineering, University of Bath. Specialising in conservation and research education, Marion is a member of National Trust Council and their Historic Environment Advisory Group. She is a Member of ICOMOS-UK Cultural Landscapes and Historic Gardens Committee, and Director of the Gardens Trust. Marion was sole researcher for *Bath: Pevsner Architectural Guides* (Yale University Press, 2003), and her publications include *Gardens and Landscapes in Historic Building Conservation* (ed.) (Wiley-Blackwell, 2014), *Place-making for the Imagination: Horace Walpole and Strawberry Hill* (Ashgate, 2013; Winner, J. B. Jackson Award 2015) and numerous other essays.

Holly Hirst is a PhD candidate in the Department of English at Manchester Metropolitan University, working on a thesis that explores the intersection of Gothic literature and contemporary theology, 1760–1830.

James Kelly is a Lecturer in English at the University of Exeter's Cornwall campus. He is the author of *Charles Maturin* (Four Courts Press, 2011) and *Ireland and Romanticism* (Palgrave Macmillan, 2011). He has written widely on Irish and Scottish literature in the long eighteenth century.

Hamish Mathison lectures in eighteenth-century literature at the University of Sheffield. His most recent work has been on the connections between print culture and patriotic sentiment in the eighteenth-century Scottish newspaper press. His publications include 'On Robert Burns: Enlightenment, Mythology and the Folkloric', in *The Voice of the People*, ed. Matthew Campbell and Michael Perraudin (Anthem Press, 2012) and 'Robert Burns and the Scottish Bawdy Politic' in *Scottish Gothic: An Edinburgh Companion*, ed. Carol Margaret Davison and Monica Germana (Edinburgh University Press, 2017).

Emma McEvoy lectures at the University of Westminster. She has published widely in the field of Gothic and Romantic studies and is the author of *Gothic Tourism* (Palgrave, 2016). With Catherine Spooner, she co-edited the *Routledge Companion to Gothic* (Routledge, 2007).

James A. McKean graduated with BA (Hons) in History from the University of Stirling, and remained at the university to complete a Masters in Environment, Heritage and Policy. He is currently a Research Postgraduate at Stirling, studying for a PhD in History. His thesis explores the effect of the Gothic on the heritage of ruined abbeys in England during the long eighteenth century.

David Punter is an academic, writer and poet, best known for his many published works on the Gothic. He is currently Professor of Poetry at the University of Bristol, and co-Director of the Bristol Poetry Institute. His work on the Gothic includes *The Literature of Terror* (Longman, 1980, revised and expanded 1996) as well as several other monographs and many essays and articles. He is partly of mid-Welsh ancestry, and has known some of these Welsh ruins for many years.

Rosemary Sweet is Professor of Urban History at the School of History, Politics and International Relations, University of Leicester. She has published widely on eighteenth-century urban and cultural history, and has a particular interest in antiquarianism and the reception of the past in the eighteenth century. *Antiquaries: The Discovery of the Past in Eighteenth-Century Britain* was published in 2004 (Hambledon and London). She is currently extending her interest in antiquarianism into the nineteenth century, concentrating on the 'invention' of the historic town and on antiquaries' interest in domestic antiquities.

Nicola J. Watson holds a Chair in English Literature at the Open University, having held posts previously at Oxford, Harvard, Northwestern and Indiana Universities. She has served as President of the British Association for Romantic Studies (BARS), and lead for European Romanticisms in Association (ERA). A specialist in the literature and culture of the Romantic period, with particular interests in travel writing, place-writing and forms of literary commemoration, she is the author of many essays and a number of monographs, most recently *The Literary Tourist: Readers and Places in Romantic and Victorian Britain* (Palgrave, 2006); her present project, *The Author's Effects*, focuses on the history and poetics of the writer's house museum from its inception to the present.

James Watt is Senior Lecturer at the Centre for Eighteenth-Century Studies at the University of York. He is the author of *Contesting the Gothic: Fiction, Genre and Cultural Conflict 1764–1832* (Cambridge University Press, 1999), and numerous other essays and chapters.

Kelsey Jackson Williams is Lecturer in Literature and Material Culture at the University of Stirling. His first book, *The Antiquary: John Aubrey's Historical Scholarship* (Oxford University Press, 2016), is an in-depth study of the biographer and polymath's antiquarian studies, and his second book, *The First Scottish Enlightenment*, is forthcoming from Oxford University Press. His current research focuses on the intellectual and material cultures of early modern Scotland.

Angela Wright is Professor of Romantic Literature at the University of Sheffield and a past co-President of the International Gothic Association (2013–17). She is the author of *Gothic Fiction* (Palgrave, 2007), *Britain, France and the Gothic: The Import of Terror* (Cambridge University Press, 2013 and [paperback] 2015) and co-editor (with Dale Townshend) of *Ann Radcliffe, Romanticism and the Gothic* (Cambridge University Press, 2014) and *Romantic Gothic: An Edinburgh Companion* (Edinburgh University Press, 2016). Her forthcoming study *Mary Shelley* will be published by the University of Wales Press in January 2018. She is currently working on a new Leverhulme-funded research study entitled *Fostering Romanticism*.

Ruined east end of Walsingham Priory Church. From Monastic Remains and Ancient Castles ... drawn on the spot by James Moore Esq. F.A.S., and executed in aquatint by G. J. Parkins Esq. *Vol. 1, London, 1792*

Introduction

The Making of Britain's Ruins: Monasteries and Castles, 1536–1650

Michael Carter

In 1510 the young King Henry VIII made the pilgrimage to the great shrine of the Blessed Virgin Mary at Walsingham Priory, Norfolk. Four years later, he visited the Cistercian abbey of Boxley, Kent, marking the occasion with pious oblations to the monastery's miraculous Rood of Grace, an animated sculpted figure of Christ on the Cross. Within thirty years, however, both of these sites of pilgrimage had been destroyed, the communities that cared for them dispersed and the monastic buildings shattered, a fate that befell the other monasteries of England and Wales between 1536 and 1540. By the time of Henry's death, approximately half the monasteries in Ireland had also been closed, while in Scotland, waves of iconoclasm and the formal adoption of the Reformation in 1560 left not only monasteries but also many cathedrals as wrecked and decaying ruins.

Even Protestant reformers acknowledged the destructiveness of the Dissolution of the Monasteries. For John Bale, Carmelite friar-turned-ardent-supporter of the new religion, it was a 'wycked age [...] muche geven to the destruccyon of thynges memorable' (quoted in Aston 1973: 246). Early seventeenth-century antiquaries, many confirmed Protestants, looked back on the Dissolution with horror and melancholy, spurring them to record the surviving documentary and physical evidence of Britain's monastic past (Aston 1973). Yet, even as these efforts were under way, the Civil Wars were to produce a whole new set of ruins, with numerous castles irreparably damaged by siege and others deliberately dismantled (or 'slighted') after the conclusion of hostilities. This introduction will examine how, in little more than a century, the vast majority of monasteries in the British Isles and a substantial proportion of the medieval castles of England and Wales were despoiled and left as ruins.

The Background to the Dissolution of the English Monasteries

At the time of the Dissolution, English monasticism had a history stretching back almost 1,000 years. There were over 800 religious houses in England and Wales when Henry VIII came to the throne in 1509 (Knowles and Hadcock 1971). The buildings of the religious houses were shaped to serve the needs of the various orders of monks, canons, friars and nuns who inhabited them, their days structured around prayer, reading, manual labour, good works and preaching. In the words of Robert Aske, leader of the Pilgrimage of Grace of 1536 that rebelled against Henry and sought, in part, to defend the monasteries, these structures fulfilled many important religious and social roles and were 'one of the great beauties of the land' (quoted in Cross 1988: 131). Despite Aske's comments, historians have not been kind to the monastic and religious orders of late medieval England. By and large, the orders have been judged against the exacting standards set by their founders, and against this yardstick often found sadly lacking. The conclusions of Benedictine monk and Cambridge don Dom David Knowles, namely that by the Tudor age the monasteries of England were, with a few exceptions, spiritually enfeebled institutions that were out of touch with changes in society and religion, have been largely accepted. Knowles argued that monks, canons, friars and nuns 'had been living on a scale of personal comfort and corporate magnificence [...] which was neither necessary, nor consistent with the fashion of life indicated by their rule and early institutions' (Knowles 1959: 256). In an equally hostile spirit, the indefatigable topographer and architectural historian Nikolaus Pevsner famously condemned the residence built by Abbot Thomas Chard (1501–39) at Forde Abbey, Dorset, as 'being on a scale to justify the Dissolution and Reformation' (Newman and Pevsner 1972: 387–8).

However, a more recent generation of scholars has questioned whether this is an appropriate way of judging the religious orders of late medieval England. Rather than being viewed as a period of decline, the two centuries before the Dissolution are now seen by many scholars as an era of vitality and renewal, during which monks, friars, canons and nuns gradually transformed their form of life to make it more compatible with the realities of contemporary religious practice and society (Clark 2002). In fact, many monasteries in early sixteenth-century England were thriving. Recruitment was at a healthy level, finances were robust, and the quality of religious observance was in many cases estimable (Heale 2009). Benedictine patronage of art and architecture reflected the widespread and self-conscious pious commitment of that order's monks and nuns at the end of the Middle Ages (Luxford 2005). Cistercian abbots in northern England, such as Marmaduke Huby, reforming abbot of Fountains, Yorkshire, between 1495 and 1526, used their patronage of art and architecture to proclaim their piety and devotion to their order (Carter 2014a).

That is not to claim that all were in universally good condition. In his capacity as *Reformator* of Cistercian monasteries in England and Wales, Huby worked hard, and not always successfully, to correct lapses in religious observance and adherence to discipline within his own order (Talbot 1964). Some small monasteries were no longer viable. In 1496, Bishop John Alcock of Ely (1485–1500) received papal permission to dissolve the decayed Benedictine Cambridge nunnery of St Radegund, using its buildings and endowments to found Jesus College for graduate priests studying for higher degrees in theology. Cardinal Wolsey dissolved over twenty religious houses, again with papal consent, for the foundation of his educational establishments at Ipswich and Oxford (Knowles 1959: 157–64).

The Dissolution of the English Houses

The immediate context for the attack on traditional religion and monasticism in England was the private life and potency of Henry VIII, the failure of his marriage to Queen Katherine of Aragon to produce a male heir, and the refusal of the Pope to annul their union. Henry took matters into his own hands and in 1531 he divorced Katherine and married Anne Boleyn. The King broke with Rome and was recognised by the English clergy as 'Supreme Head of the Church in England [...] in so far as the law of Christ allows', a position confirmed by Parliament in 1534 (quoted in Coppack 1998: 124). Monastic superiors were required to swear the Oath of Succession, recognising the legitimacy of any offspring from Henry's marriage to Anne. The resistance of the Observant Franciscans led to the dispersal of their communities, with many of the friars dying for their refusal to subscribe. Ten Carthusians were executed or starved to death for their obstinacy (Knowles 1959: 206–40). Members of the religious orders can have had little doubt of the likely deadly consequences of defying the royal will.

The death-knell for the monasteries came in the spring and summer of 1535, when commissioners were dispatched to conduct a valuation of church property, the *Valor Ecclesiasticus*. In parallel, a second set of commissioners was appointed by Thomas Cromwell in his capacity as Vicar General, and charged with the specific task of assessing the quality of religious observance in the monasteries and the moral condition of their inmates. While in the service of Cardinal Wolsey, Cromwell had seen the riches that could accrue from the suppression of religious houses, and in December 1534, he boasted to the Holy Roman Empire's ambassador to England, Eustace Chapuys, that he would make Henry richer than all other kings in Christendom. The visitations of 1535 were notably more critical than similar exercises conducted under episcopal authority, in some cases only one year before. Many of the allegations made by the commissioners against the monks and nuns do not stand up to even cursory scrutiny, and the monasteries were given no opportunity to institute reforms before an Act of Parliament was passed in 1536. This demanded the suppression of all religious houses with an income of under £200 a year and fewer than twelve inmates: monastic institutions in which, as the preamble put it, 'manifest sin, vicious and abominable living' were practised on a daily basis (quoted in Knowles 1959: 12). However, the motives were as much financial as they were theological: Knowles's conclusion that 'neither the desire nor the hope of reforming the religious of England had any part in determining the actions of Henry and Cromwell in the years preceding the Act of Suppression in 1536' (Knowles 1959: 205) has much to recommend it.

Under the terms of the 1536 Act, monastic presidents were pensioned off, while the inmates were given the option of either leaving the monastic life with the grant of a 'capacity' and a small cash reward, or transferring to a larger monastery, 'wherein, thanks be to God, religion is right well kept and observed' (quoted in Knowles 1959: 125). The suppressed monasteries passed into the ownership of Henry in his role as head of the Church, and a new body, the Court of Augmentations of the Revenues of the King's Crown, was established to oversee the administration of the seizing of property. Commissioners took the surrender of individual houses, the buildings of which were surveyed, their possessions accounted for and the moveable assets sold by auction. With an eye to future use or sale, the buildings escaped serious damage at this stage, though lead was stripped from the roofs and glazing and bells were removed to be melted down.

The assault on the smaller monasteries, worries about wider reforms in the Church and economic grievances led to two major revolts: the Lincolnshire Rising and the above-mentioned Pilgrimage of Grace, which affected the northern counties. Several religious houses were implicated. All benefited from the general pardon granted in late 1536, but the minor role that some houses played in the further outbreak of rebellion in early 1537 led to the condemnation and execution of the abbots and priors of several monasteries and the forfeiture of their houses to the Crown (Hoyle 2001). The abbot and community of Furness Abbey, Lancashire, terrified that a similar fate would befall them, voluntarily surrendered their monastery to the King's commissioners, creating a precedent for the closure of monasteries without the need for further legislation (Woodward 1966: 101). All pretence of reform and selective closure was now abandoned. Between late 1537 and 1540, monasteries throughout England and Wales, great and small alike, surrendered to the Crown. The religious left the cloister with pensions and small cash gifts for their compliance. The brutal executions of the abbots of Colchester in Essex, Glastonbury in Somerset, Reading in Berkshire and Woburn in Bedfordshire served as bloody examples of the consequences of resistance (Knowles 1959: 367–82).

Stripping the Assets

The work of despoiling the monasteries of their riches began almost immediately. The gold and silver altar plate, jewels and precious metal thread from vestments were sent to the King's receiver at the Tower of

London. The great Benedictine monastery of Bury St Edmunds, Suffolk, had already been relieved of 5,000 marks' worth of gold and jewels in early 1538, when the shrine of the abbey's titular saint was taken down. The abbey itself was suppressed in November 1539, yielding well over 2,400 ounces of precious metal altar plate, including 'a mitor [mitre] of white silke, garnished wt siluer, and sett with diuerse counterfeete stones' (quoted in Turnbill 1836: 28).

Lead was stripped from the roofs, with the buildings of Strata Florida Abbey, Ceredigion, yielding ten tons (Robinson 2007: 31). For convenience's sake, the lead was melted into ingots or fothers; one survives at Rievaulx Abbey, Yorkshire, stamped with the King's badge, unmistakable proof of his ownership of the suppressed monastery's assets. Rievaulx was sold to Thomas Manners, Earl of Rutland, patron of the monastery, who had been meddling in its internal affairs since the early 1530s. He was eager to maximise the full monetary potential of his acquisition, inventorying the contents of the abbey and listing everything saleable, from the 'little shryne over the [high] altar gilded', almost certainly that of St Aelred (d. 1167), the abbey's third abbot and the focus of veneration until the eve of the Dissolution, to 'diverse old naylys' recovered from the window frames (quoted in Coppack 1999: 227, 229). The contents of other monasteries were similarly inventoried before sale, the contents of the church and chapter house at Merevale Abbey, Warwickshire, including alabaster altarpieces, choir-stalls and base-metal altar vessels, together yielding £4 14s 8d (Austin 1998: 152–5). Even funerary monuments were fair game, the inventory for the Dominican friary in Chelmsford, for instance, listing 'the pathement with gravestones in the quere chapellis and cherche with ye eyarne [iron] and glase in those placeis xxxs[30s]' (quoted in Bertram 1976: 16).

There is evidence to suggest that the commissioners who oversaw the despoiling were sometimes capable of appreciating the buildings that they were destroying. In 1537, Sir Arthur Darcy arrived at Jervaulx Abbey, Yorkshire, and was moved to comment that the monastery possessed 'oon off the fairest chyreches that I have seen' (quoted in Knowles 1959: 384). Destruction, nonetheless, was the order of the day. The commissioners received instructions to 'pull down to the ground all the walls of the churches, stepuls, cloysters, fraters, dorters, chapter howsys' (quoted in Knowles 1959: 384). The explicit intention was to make it impossible for the communities to return to, and resume, their

'Kirkstall Abbey, from an original drawing in the Possession of Abraham Rhodes Esq.'
Print by F. Jukes Howland, 1 November 1798

religious life; the buildings at the impoverished Franciscan friary at Aylesbury, Buckinghamshire, for example, were damaged to ensure they 'shuld nott lythtly be made Fryerys agen' (quoted in Knowles 1959: 363).

The dismantling of Lewes Priory, Sussex, is particularly well documented. The destruction of the monastery's great Romanesque church was carefully planned by Giovanni Portinari, and required the assistance of seventeen workmen from London. Regular progress reports were dispatched to Thomas Cromwell (Aston 1973: 239). In the spring and early summer of 1538, masons, carpenters, bricklayers and plumbers were employed to take down Chertsey Abbey, Surrey, and they were assisted in their work by ninety labourers (Aston 1973: 238). Meaux Abbey, Yorkshire, was 'taken down' by twenty masons in 1542, resulting in the near-total destruction of the standing fabric, with masonry and rubble used to build the defences at nearby Hull (Carter 2015: 77). But demolition could be an expensive job. Rather than spending £1,000 on the 'plokynd down' of the monastic churches in Lincolnshire, the decision was made to 'deface' them instead, removing the roofs and stairs to make them uninhabitable (quoted in Knowles

Roche Abbey. John Buckler, watercolour, 1803

1959: 384). Kirkstall Abbey, Yorkshire, was also unroofed in this way, many of its buildings still standing to their full height today. As will be seen, this state of preservation may have been significant during the restoration of Catholicism under Queen Mary Tudor, when some former monks hoped for the refounding of their abbeys.

Plundering added to the destruction. Michael Shirebrook's well-known late-sixteenth-century description of the ruination and despoiling of Roche Abbey, Yorkshire, presents a picture of the meticulous and calculated seizure of anything of value. Shirebrook was the Anglican rector of Wickersley, five miles west of Roche, between 1567 and c. 1610. However, it is clear from his account that he was sympathetic to monks. His uncle had witnessed the dissolution of the house, and he described how the lead was 'cast down into the church', destroying the tombs beneath. The lead was then melted using the choir-stalls as fuel. The church was 'all broken [...] and all things of price, either spoiled, carped away or defaced to the uttermost'. The local population participated in the plundering of the house, and 'it seemeth every person bent himself to filtch and spoil what he could'. Shirebrook's father thought well of the monks 'and their religion', but this did not prevent him acquiring timber from the bell tower, explaining 'might I not as well as others have some Profit of the Spoil of the Abbey? [...] therefore I did as others did' (quoted in Dickens 1959: 123–5). Michael Shirebrook himself obtained property from the abbey, his ownership inscription recently identified in one of the few surviving books from Roche (Carter 2016). At Reading Abbey, Berkshire, 'the multitude of the poverty of the tone resortyd thedyr, and all things that might be hadde they stole away, insomyche that they hadde covayd the very clapers of the bellys' (quoted in Knowles 1959: 385). Hailes Abbey, Gloucestershire, was plundered on such an enormous scale by local gentry, farmers, artisans and even priests that a special commission was convened in 1541–2 to investigate the events (Shagan 2003: 162–96).

Nevertheless, a significant number of former monastic churches and conventual buildings survive intact to this very day. Among the best preserved are the eight cathedrals served by monastic communities: Canterbury, Carlisle, Durham, Ely, Norwich, Rochester, Winchester and Worcester. At the Dissolution, they ceased to be monasteries, but continued as cathedrals, the monastic communities secularised and many of the former monks remaining as canons and prebendaries. Though almost totally stripped of their imagery, stained glass and other accoutrements of Catholic worship during the reigns of Edward VI and Elizabeth I, the churches, in many cases with the claustral buildings attached, were left largely unscathed. Six former monastic churches – Bristol, Chester, Gloucester, Oxford, Peterborough and, briefly, Westminster – survived thanks to their conversion into cathedrals.

Several monastic churches were preserved because they also functioned as, or were converted into, parish churches. The entire churches at St Albans in Hertfordshire and Tewkesbury in Gloucestershire, and parts of those at Pershore in Worcestershire and Malmesbury in Wiltshire, were saved after their purchase by the townspeople for parochial use. The church at the Cistercian abbey of Holm Cultram, Cumberland, also initially survived intact. At the time of the abbey's suppression in 1538, the 'eighteen hundred houselynge people' of Holm Cultram petitioned Thomas Cromwell for the preservation of the monastic church, explaining that it was 'not only unto us our parish Churche [...] but also a great ayde, socor and defence for us agent our neghbors the Scots' (quoted in Gilbanks 1899: 130). However, the parish was unable to maintain the fabric of the church, which was equal in size to Carlisle Cathedral. The crossing tower collapsed in 1600, destroying much of the chancel (Gilbanks 1899: 130, 138).

Elsewhere, the churches were allowed to fall into decay, with the former claustral buildings converted into dwellings. Sir Anthony Browne (c. 1500–48) acquired Battle Abbey after its suppression in 1538. He rapidly eradicated the monastic church, despite its being built 'on the very spot' where William the Conqueror secured his great victory in 1066. Browne converted the palatial abbatial residence in the former west range of the monastery into a mansion (Coad 2007: 42). Browne was one of the many religious conservatives who profited from the Dissolution. He made a traditional Catholic will, requesting the saying of Masses and dirges by the priests of Battle parish church, where he was buried in 1548. His eldest son, Sir Anthony (1528–90), was created 1st Viscount Montague by Queen Mary, who refounded several monasteries. Following the accession of the Protestant Queen Elizabeth in 1558, Viscount Montague was the only secular peer to vote against the suppression of these refounded houses, and in the late sixteenth and early seventeenth centuries Battle acquired so strong a reputation for Catholic recusancy that it became known as 'little Rome' (Questier 2008).

Titchfield Abbey, Hampshire, was granted to Thomas Wriothesley (1505–50), a loyal servant of Henry VIII who had played a key role in the closure of the monasteries. He transformed the site into a home fit for a rising courtier, with an imposing great gate sited in the middle of the former nave of the abbey church with lodges inserted into the bays to the east and west. The redundant choir and presbytery were demolished (Knowles 1959: 386).

Netley Abbey, Hampshire, a royal foundation dating to the thirteenth century, was closed in 1536 and given to Sir William Paulet (1483–1572), who converted the claustral nucleus into his private mansion, reusing many of the former abbey buildings to create a fashionable courtyard house (Robinson 1998: 153). Elsewhere, the buildings were put to more mundane uses. The great church at Bury St Edmunds, for instance, was converted into tenements, and the Charterhouse in London was used as storage for the King's garden gear, while the nave and aisles at Gloucester Greyfriars were converted into a brewery.

Survival and Preservation

Despite this destruction and reuse, some books, liturgical furnishings, sculpture, vestments and even liturgical vessels of precious metal escaped the attention of the Dissolution commissioners, and continue to survive to this day. In some instances, this was due to deliberate concealment. Richard Layton, a commissioner for Thomas Cromwell, was unimpressed by the possessions of Battle Abbey, 'so beggary a house I never see, nor such filthy stuff [...] the revestry is the worst and poorest that is [...] so many evil I never see' (quoted in Coad 2007: 41). It is difficult to square this damning description with the expenditure on vestments and other liturgical paraphernalia detailed in the abbey's early-sixteenth-century accounts (Evans 1942). The answer is surely that the best vestments had been taken away or sold prior to the removal by the King's men. Images were also deliberately concealed. Three alabaster panels were discovered buried under the floor at Plas yn y Pentre, a grange of Valle Crucis Abbey, Denbighshire, in 1834 (Vernon Price 1952: 212–14). The monks themselves also carried away vestments, chalices and books from their former abbeys. Abbot Henry Cundall of Roche was awarded a pension of fifty marks and allowed to take away 'his books, and the fourth part of the plate, the cattle [...] the household stuff, a chalice, a vestment and £30 in money at his departure' (quoted in Carter 2015: 96).

The monastic libraries were ransacked and rapidly dispersed (Carley 2006). John Leland, Henry VIII's antiquary, who toured the monasteries shortly before their suppression, later commented that he had 'conservid many good autors, the which other wise had beene like to have perished' (quoted in Coppack 1990: 13); these books were destined for the royal library. Nevertheless, enormous numbers of books were destroyed; the service books of Roche Abbey were used to repair carts (Dickens 1959: 124). However, several books were salvaged by the departing religious. In most instances, this involved carrying away no more than a few volumes, such as liturgical and devotional books for use during the priestly careers that most monks adopted after leaving the cloister. A recently discovered printed missal from a Yorkshire Cistercian house (Carter 2014b) and a Bible owned by one of the last monks of St Mary's Abbey, York, are likely to have survived in this way (Carter 2013).

More ambitiously, the final prior of Byland Abbey, Yorkshire, appears to have saved a substantial portion of his monastery's library (Cross 1989). A similar attempt was made to preserve the library of Kirkstall Abbey, the will of Edward Heptonstall (a former monk who died in 1558) specifying that the books that had once belonged to Kirkstall be restored to the abbey by his executors 'if it go up in their times' (quoted in Cross and Vickers 1995: 146). Members of the Benedictine priory of Monk Bretton attempted to maintain a communal life after the Dissolution, with at least three former monks and the prior, William Brown, settling at Worsborough Hall, near the site of their priory. At his own expense, Brown acquired thirty-one books from the priory's library, instructing in his will of 1557 that his books, together with a vestment and other property, should be returned to Monk Bretton in the event of the priory's restoration (Cross and Vickers 1995: 22).

The monks of Monk Bretton were not alone in their attempt to continue some form of religious life after the Dissolution of the Monasteries. According to a nineteenth-century antiquarian source, the monks of Whalley Abbey, Lancashire, clung to their ruinous buildings 'like a few surviving bees about a suffocated hive' (Whitaker 1818: 107). The prioress and four nuns of Kirklees Priory, Yorkshire, moved to nearby Paper (or Papist) Hall (Cross and Vickers 1995: 577). Elizabeth Throckmorton, last abbess of Denny Abbey, Cambridgeshire, retired with two of her fellow ex-nuns and continued the religious life at her family's manor house at Coughton, Warwickshire (Oliva 1998: 59).

The Dissolution enriched the private chapels of the gentry, as shown by the survival of a complete set of Mass vestments from Whalley Abbey, Lancashire, which were acquired by the recusant Towneley family at the time of the abbey's suppression and remained at their seat at Towneley Hall, near Burnley, until the early twentieth century. Manuscripts and printed books also found their way into the libraries of the Catholic gentry, and the dissolved monasteries provided a handy source of ornamental stonework with which to rebuild their manor houses (Carter 2015: 98–9). Other monastic artworks survived because of their acquisition by parish churches. Whole windows were removed from Hailes Abbey and recycled at churches in the vicinity. Choir-stalls from Whalley Abbey made the short journey to the local parish church, whereas the pulpitum loft and screenwork from Bridlington Priory, Yorkshire, migrated to the nearby parish church at Flamborough, and the stalls from Basingwerk Abbey, Flintshire, were bought by St Mary's church, Chester (Carter 2015: 101).

For the dispossessed monks, canons, friars and nuns, the ruined buildings, the fragments of the fittings of monastic churches and the salvaged books and liturgical vessels in their personal possession must have been vivid reminders of their former existence. Some successfully adjusted to their new life outside the cloister, marrying and embracing the new Protestant settlement. But for others, the closure of the monasteries was a lasting trauma. Many former monks – abbots and priors included (Heale 2016: 364–76) – bitterly regretted the suppression of their monasteries and hoped for, even expected, the restoration of the monastic life. This became a reality during the reign of Queen Mary (1553–8), when six religious houses, all in or around London, were refounded (Knowles 1959: 421–3). There is evidence that further foundations were anticipated by ex-religious. In 1554, the surviving monks of Roche Abbey and Rufford Abbey, Nottingham, once again assumed their monastic titles (Cross 1993). This hope or expectation that their houses would 'go up again' calls into question the thoroughness of the destruction of the churches and claustral buildings during their suppression. Clearly, enough was left for individual ex-religious and the remnants of entire communities to believe that the repair and repopulating of their monasteries was viable, and it is significant that the chancel and transepts of Abbey Dore, Herefordshire, were in a sufficiently sound state of preservation in the early seventeenth century for them to be repaired and rededicated as an Anglican parish church (Robinson 1998: 104). Some of the surviving medieval buildings at the Carmelite friary at Aylesford, Kent, were repaired and reoccupied by friars of that order in 1949.

The widespread restoration of the monastic life, however, was never a realistic possibility. The legal validity of the sale of the monastic estates was recognised by the Marian regime and, as has already been seen, even religiously conservative nobles and gentry had acquired large swathes of monastic property. The accession of the Protestant Queen Elizabeth I in 1558 put an end to the monastic revival, ensuring that the monastic remains that populated the landscape continued to decay, becoming those 'bare ruin'd choirs' so movingly evoked in the verse of Shakespeare.

The Irish Monasteries

Henry VIII as Lord and, after 1541, King of Ireland attempted to implement a similar policy of religious reform and monastic suppression there. His attempts, however, were to be hampered by political, religious and social circumstances. Full royal control was limited to the relatively small area in the Pale around Dublin and a few areas loyal to the Crown in the south of the country. As one scholar has commented, 'more was accomplished in the seven years in England between 1535 and 1542 than in the seventy years between 1536 and 1606 in Ireland' (Bradshaw 1974: 206).

There were approximately 400 religious houses in late medieval Ireland, a greater density of settlement relative to the population than in England and Wales. Lay support for their closure was limited, and Observant reform of the friaries ensured that they enjoyed considerable popular support. In 1534, Eustace Chapuys, the imperial ambassador to Henry's court, commented that the Observants in Ireland were feared, obeyed, and almost adored by peasants and lords alike (Bradshaw 1974: 11). Some Cistercian and Augustinian houses continued to thrive, and even those where religious observance was moribund enjoyed the support of the Irish gentry, who often had large estates vested in them, and who sentimentally valued the monasteries as family sepulchres and burial sites.

A Suppression bill was introduced in the Irish Parliament in 1536, but it was met with such strong opposition that it did not pass into law until the autumn of the following year, its scope limited to thirteen smaller houses in the east of the country. By this time, many of the affected monasteries had already been closed, the legislation merely providing a legal basis for the confiscation of their property. There were further closures in 1538, and a campaign against pilgrimage shrines and images was initiated in the winter of 1538–9, netting the Crown £326 2s 11d in spoils. A campaign for general suppression was initiated in the summer of 1539, but its scope was restricted to the areas under Crown control. The appointment of Anthony St Leger as Lord Deputy in 1541 initiated a more vigorous policy of dissolution, one that was characterised by the appointment of commissioners to value monastic properties and make recommendations for their disposal. A limited number of suppressions also took place in areas controlled by the Gaelic lords. However, by the time of Henry's death in 1547, only about half of the Irish monasteries had been closed; many continued to function into the seventeenth century, and even some friaries were able to maintain a somewhat precarious existence (Moss 2012: 116–17).

In Ireland, the policy of Henry's commissioners towards the buildings of the monasteries that they could close was guided by pragmatism rather than iconoclastic zeal. Of the 172 properties surveyed in 1541, only 21 were targeted for complete or partial demolition. As in England, the spoils extracted from the dissolved houses were sold. In 1537, Lord Deputy Grey bought substantial quantities of window glass from Killeigh Abbey, Co. Offaly, for the college at Maynooth, Co. Kildare. Timbers from Clane Friary, Co. Kildare, also found their way to Maynooth. Stonework was still being removed from monastic ruins well into the seventeenth century (Moss 2012: 118–20).

Several Cistercian monasteries in Ireland had a short-term posthumous existence due to their conversion into secular colleges of priests, the former abbots remaining in place as provosts or wardens. The buildings of dissolved monasteries were also often considered suitable for conversion into educational establishments: in 1541, for example, lawyers in Dublin received permission to transform the former Dominican friary there into King's Inn. The site of All Hallows, Dublin, was converted into a university in 1591, the earliest college buildings following the footprint of the church and claustral buildings (Moss 2012: 125–6). Former religious buildings were also reused as hospitals, including the nave and south transept of the church of the Franciscan friary in Waterford. A wooden floor was inserted to create an upper storey where the sick and vagrant poor were accommodated, while the body of the church beneath was used for burials. Franciscans unofficially maintained worship at the hospital's chapel. At Ennis Friary, Co. Clare, the west range of the cloister was used as a lodging for the 'English'. The Dominican friary at Carlingford, Co. Louth, was used to accommodate English fishermen. Other houses were transformed into garrisons, including Boyle Abbey, Co. Roscommon. The Franciscan church at Galway was used as a courtroom, with the judge's seat on the site of the high altar. The church at the former priory dedicated to Saints Peter and Paul at Athlone found a more prosaic function: by 1572, it was being used as a store for malt biscuits and beer made on the site (Moss 2012: 126–8; 136).

The suppressed Irish monasteries were also used to house loyal royal servants and officials. In 1545, Dunbrody Abbey, Co. Wexford, was granted to Sir Osborne Etchingham with the express intention of furthering royal control over the locality. Several former monasteries were converted into mansions, though with an eye to defence as much as splendour (Moss 2012: 136–42). In 1541, royal commissioners suggested the remodelling of the strategically located Moore Abbey, Co. Kildare, for use by the Lord Deputy 'either for his pleasure and relaxation, or for the defence of the countries' (quoted in Moss 2012: 142).

A substantial number of monastic churches continued to be used for religious services, both Protestant and Catholic. Of the 172 monastic churches surveyed in 1541, 35 also had a parochial function. But rarely did the fabric survive intact, with usually only a portion of the building, typically the chancel, preserved for Protestant worship. A posthumous monastic presence was maintained at a number of houses. The church and claustral buildings at the Augustinian friary of Clontuskert, Co. Galway, were ruinous by 1569, but in the 1630s the buildings were reoccupied, possibly by Augustinian canons, and used once again for Catholic worship. In other instances, monastic ruins provided the setting for Mass houses – homes used for the celebration of the Mass – and the sites of former religious houses were the location of Catholic burials, occasionally maintaining family traditions of interment dating back to the Middle Ages (Moss 2012: 149–58). These survivals soon melded into revival. The Irish Observants quickly established links with continental Catholic reform movements. By the second decade of the seventeenth century, the Counter-Reformation orders of friars had become firmly entrenched in the religious life of the Catholic Irish (Bradshaw 1974: 230). The suppression of the Catholic religious life in Ireland was thus never fully achieved.

INTRODUCTION

The Scottish Reformation

Of the constituent nations of the British Isles, it was undoubtedly Scotland that experienced the most destructive religious Reformation. By the time the Reformation was formally adopted in Scotland in 1560, warfare with England and the actions of iconoclasts had ensured that most of the great churches of medieval Scotland had already been plundered, despoiled or ruined, the zeal and thoroughness of the reformers arguably achieving a level of destruction beyond that accomplished by European Protestants.

Pre-Reformation Scotland could boast thirteen cathedrals, forty college churches, fifty-five abbeys, priories and friaries and a dozen nunneries (McRoberts 1962: 417). The battered sculpture encrusting the church at Melrose Abbey, Roxburghshire, the choir-stalls at King's College, Aberdeen, and the surviving panels of the altarpiece painted in the late fifteenth century by the leading Netherlandish artist Hugo van der Goes for the church of Trinity College, Edinburgh, hint at the magnificence of the late Scottish church. Artworks of this kind were targeted by iconoclasts a full generation before the formal adoption of the Reformation. In 1533, the image of Our Lady at the Observant friary in Ayr, Ayrshire, suffered malicious damage, and by 1540–1, there was sufficient concern about the violence directed towards images that the Scottish Parliament decreed that no one should cast down images of saints or treat them with dishonour. It had little effect. Dundee was an early centre of Protestantism: riots broke out there in August 1543, with the rioters 'breaking and destroying the ornaments, vestments, images and candlesticks and carrying off the silver of the alters' (quoted in McRoberts 1962: 419). A mob from the city ransacked Lindores Abbey, Fife, and turned out the monks, though they subsequently returned (McRoberts 1962: 417–22).

English invasions in 1544, 1545 and again in 1547 caused serious damage at Border monasteries, including Dryburgh, Jedburgh, Kelso and Melrose, with some plundered on more than one occasion (McRoberts 1962: 421–5). The neglect of commendators (usually high-ranking lords who enjoyed the revenues of a monastery without being members of the community or having any responsibility for monastic discipline) added to the decay. Nevertheless, religious life continued, and the monks at Melrose were not alone in attempting

Ruins of St Andrews Cathedral. From Thomas Pennant, A Tour in Scotland, *1776*

repairs in the face of indifference from their commendator (Fawcett and Oram 2004: 59–64)

But the great churches were soon to suffer attacks from which there would be no recovery. A tidal wave of iconoclasm in 1558–9 left a trail of destruction. The Charterhouse at Perth, described by firebrand reformer John Knox (1513–72) as 'a building of wonderous cost and greatness', was wrecked to such an extent 'that the walls only remain' (quoted in McRoberts 1962: 429). Knox incited his followers to despoil St Andrews Cathedral, stripping it of its furnishings but probably, at this stage, leaving the fabric untouched. In central Scotland, the altars, statues, windows, shrines and royal tombs at Dunfermline Abbey, Fife, were destroyed, with the choir unroofed and left as a ruin. Aberdeen Cathedral in the north was pillaged and its chancel wrecked, though an armed band of defenders was able to save the chapel of King's College, thus preserving its gorgeous choir-stalls. Petty thievery added to the melancholy trail of destruction (McRoberts 1962: 429–41).

In August 1560, Protestantism was formally adopted as the religion of the land, signalling a further assault on the fabric of the great medieval churches of Scotland. Episcopacy was abolished, and all the larger churches became redundant. At St Andrews, the parish church sufficed for Protestant worship and the wrecked cathedral was scheduled for demolition in 1561 and probably unroofed at this time. The nave of Dunblane Cathedral, Perthshire, was unroofed, with only the smaller choir retained for use by the parish. Glasgow Cathedral was more fortunate and remained intact, though in 1574 it was described as being in a state of 'greit dekaye and ruyne' (quoted in McRoberts 1962: 436). Rather than being actively suppressed, the monasteries of Scotland were left to die a natural death. Recruitment of novices ceased, as did the singing of the Divine Office and the public celebration of the Catholic liturgy. However, the communities were allowed to remain in place with their incomes intact, and it was only in 1573 that holders of Church benefices were required to subscribe to the Kirk – the Protestant Church of Scotland – or suffer deprivation (Dilworth 1995: 78-9).

Some form of religious life was maintained at Sweetheart Abbey, Dumfries and Galloway. Gilbert Brown, the commendator appointed in 1565, had a lifelong attachment to the abbey and permitted Catholic worship to continue. As late as 1579 there was still a high altar in the church (Robinson 1998: 181). Some monks of Dunfermline served

Sweetheart Abbey, engraved by Archibald Robertson, 1 July 1812

in the Kirk, but as late as 1580, the Divine Office was still being said privately and the relics of St Margaret were being protected (Dilworth 1995: 80). These, however, were rare – and temporary – survivals. The majority of the religious conformed to the new Protestant religion, their monasteries at least partially ruined, with, at best, part of the church retained for parochial worship (the nave at Jedburgh, and the transepts at Kelso). Elsewhere in Scotland, buildings were recycled. In 1561–2, the Privy Council ordered that the 'undemolissit' friaries in Aberdeen, Elgin, Inverness and Glasgow be used as schools and hospitals. In several instances, the conventual buildings provided homes for those who profited from the fall of the monasteries; the first lay owner of Scone Abbey, Perthshire, built a palace in the ruins of the burnt-out abbey, much to the disgust of a later antiquarian. Elsewhere, the ruins were cannibalised for building materials, with dressed stone from Incholm Abbey used to build the Edinburgh tollbooth in 1581. By this time, almost every one of the larger Scottish churches was in a state of complete or partial ruin (McRoberts 1962: 447–51). The ruination was poignantly described by Quintin Kennedy, abbot of Crossraugel (1548–64): 'antiquities ande monumentis of this realme bene schaim-fullie dstroyit' (quoted in McRoberts 1962: 460).

Destruction During the Civil Wars and their Aftermath

A century later, ecclesiastical architecture in England and Wales suffered further damage during the Civil Wars (1642–51). The conflict had religious as well as political causes, but rather than being a war between Catholics and Protestants, it was different visions of Protestantism that drove the two sides to take up arms. Puritan iconoclasts smashed large portions of the stained glass and broke much of the medieval religious imagery that had survived the attention of sixteenth-century reformers. The fabric of churches great and small suffered too. Lichfield Cathedral was badly damaged during the Parliamentary sieges in 1643 and 1646. Parliamentarians and Royalists alike wrecked and burnt parish churches (Porter 1994: 64–89). Several episcopal residences were severely damaged during sieges or at the hands of victorious Parliamentarians after the abolition of episcopacy. The medieval Bishops' Palace at Lincoln was used to accommodate prisoners, then stormed and set ablaze, the roofs stripped of their leads and large parts of the fabric demolished (Coppack 2000: 20–2).

However, it is the ruins of castles that were wrecked or slighted – that is, deliberately damaged so as to make them indefensible – that are the most vivid and enduring architectural legacy of the violence and destruction caused by the Civil Wars. The process and extent of the destruction can be analysed by examining three castles with especially striking ruins and rich contemporary documentation: the castles of Scarborough, Goodrich and Kenilworth.

Scarborough Castle, Yorkshire, stands on a headland overlooking the port on a site intermittently inhabited and fortified for the best part of 3,000 years. A castle was first established there in the mid-twelfth century, the great keep built between 1159 and 1169. By the late Middle Ages, the castle was in poor repair, and by the reign of James I, its military function appeared to be at an end. However, on the outbreak of hostilities in August 1642, Sir Hugh Cholmley (1600–57), a prominent local gentleman and sometime MP for Scarborough, occupied the castle for the Parliamentary cause. Cholmley quickly changed sides. In the spring and summer of 1645, the castle endured a five-month siege.

'A drawn View of the Keep of Goodrich Castle', 1829

The Parliamentary artillery included a gun capable of firing a 64-pound ball. The castle was subjected to an intense bombardment, and within three days the great keep split in half and collapsed. Cholmley described the fall of the tower as 'a very terrible spectacle, more sudden than expected' (quoted in Goodall 2013: 35). The castle suffered further bombardment from land and sea, finally surrendering in July 1645. It endured a further siege in 1648, after which instructions were given by Parliament for the defences to be slighted. Opposition from the town, however, preserved it from destruction. It was subsequently garrisoned by Parliament, retaining a military function well into the nineteenth century (Goodall 2013).

The twelfth- and thirteenth-century fortifications of Goodrich Castle, Herefordshire, provided a base for Royalist forces from 1644. A thorn in the side of the Parliamentarians, it was besieged in the summer of 1646. A mortar, nicknamed 'Roaring Meg', pounded the castle walls, with the attack focused on the northwest tower, a perceived weak point. A combination of artillery fire and undermining caused much of the tower to collapse. The castle was stormed on 31 July 1646, forcing the surrender of the Royalist garrison. The siege left the castle ruined, with, in the words of the victorious Parliamentarian commander, 'noe whole room in it' (quoted in Ashbee 2005: 44). The surviving defences, however, were considered to be sufficiently strong for Parliament to order their slighting, the battlements being duly removed and the main fortifications rendered useless. The dowager Countess of Kent, owner of the castle and supporter of the Parliamentarian cause, received £1,000 in compensation (Ashbee 2005).

The magnificent royal castle-turned-Renaissance-palace at Kenilworth, Warwickshire, was occupied by Parliamentarian forces for much of the wars and suffered no serious damage during the conflict. However, several commissions for its slighting were issued in 1649. Aware of the impending destruction, the antiquary William Dugdale made several sketches of the castle, which were engraved by Wenceslaus Hollar and published in Dugdale's *The Antiquities of Warwickshire* (1656). The slighting of Kenilworth eventually took place in 1649–50. The north side of the twelfth-century great tower was taken down, along with portions of the curtain wall. The Parliamentary commander who oversaw the destruction, Colonel Joseph Hawkesworth, acquired the estate in lieu of back-pay for the local militia, but retained the castle

INTRODUCTION

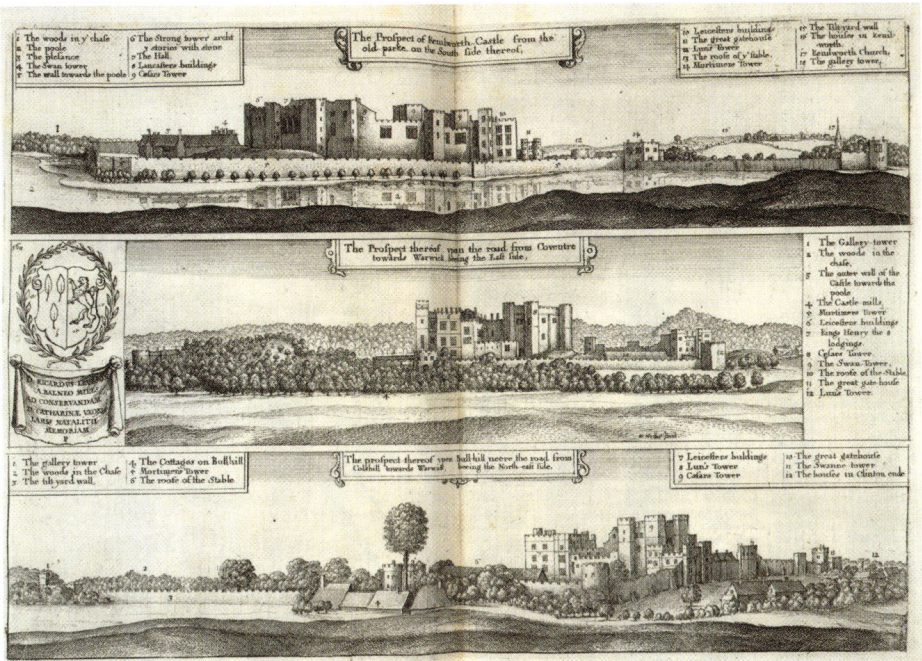

Kenilworth Castle. From The Antiquities of Warwickshire illustrated [...] *by William Dugdale, 1656*

for himself. The gatehouse, built by Robert Dudley, Earl of Leicester, in the 1570s, was converted into a lodging for Hawkesworth. The estates were divided between his officers. The residential buildings in the inner court were wrecked by pillaging, rapidly becoming roofless ruins. The castle's ornamental landscape was also destroyed and its mere or lake drained around this time (Morris 2010). The destruction of the aristocratic pleasure grounds at Kenilworth is evidence of the wider social and political reasons for the dismantling: of deliberate aesthetic impact, slighting was also a visible assault on the culture and chivalric ethos of the Royalist nobility (Goodall 2011: 490).

As was the case with the despoiling of the monasteries, the slighting of castles was well planned and intended to yield a profit. The dismantling of Pontefract Castle, Yorkshire, in 1649 shows that both military and economic interests were at stake. Pontefract had played an important role during the wars and was badly damaged in three prolonged sieges. Its slighting was ordered by Parliament in early 1649. The instructions issued by the West Riding Committee for the dismantling of the defences can leave no doubt that there were economic considerations from the outset; they directed and specified 'the manner and order how the Lead, Timber, Iron, and other materials of the said castle shalbee pulled downe, sold, and disposed of' (quoted in Rakoczy 2008: 263). Gangs of specialist stonemasons were employed, and timber and glazing were removed with care. Sale of the lead yielded over £1,640; some of it was ultimately traded as far away as Rotterdam. Spoils from the castle were also put to civic use, including augmenting the defences of Hull. Overall, the sale of stonework, timber, glass and metal netted Parliament in excess of £1,779, out of which £777 went on wages and £1,000 was given to the Pontefract Corporation for a new church, since the medieval parish church had been badly damaged during the fighting. Both individuals and civic institutions therefore profited from the slighting (Rakoczy 2008).

It is true that many castles survived the wars and their aftermath without serious damage, and there is evidence that, even amidst the chaos, a consciousness prevailed concerning the need to curtail the destruction. As early as 1646, for example, the Shropshire Committee was told that 'we do not think it fit that all houses of situation and strength render them capable of being garrisons should be pulled down. There would then be too many sad marks left of the calamity of this war' (quoted in Thompson 1987: 152). Certain castles continued to be used as fortifications against foreign invasion, as at Dover; Berkeley Castle in Gloucestershire, where the defences suffered no more than token slighting, was appropriated as an aristocratic residence. Even so, the destruction caused to castles in the middle of the seventeenth century by warfare and slightings has rightly been described as the single most radical change violently inflicted on the English and Welsh landscape between the Reformation and the Second World War (Goodall 2011: 490).

For nineteenth-century Whiggish historians, the Reformation, the Dissolution of the Monasteries and the Civil Wars were key markers of Britain's progress towards liberty and enlightenment, national progress that was hard won through bloodshed and public burnings, beheadings and disembowelments. The spread of the spirit of British liberty, it was thus believed, was written in the ecclesiastical and military ruins that populated the landscape. The essays and case studies in this book continue to explore the legacy of Britain's ruins in later centuries, focusing particularly on the lively antiquarian, historical, literary, artistic and political interest that they attracted in the period 1700–1850. Approaching Britain's ruins with a broad conceptualisation of 'writing' at hand, this collection surveys the ways in which the ruins of England, Wales, Scotland and Ireland became the subjects of concerted cultural 'inscription' in the long eighteenth century, be this in the form of scholarly antiquarian enquiry; the poetic musings of topographical poets and novelists; the diaries, journals and sketches of picturesque travellers and artists; metaphorically in the political discourses of the day; or literally in the rise of a spirit of conservation from the late eighteenth century onwards. Including between each of its seven chapters case studies of British ruins of particular interest, this volume offers an informed yet accessible account of the ways in which Britain's ruins were 'written', 'written about' and 'read' in the eighteenth and nineteenth centuries, tracing the origins of impressions and practices that are still very much a part of British cultural heritage today.

Further Reading

Knowles, David. 1976. *Bare Ruined Choirs: The Dissolution of the English Monasteries* (Cambridge: Cambridge University Press).

Phillips, John. 1973. *The Reformation of Images: The Destruction of Art in England, 1535–1660* (Berkeley: University of California Press).

Walsham, Alexandra. 2011. *The Reformation of the Landscape: Religion, Identity, and Memory in Early Modern Britain and Ireland* (New York: Oxford University Press).

References

Ashbee, Jeremy. 2005. *Goodrich Castle* (London: English Heritage).

Aston, Margaret. 1973. 'English Ruins and English History: The Dissolution and the Sense of the Past', *Journal of the Courtauld and Warburg Institutes* 36: 231–55.

Austin, John. 1998. *Merevale Church and Abbey* (Studley: Brewin Books).

Bertram, Jerome. 1976. *Lost Brasses* (Newton Abbot: David & Charles).

Bradshaw, Brendon. 1974. *The Dissolution of the Religious Orders in Ireland Under Henry VIII* (Cambridge: Cambridge University Press).

Carley, James. 2006. 'The Dispersal of the Monastic Libraries and the Salvaging of the Spoils', in *The Cambridge History of Libraries in Britain and Ireland*, I: *to 1640*, edited by Elisabeth Leedham-Green and Teresa Webber (Cambridge: Cambridge University Press), 265–91.

Carter, Michael. 2013. 'Brother Grayson's Bible: A Previously Unrecorded Printed Book from St Mary's Abbey, York', *Nottingham Medieval Studies* 57: 287–302.

Carter, Michael. 2014a. 'Cistercian Abbots as Patrons of Art and Architecture: Northern England in the Late Middle Ages', in *The Prelate in England and Europe, 1300–1560*, edited by Martin Heale (Woodbridge: York Medieval Press), 215–39.

Carter, Michael. 2014b. 'A Printed Missal from an English Cistercian Abbey', *Cistercian Studies Quarterly* 49: 243–59.

Carter, Michael. 2015. '"It would have pitied any heart to see": Destruction and Survival at Cistercian Monasteries in Northern England at the Dissolution', *Journal of the British Archaeological Association* 168: 77–110.

Carter, Michael. 2016. 'Michael Sherbrook, the Fall of Roche Abbey and the Provenance of Cambridge University Library MS GG. 3. 33', *Notes and Queries* 63: 19–22.

Clark, James. 2002. 'The Religious Orders in Pre-Reformation England', in *The Religious Orders of Pre-Reformation England*, edited by James Clark (Woodbridge: Boydell), 3–34.

Coad, Jonathan. 2007. *Battle Abbey and Battlefield* (London: English Heritage).

Coppack, Glyn. 1990. *Abbeys and Priories* (London: Batsford).

Coppack, Glyn. 1998. *The White Monks: The Cistercians in Britain, 1128–1540* (Stroud: Tempus).

Coppack, Glyn. 1999. 'Suppression Documents', in *Rievaulx Abbey: Community, Architecture and Memory*, by Peter Fergusson and Stuart Harrison, with contributions from Glyn Coppack (New Haven and London: Yale University Press), 226–37.

Coppack, Glyn. 2000. *Medieval Bishops' Palace, Lincoln, Lincolnshire* (London: English Heritage).

Cross, Claire. 1988. 'Monasticism and Society in the Diocese of York, 1520–1540', *Transactions of the Royal Historical Society* 5th series, 38: 131–45.

Cross, Claire. 1989. 'A Medieval Yorkshire Library', *Northern History* 25: 28–90.

Cross, Claire. 1993. 'The Reconstitution of Northern Monastic Communities in the Reign of Mary Tudor', *Northern History* 29: 200–204.

Cross, Claire and Noreen Vickers. 1995. *Monks, Friars and Nuns in Sixteenth-Century Yorkshire*, Yorkshire Archaeological Society Record Series 150.

Dickens, Geoffrey (ed.). 1959. *Tudor Treatises*, Yorkshire Archaeological Society Record Series 125.

Dilworth, Mark. 1995. *Scottish Monasteries in the Late Middle Ages* (Edinburgh: Edinburgh University Press).

Evans, Allan. 1942. 'Battle Abbey at the Dissolution: Expenses', *Huntington Library Quarterly* 6: 53–101.

Fawcett, Richard and Richard Oram. 2004. *Melrose Abbey* (Stroud: Tempus).

Gilbanks, G. E. 1899. *Some Records of a Cistercian Abbey: Holm Cultram, Cumberland* (London: Walter Scott).

Goodall, John. 2011. *The English Castle* (New Haven and London: Yale University Press).

Goodall, John. 2013. *Scarborough Castle* (London: English Heritage).

Heale, Martin. 2009. *Monasticism in Late Medieval England, c. 1300–1535*, (Manchester: Manchester University Press).

Heale, Martin. 2016. *The Abbots and Priors of Late Medieval and Reformation England* (Oxford: Oxford University Press).

Hoyle, R. W. 2001. *The Pilgrimage of Grace and the Politics of the 1530s* (Oxford: Oxford University Press).

Knowles, David. 1959. *The Religious Orders in England*, III. *The Tudor Age* (Cambridge: Cambridge University Press).

Knowles, David and Neville Hadcock. 1971. *Medieval Religious Houses: England and Wales*, revised edn (London: Longman).

Luxford, Julian. 2005. *The Art and Architecture of English Benedictine Monasteries, 1300-1540: A Patronage History* (Woodbridge: Boydell).

McRoberts, David. 1962. 'Material Destruction Caused by the Scottish Reformation', in *Essays on the Scottish Reformation*, edited by David McRoberts (Glasgow: Burns), 415-62.

Morris, Richard. 2010. *Kenilworth Castle* (London: English Heritage).

Moss, Rachel. 2012. 'Recuse, Reuse, Recycle: Irish Monastic Architecture, c. 1540-1640', in *Irish Gothic Architecture: Construction, Decay and Reinvention*, edited by Roger Stalley (Dublin: Wordwell), 115-59.

Newman, John and Nikolaus Pevsner. 1972. *The Buildings of England: Dorset* (Harmondsworth: Penguin).

Oliva, Marilyn. 1998. *The Convent and Community in Late Medieval England: Female Monasteries in the Diocese of Norwich, 1350-1540* (Woodbridge: Boydell).

Porter, Stephen. 1994. *Destruction and the English Civil War* (Stroud: Sutton).

Questier, Michael. 2008. *Catholicism and Community in Early Modern England: Politics, Aristocratic Patronage and Religion, c. 1550-1640* (Cambridge: Cambridge University Press).

Rakoczy, Lila. 2008. 'Out of the Ashes: Destruction, Reuse, and Profiteering in the English Civil War', in *The Archaeology of Destruction*, edited by Lila Rakoczy (Newcastle upon Tyne: Cambridge Scholars Press), 261-86.

Robinson, David (ed.). 1998. *The Cistercian Abbeys of Britain: Far from the Concourse of Men* (London: Batsford).

Robinson, David. 2007. *Strata Florida Abbey, Talley Abbey* (Cardiff: Cadw).

Shagan, Ethan. 2003. *Popular Politics and the English Reformation* (Cambridge: Cambridge University Press).

Talbot, Charles. 1964. 'Marmaduke Huby, Abbot of Fountains (1495-1526)', *Analecta Sacri Ordinis Cisterciensis* 20: 165-84.

Thompson, M. W. 1987. *The Decline of the Castle* (Cambridge: Cambridge University Press).

Turnbill, William (ed.). 1836. *Account of the Monastic Treasures Confiscated at the Dissolution of Various Houses in England by Sir John Williams Kt* (Edinburgh: Abbotsford Club).

Vernon Price, G. 1952. *Valle Crucis Abbey* (Liverpool: H. Evans).

Whitaker, Thomas Dunham. 1818. *An History of the Original Parish of Whalley, and Honor of Clitheroe, in the Counties of Lancaster and York*, 3rd edn (London: Printed by and for Nichols, Son, and Bentley, and Thomas Edwards).

Woodward, George. 1966. *The Dissolution of the Monasteries* (London: Blandford).

RUINS IN FOCUS

CAERNARFON CASTLE

David Punter

> Out of the ruins of this city arose the present town, justly the boast of North Wales for its situation, buildings, harbour, &c. but above all for the grandeur of its castle. (Evans 1800: 165)

As a town and as a fortified site, Caernarfon, Gwynedd, has been of great importance to the Welsh people for many centuries; like Conwy, the whole town is walled, and the castle itself is only one part of the fortifications. Here is John Taylor, the self-dubbed English 'Water poet', writing of Caernarfon in 1652:

> to Caernarvon, where I thought to have seen a Town and a Castle, or a Castle and a Town; but I saw both to be one, and one to be both; for indeed a man can hardly divide them in judgement or apprehension; and I have seen many gallant fabrics and fortifications, but for compactness and completeness of Caernarvon, I never yet saw a parallel. (Taylor 1870: 14)

'Caernarvon Castle'. J. M. W. Turner, watercolour, c. 1832

INTRODUCTION

Yet Caernarfon, as is the case with so many of the Edwardian castles of North Wales, was never completed; it was, we might say, the greatest of all the Welsh ruins, or at least of those ambitious constructions that never survived to the point where they might become the defensive fortress regarded as needed.

Samuel Johnson was particularly impressed; he says that he had not imagined that, in medieval times, there had been any such buildings; he was perhaps, as we may still be, amazed at the level of engineering skill required to construct such a monument of magnificence. But Caernarfon Castle was, in a sense, haunted from the start; it is haunted by King Edward's 'great myth' which would allow him, so he hoped, to rule Wales, as it were, from within, as a Welshman, and which thus required him to invent a whole set of myths. These myths centred on the Macsen Wledig romance in the *Mabinogion* (c. 1350–1410), which was taken to substantiate a connection between Caernarfon and imperial Rome, or rather the Roman city of Constantinople; Caernarfon Castle's 'great towers of many colours' were supposed to represent, repeat or echo an earlier imperial heyday.

'Ruynous' from the sixteenth century, as the records assure us, Caernarfon nevertheless did its obligatory tour of duty during the Civil Wars; after this, in 1660, there were attempts at demolition, which clearly failed, although it might be argued that the grandeur of Caernarfon was eventually overwhelmed in more prosaic ways by the incursion of industry and of the railways in 1827, which clearly rendered the 'strongest of all gateways' less relevant and effective than before.

The prolific brothers Buck, as well as Boydell of Hawarden, produced engravings of Caernarfon in the 1740s; but, as so often, it was J. M. W. Turner who produced in c. 1832 the masterpiece which enshrined Romantic-era Caernarfon. As a painter of the sea, perhaps it was inevitable that he should portray the castle – triangular in shape, poised on its supposedly impregnable headland – from the water. It is seen from low down in the water, too; from the very surface of the sea, where neighbouring oars plash and the castle soars, half-hidden in a golden mist, signifying a lost era, a grandeur which was never foolish even if its values have now been sunk, reduced to ruin, half-covered in a misty nostalgia that may, after all, do more to support the persistence of Celtic legendry, even if in English hands, than to allow it to slip beyond reach.

References

Evans, John. 1800. *A Tour Through Part of North Wales, in the Year 1798, and at Other Times* (London: Printed for J. White).

Taylor, John. 1870. 'A Short Relation of a Long Journey', in *Works of John Taylor the Water Poet Not Included in the Folio Volume of 1630, Vol. I* (London: Printed for the Spenser Society), 5–28.

Chapter 1:
Antiquaries and Ruins

Rosemary Sweet

A taste for ruins became the height of fashion in the eighteenth century: ruins were depicted in art, celebrated in poetry and incorporated into landscape gardens. The fashion drew on picturesque theory and the vogue for things 'Gothic', and was fuelled by the growth in domestic tourism and the popularity of the Gothic novel. But it drew first and foremost upon the practice of antiquarianism and the efforts of antiquaries to describe, record and preserve the monuments of the past. It was the antiquaries of the seventeenth and eighteenth centuries who first drew attention to ruins in the landscape and made the case for their social and cultural value, transforming ruins from structures of little worth into sites replete with meaning and historical significance. It was their observations and publications that provided essential information on which many other travellers, writers and artists could build in more imaginative ways. The antiquarian community also led the way in arguing for the preservation of ruins as an essential part of the nation's heritage. If we are to understand why particular ruins seized the wider public imagination in the eighteenth century, we need first to understand why antiquaries accorded such significance to them.

Antiquaries and Antiquarianism Before 1700

Who or what were the antiquaries? Few people today would describe themselves as antiquaries: fellows of organisations such as the Society of Antiquaries of London or of Scotland would generally identify as archaeologists, architectural historians or simply historians. In the seventeenth and eighteenth centuries, however, the term 'antiquary' or 'antiquarian' was applied to anyone who had an interest in the material or textual remains of the past. Whereas historians in the seventeenth and eighteenth centuries typically wrote histories of empires, dynasties or wars which were more concerned with the military, political or moral lessons of the past, the antiquary looked to validate and corroborate the facts of history through the material evidence of antiquities, whether manuscripts, inscriptions, coins or physical remains. Such objects were survivals from the 'deluge of time', the authenticity of which provided the evidential base for historical narrative and which offered a direct and tangible point of contact with the past (Sweet 2004). Antiquarianism was seen as the 'handmaid' to history, and antiquaries, who were concerned with detail and evidence rather than narrative and argument, were regarded with rather less scholarly esteem. Indeed, they were frequently the butt of ridicule and satire for their supposed pedantry and indiscriminate appetite for anything old: to write history required judgement and taste, but antiquaries were merely 'criticks in rust' (Addison 1726: 10).

In practice, most antiquaries were gentlemen of education, and without exception they were men. Many were landed gentry, educated in the Classics, with sufficient time and leisure to investigate the antiquities of their localities, and for whom the study of antiquities relating to the history of their families and their county was an expression of patriotism and public spirit. Clergy were likewise well represented: they too, generally, had leisure and education and a professional interest in what were often called 'ecclesiastical antiquities'. But increasing numbers of antiquaries were also autodidacts or individuals who had an occupational or professional interest in studying the remains of the past – surveyors and lawyers, for example, but also, increasingly, artists and architects who drew, studied and described architectural antiquities for a living. The Society of Antiquaries of London (established 1707) provided a focus for antiquarian activity and included the study and preservation of the nation's monuments (or ruins) among its founding principles, but its membership only ever included a small proportion of those who claimed an interest in the nation's antiquities.

Of course, antiquarianism as a field of study did not suddenly emerge, fully formed, in around 1700. It had long antecedents going back to the humanist Renaissance of the fifteenth century, when scholars, architects and artists began seriously to record and recover the textual and physical remains of Classical antiquity, particularly in Italy. Antiquaries such as Poggio Bracciolini, Andrea Palladio or Pirro Ligorio described and drew the monuments of ancient Rome and lamented their destruction, as cardinals plundered their remains to ornament their grandiose building projects or, more prosaically, as a source of lime. Antiquarianism was never simply the study of ruins, but awareness of their importance and of their vulnerability was always one of its hallmarks. The ruins of ancient Rome were visible in medieval and early modern England, too, albeit on a lesser scale. They were vivid reminders of a lost civilisation, a time that once was: for example, in the fourteenth century, Gerald of Wales famously described the ruins of the Roman fortress of Caerleon in highly evocative terms, referring to the 'vestiges of its former splendour' evident in the 'immense palaces, ornamented with gilded roofs', the 'remarkable' hot baths, the tower of 'prodigious size' and the 'relics of temples, and theatres' enclosed by walls (Colt Hoare 1806: vol. 1, 103). In sixteenth-century Britain the influence of Renaissance humanism inspired antiquaries such as William Camden to 'restore antiquity to Britaine and Britain to his antiquity' as he sought out the ruins that provided the tangible evidence that the Romans had indeed brought civilisation to the country (Camden 1610). Antiquaries were intrigued by the mystery inherent in ruins and recognised them as puzzles which, if unlocked, could provide information about an earlier age. Such 'visible superviving evidences of antiquitie', wrote the seventeenth-century scholar Meric Casaubon, 'represent unto their [antiquaries'] minds former times, with as strong an impression, as if they were actually present, and in sight' (Casaubon 1638: 97–8).

If the antiquaries of Rome deplored the destruction of the monuments of Classical antiquity by the modern Catholic Church, in Britain the great stimulus to antiquarian interest in ruins was the impact of the religious, political and social upheavals of the Reformation and the Civil Wars. British society had been fractured and tradition overturned; in the process the rural and urban landscapes in which religious and monastic buildings had been so prominent were transformed. These events precipitated a radical disjuncture with the past and a widespread sense of loss that lingered on through the eighteenth and nineteenth centuries. In England and Wales the Dissolution of the Monasteries led to the secular appropriation, demolition or simply gradual decay of hundreds of monastic buildings. The Dissolution and the Reformation were never uncontested, and within a generation antiquarian literature was replete with expressions of indignation at the cynical rapacity of Henry VIII and Thomas Cromwell, and nostalgic regret for a monastic way of life and traditions of religious piety and learning (Aston 1973). In Scotland, the devastation wrought by the Reformation was even more complete. The Civil Wars continued the destruction inflicted upon many religious buildings but also spawned a different category of ruin – that of castles, fortifications and city walls, which were frequently damaged beyond repair. Such ruins were as pregnant with moral and political lessons as were those of the Roman Catholic Church, and just as closely associated with the memories of local families and communities. By the period of the Restoration (1660), therefore, Great Britain could boast a unique landscape of ruins, both religious and secular, all a potent reminder of events that had transformed the nation. They were signifiers of the transience of human affairs, the vagaries of political power and the hubris of human ambition in the face of divine Providence. And in a society where the memorialisation of the dead was still a pressing obligation, they offered a monument to those who had lost their lives and their property. Indeed, the terms 'monument' and 'ruin' were often used synonymously; ruins were nothing if not a mnemonic device. They were the tangible reminders of families and individuals, of the ownership of the rights, privileges and property that held society together and which it was the duty of the antiquary to record.

It was this sense of social dislocation and a corresponding search for continuity and the preservation of memory that underpinned the researches of many of the antiquaries of the later seventeenth century, scholars whose publications and manuscript collections provided the foundations on which eighteenth-century antiquaries would build. Today the dusty and weighty volumes of the seventeenth-century antiquaries are decidedly off-putting. They are sparingly illustrated, with small and dense typefaces, and the information they contain is dry and factual: copies of charters, dates of benefactions and lists of office-holders. 'Of the Religious Houses, hospitals, Chantries (those signall Monuments of our Forefathers Pieties)', wrote Sir William Dugdale, 'I have shewed their Foundations, endowments, and continuance, with their dissolutions and ruine, which gave the greatest blow to Antiquities that ever *England* had' (Dugdale 1656: sig. b3v). Dugdale confined himself to the collation of facts – his was the age of the empiricism of the scientific revolution – rather than the evocation of a sense of place. But the cumulative influence of these publications was to provide legitimacy to a belief among antiquaries and their readers that ruins had an intrinsic value – they were not simply a source of masonry or additional storage space – and deserved actively to be preserved. Antiquaries had also begun the process of collating the records and information that related to particular ruins, thereby endowing them with a textual presence in the antiquarian imagination. Thus, by the early eighteenth century, there was a growing body of information to which antiquaries and other interested readers could refer in order to find information relating to the history of antiquities and ecclesiastical ruins in particular.

The Eighteenth Century: Politics, Religion and Nation

Early eighteenth-century antiquaries, such as the Buckinghamshire gentleman and high church Tory Browne Willis, followed in the path set by Dugdale and saw ruins as a powerful reminder of the iniquitous conduct of Henry VIII, 'the pulling down and desecrating of which [monasteries] was the chief Blemish of the Reformation, and what our Nation stands greatly censured for' (Willis 1718–19: vol. 1, p. 2). In his survey of the *Mitred Parliamentary Abbies* he quoted John Denham's poem, *Cooper's Hill* (1642):

> Who sees these dismal Heaps, but would demand
>   What barbarous Invader sacks the Land;
> But when he hears no *Goth*, no *Turk*, did bring
>   This Desolation, but a Christian King;
> When nothing but the Name of Zeal appears,
> 'Twixt our best Actions, and the worst of theirs;
> What does he think our Sacrilege would spare,
>   When such th' effects of our devotion are?
> (Willis 1718–19: vol. 1, 2)

Yet, for all Willis's evident disgust at the damage inflicted upon such ornaments to the kingdom, the reader of *Mitred Parliamentary Abbies* or any other publication from this date will not find a detailed description of the ruin *qua* ruin. The kind of sophisticated descriptive vocabulary that we associate with, for example, a Pevsner guide today simply did not exist. Typically the dimensions might be provided – antiquaries, as good empiricists, liked to measure a ruin. The material from which the structure had been built would be identified, with brief comments upon the size, ornaments, style and age of the building. Thus, the non-juring bishop and antiquary, Richard Rawlinson, excused himself for the inadequacy of his description of the ruins of the abbot's apartment at Glastonbury on the grounds that he had not *measured* it when he visited ten years earlier. The kitchen – the most impressive standing remains of the complex – was reduced to a summary of its dimensions and a catalogue of doors, windows and hearths (Rawlinson 1722: 55, 73–6, 79–80). Meanwhile, the kinds of qualitative adjectives that antiquaries used to convey the appearance of ruins in this period were vague and imprecise: 'venerable' and 'ancient' or 'mean' and 'barbarous'. John Farmer, for example, described the remains of the monastic church at Waltham as 'built after a Gothick Manner, in which the Columns are either too Massey, in form of vast Pillars, or as slender as Poles, having Capitals, without any certain Dimensions'. It was, he continued, 'rather large than neat, firm than fair, very dark' (Farmer 1735: 7). Rather than describing the ruins in their own right, antiquaries tended to use them as a prompt to summarise the original extent or plan of the building: thus Rawlinson gave a verbal summary of the different elements of the monastery at Glastonbury as it would originally have been built, rather than describing what still remained. Nor do we find attempts to evoke the atmosphere of place; specifying location was important to antiquaries in their campaign accurately to describe and record, but landscape appreciation, like the study of Gothic architecture, had not, in the early eighteenth century, evolved as a language.

Such brevity of description also reflects the fact that the ruined quality of such buildings at this time was not something that held value in itself. Of greater interest were the names of the people associated with the ruin – that is, the owners of the property – or the events that had taken place there. Thus Rawlinson's description of the ruins at Glastonbury concluded with a lengthy list of all the abbots who had held office there. Antiquaries such as Willis, Rawlinson and Farmer were not insensible to the beauty of such structures, but their beauty lay principally in the memories of former magnificence and splendour that they evoked, rather than being inherent in the ruinous state itself. Moreover, for such religiously inspired antiquaries, the ruins of any ecclesiastical building could lay claim to the beauty of holiness that derived from having been built as an act of faith dedicated to God. And underpinning the descriptions was a belief that the ruins, and more particularly the memories associated with them, were essential to the collective good; the mark of a civilised society was to preserve such ruins – civil and ecclesiastical – and to respect the lessons of the past that they represented, both religious and political. Among antiquaries there was an assumption that it was a mark of philistinism or barbarism wilfully to destroy such structures purely for convenience or financial gain.

Even in the early eighteenth century not all antiquaries shared Willis's or Rawlinson's high church sympathies. William Stukeley, for example, probably the most influential antiquary of the first half of the eighteenth century, was less than orthodox in his religious beliefs, but he was fiercely critical of the unmindful destruction of any monument of antiquity and described the Dissolution of the Monasteries as a 'terrible' stroke to the nation's history and antiquities (Stukeley 1770b: 53). Stukeley's descriptions of the ruins of monastic architecture, like those of his antiquarian contemporaries, were brief, but he had an eye for the place of a ruin in the landscape (the abbey at Reading stood in a 'charming situation'). He noted the poignant contrast between the vigorous growth of ivy and the decaying state of the ruins at Malmesbury, while the soaring height of Gothic arches was compared to the effect of the interlocking branches of a grove of trees – which offered him both an explanation of the origins of the Gothic pointed arch and a link between Christianity and the sacred groves of druidical religion (Stukeley 1724: 59, 145; 1770a: 43). In Stukeley's antiquarianism we find a suggestion of the potential of ruins as imaginative prompts, as spurs to curiosity and to meditation, and of the possibilities that their very incompleteness opened up for the play of fancy. Observing the abundant evidence for the ruins of Roman buildings in the north of England, he conjured up visions of a flourishing Romano-British civilisation: 'We may imagine the glorious show of towns, cities, castles, temples, and the like [...] by contemplating the prodigious quantities of their ruins and memorials beyond that of any other part of Europe' (Stukeley 1776: 66). As a later antiquary, Joseph Forsyth, remarked of

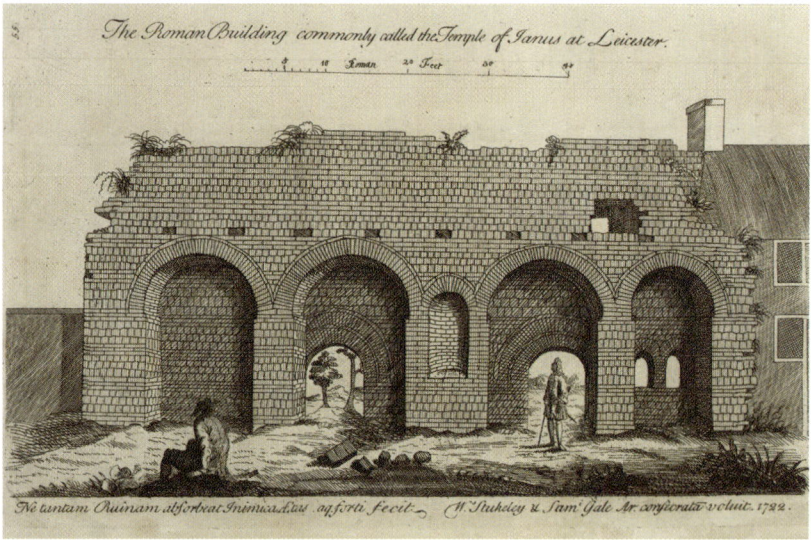

'The Roman Building commonly called the Temple of Janus at Leicester'. From William Stukeley, Itinerarium curiosum, *1776*

the imaginative power of ruins, 'we trace and we lose its design, we rebuild, re-people it, we call in history, we compose, we animate, we create, and man ever delights in his own creation' (Forsyth 1816: 251).

Stukeley, who had never journeyed outside Britain, expressed a patriotic disdain for the ruins of continental Europe that so many well-heeled young men travelled to see at great expense as part of the Grand Tour. He was highly critical of those who travelled and spent their money abroad without travelling within or knowing their own country first. His celebration of the monuments, antiquities and ruins in *Itinerarium curiosum* was a chauvinistic riposte to the descriptions of Roman antiquities that were so popular among architects and gentlemen of taste: 'Hither let the young noblemen and gentry travel, to admire the wonders of their native country, thick sown by that great, wise and industrious people, and learn with them how to value it' (Stukeley 1776: 67). The shadow of neglect cast over domestic Roman and Gothic ruins by those of Greece and Italy would prove a constant lament by antiquaries down the century. 'It is the glory of this age and nation to penetrate the wilds of Europe and the desarts of Asia and Africa for the remains of Grecian, Roman and earlier architecture', wrote Richard Gough, the leading antiquary of the later eighteenth century, 'yet no artist offers himself a candidate for fame in preserving those of our forefathers in their own country' (Gough 1780: vol. 1, xiii–xiv).

The patriotism that William Stukeley expressed in *Itinerarium curiosum* can be traced in many other publications from this period that provided readers with a description of their native country in both its ancient and modern state, such as Daniel Defoe's *Tour through the Whole Island of Great Britain* (1726) or the various editions and abridgements of William Camden's *Britannia*. Even Defoe, who 'studiously avoided' antiquities, preferring to focus instead upon modern commercial society, was unable to avoid all references to the material fabric of the past (Defoe 1971: 43). Stukeley had written nothing about Scotland: despite visiting the Roman wall he never ventured north of the border. In 1718, however, John Slezer published *Theatrum Scotiae*, a volume that illustrated not only the castles, palaces, towns and colleges of Scotland, but also the *ruins* of abbeys, churches, monasteries and convents. In actual fact, Slezer had very little of consequence to say about ruins, most of which were the ruins of Scotland's Reformation – cathedrals, abbeys and churches – beyond reference to their existence. The Catholic legacy in Scotland in the early eighteenth century was far more contentious than it was south of the border, a reality that would

Fountains Abbey. From Samuel and Nathaniel Buck, Views of the Ruins of Castles and Abbeys in England and Wales, *1726*

have inhibited the kind of sentiments expressed by Browne Willis. Moreover, in publications such as this the primary value of the work in terms of ruins lay in the accompanying plates.

In a similar spirit, the topographical artists Samuel and Nathaniel Buck commenced publication of *Views of the Ruins of Castles and Abbeys in England and Wales* (1726). This is a landmark publication in many ways, not least because it was the first such volume to make *ruins*, rather than a particular type of building or institution, its primary focus. The brothers' motivations, which were laid out in the Preface, emphasised the importance of ruins in commemorating both the piety of ancestors and the memory of men, as well as their historic value in transmitting information about the past to the present and to future generations. In their prospectus for publishing by subscription a follow-up volume they argued that ruins were the repositories of the nation's history:

> The Antiquity of such *Edifices*, together with the pious Intention of the *Founders*, having made the Memory of them justly venerable; and as most of those valuable *Structures* are now mould'ring in *Ruins*, they being already no more than the defac'd *Remains* of what they originally were: The best *Perspective Views* they are at this Day capable of, we find by Experience do not fail of being acceptable to this curious Age: as they greatly contribute to illustrate the History of the former State of this *Island*, and to transmit those things to Posterity, which must otherwise be irretrievably lost: the *Undertakers* have for these Reasons made it their principal Business, at no small Expence, to visit them, and take *Perspective Views* of whatever remains remarkable. (Buck and Buck 1737: n.p.)

This proposal suggests that the primary interest in ruins was still seen to lie in the reminder that they provided of the piety of former ages and the illustration that they offered of the nation's history. The final rationale – that the engravings would preserve a memory of the buildings for future generations that would otherwise be lost – was an increasingly common sentiment in an age that was keenly aware of the rapidity of change; it contains within it the germ of the ethos of preservationism. The idea that the inevitable process of decay should be halted, or that buildings should be preserved at the expense of improvement, was at this time only rarely expressed by antiquaries, but the preservation of a memory or memorial was a different matter, and it was in this way that many descriptions and engravings of ruins were presented to the public. The letterpress accompanying the plates in the Bucks' volumes was laconic and hardly expansive, drawn from other antiquarian authorities including Stukeley, but the selling point of the *Views of the Ruins* was always the large copperplate engravings. Gentlemen of taste had been collecting prints of the ruins of Rome since the seventeenth century; by the 1720s, prints of ruined abbeys and castles in Britain were coming into fashion for the first time. It was the visual image and the partnership of image and text that combined to establish the cultural importance of the ruin beyond narrowly antiquarian circles.

Popular Antiquities and Picturesque Tourism

The fashionable taste for ruins was, meanwhile, becoming evident elsewhere: the first 'Gothic' ruins were being constructed for landscape gardens at Cirencester Park (1732) and Stowe (1734). The 'Gothic' – and artificial ruins were almost always Gothic – acquired heightened political salience in the early eighteenth century as the architectural expression of the ancient Gothic constitution and the symbol of political liberty, arguments that were underpinned by antiquarian research. At the same time the aesthetic properties of the Gothic began to be explored. Gothic, which had formerly carried connotations of gloom, heaviness, darkness and barbarism, was being redefined in more positive terms. By the 1740s the Gothic style was widely seen as airy, light, elegant or picturesque. 'I must not omit Riveaulx Abbey which is a more charming Ruin than Fountains, the stile of Building being of the lightest kind', wrote the future president of the Society of Antiquaries, Charles Lyttelton, to his nephew and fellow antiquary Jeremiah Milles in August 1749 (Lyttelton 1749: fol. 24v). Fashionable gentleman architects such as Sanderson Miller were creating a 'Gothick' style for their wealthy clients, while Horace Walpole's antiquarian tastes, driven by his sense of Gothic 'gloomth' rather than light, inspired him to transform a suburban villa in Twickenham into the 'castle of my Ancestors'.

A taste for visiting ruins, reading about them and purchasing illustrative engravings went hand in hand with the growth of domestic tourism and the burgeoning popularity of topographical literature.

After the religious and political upheavals of the seventeenth century, the political stability of the eighteenth encouraged the growth of trade and the improvement of agriculture. This rising prosperity encouraged investment in the transport infrastructure, which meant that travel grew swifter, safer and cheaper; at the same time a fall in the cost of paper and the rapid expansion of the print trade helped drive a growing market for books, including those describing ruins and antiquities. As William Stukeley had suggested, a knowledge of the history of one's locality or one's nation was evidence of patriotism and public spirit, and satisfied people's curiosity to discover more about the places in which they lived and which they visited. Thus antiquities – and books about antiquities and engravings of antiquities – exercised steadily increasing appeal.

The most important factor behind the popularisation of ruins, however, was the deepening influence on British taste of theories of the picturesque and the sublime. The picturesque was nothing without a ruin: William Gilpin, the medium through which many readers gained their appreciation of the picturesque, informed his public that 'among all the objects of art, the picturesque eye is perhaps most inquisitive after the elegant relics of ancient architecture; the ruined tower, the Gothic arch, the remains of castles, and abbeys' (Gilpin 1792: 46). Crumbling masonry, ivy-clad walls and broken arches were prized as a pleasing contrast to the regularity of Classicism, as an exercise in *chiaroscuro* (the contrast of light and shade), and for the imaginative associations they provoked. Alternatively, ruins might conjure up notions of the sublime described in language that was both personal and emotional: Gothic ruins inspired wonder and reverence; their gloom and obscurity heightened the sense of mystery. 'One must have taste to be sensible of the beauties of Grecian architecture', wrote Walpole; 'one only wants passions to feel Gothic' (Walpole 1765–71: vol. 1, 107–8). For the traveller of taste and feeling in search of heightened emotional impact, the sight of a ruined abbey such as Tintern was enough to initiate transports of delight: 'Heavens what a noble pile of Gothic Architecture is Tintern Abbey. I was in extase and speechless' wrote Edward Haistwell in a letter to Richard Gough (Haistwell 1765).

What we might call the aestheticisation of the ruin, therefore, was a powerful factor in the expansion of the market for antiquarian publications, as demonstrating one's appreciation of the picturesque became an increasingly important marker of taste and social status. Traditionally, antiquarian volumes had been aimed at the learned or the gentry elite of county society, but from the 1770s there was a swelling tide of volumes designed principally for a middling audience with an appetite for knowledge and entertainment. Antiquities were represented to these readers as instructive with regard to the nation's past, morally improving (by dint of encouraging reflection upon the deeds of men) and pleasing in the picturesque qualities of their engravings and the opportunities they offered to the imaginative faculty.

This was the rationale behind publications such as Francis Grose's *Antiquities of England and Wales* (1772–6). Grose undertook the project in order to rescue his precarious finances: unlike so many antiquarian publications, which relied on heavy subsidies from the pockets of the author or of patrons, these volumes were intended to turn in a profit. Grose's intentions were stated in the Preface: he did not pretend to inform the 'Veteran Antiquary', but had written with readers in mind who wished to acquire a general rather than a specialist knowledge of antiquities (Grose 1772–6). But although he presented the *Antiquities* to a non-specialist market, it was still one in which a familiarity with Latin and French was assumed. Published in parts, the volumes were relatively affordable (although still beyond the means of the majority of the population), costing one shilling and six pence for twenty-four pages plus three plates. This worked out as 6d a plate: half the price, or less, of any of the comparable publications available at the time – although few purchasers, it must be allowed, would have bought only a single plate (Farrant 1995). Moreover, *The Antiquities of England and*

Pevensey Castle. Drawing by Francis Grose, August 1782

Wales was also frequently found in the subscription libraries and book clubs that were springing up across the country.

The Antiquities of England and Wales was far more successful than most antiquarian publications, and it was republished in a second edition in 1783–7. Grose published follow-up surveys of *The Antiquities of Scotland* (1789–91), capitalising on the increasing popularity of the Scottish Highlands as a destination for domestic tourism, and *The Antiquities of Ireland* (1791–5), although he died before the latter could be completed. *The Antiquities of England and Wales* was also much imitated, even plagiarised, spawning a series of similar publications that illustrated the nation's ruins and antiquities for a growing middle-class readership. The editor of the *Historical Descriptions of New and Elegant Picturesque Views of the Antiquities of England and Wales* appealed to the innate 'Propensity to admire every Thing relative to the Antiquities of Ruins and Antient Buildings' that, he suggested, subsisted in every individual (Boswell 1786: i). Antiquities and ruins were not just for the elite, on whose land the ruined castles and monasteries stood: however rude a person's manners, they would still wish to be informed of a building's 'History and several Possessors, to hear with Avidity, if it has been the Scene of any memorable Transaction, and to learn every interesting Circumstance relative thereto' (Boswell 1786: i). Without such knowledge, the editor added, it would be impossible to cut a proper figure in the world. Special pleading, perhaps, but such confident assertions of the irrefutable value of antiquities and ruins were an essential foundation upon which more imaginative responses to ruins could be constructed. *The Antiquarian Repertory*, a periodical which appeared in the 1770s, was similarly targeted at those in the 'middling walk of life'. Here the editor suggested that the ruins of castles, described as the evidence of 'violent convulsions and sudden reverses, to which men of a more elevated rank are frequently subjected', were less likely to appeal to this class of readers, who would have been 'happily' removed from such events; religious ruins, by contrast, excited ideas of melancholy, piety and veneration which were 'equally applicable to all ranks and opinions' (Grose and Astle 1775: 244). Other editors were more sanguine regarding their readers' ability to take instruction from the contemplation of the 'ruins of ancient structures': the compilers of *England Displayed* reminded their readers of how such ruins were 'pregnant' with instruction regarding the invaluable blessings of civil and religious liberty they enjoyed in the present. It was the 'iron hand of tyranny, and the insatiable sword of religious bigotry' that had reduced the buildings to heaps of rubble 'and laid the splendour of their inhabitants in the dust' (Russell 1769: advertisement).

The growing taste for medievalism and the cult of chivalry in the later eighteenth century, however, conferred an additional, and far more romantic, layer of meaning upon the ruins of castles, one far more powerful than simply the memories of violent convulsions. Richard Hurd's *Letters on Chivalry and Romance* (1762) had insisted upon the poetic importance of the cult of chivalry and the 'old Romances' through which it had been celebrated, which in turn had inspired poets such as Edmund Spenser and John Milton. Feudal society provided the warlike context to deeds of knight errantry, and castles provided the settings for the jousts and tournaments through which chivalric honour was cultivated. Responding to such sentiments, the antiquary Thomas Burgess suggested in *An Essay on the Study of Antiquities* that ancient castles displayed the very genius of chivalry:

> Amid such a scene the manly exercises of knighthood recurr [sic] to the imagination in their full pomp and solemnity; while every patriot feeling beats at the remembrance of the generous virtues which were nursed in those schools of fortitude, honour, courtesy and wit, the mansions of our ancient nobility. (Burgess 1781: 16)

Burgess's comment reflects the fact that many who contemplated ruins in the later eighteenth century did so less in search of rational moral or political instruction than, in true picturesque style, as a spur to imaginative reverie. Burgess described the 'irrational impact', a 'natural and irresistible impulse' evoked in response to the individual's confrontation with what he called the 'hoary honours' of age. In such contemplation, the visitor might forget the refinements of modern life and feel themselves transported into the past and the 'romantic and poetical simplicity of former ages' (Burgess 1781: 4). Another antiquarian periodical, the *Topographer*, similarly highlighted the romantic potential inherent in the study of antiquities, conjuring up the 'exquisite pleasure' to be experienced in rescuing the memory of past days. The antiquary of true taste shared the 'melancholy delight' of poets in 'revivifying the features of the dead and the manners and arts of ages that are gone' (Shaw and Brydges 1790: i-ii).

These comments remind us that by the end of the eighteenth century the sense of a break with the past and the feelings of regret and nostalgia, originally triggered by the Dissolution of the Monasteries, had become much sharper. Ruins were a reminder of an earlier age – of 'olden time' – frequently imbued with qualities such as charity, harmony and piety that the modern age had lost. The medieval past demanded an act of empathetic imagination to understand, but it was a period that could be used both to affirm the values of the present (by illustrating the roots from which modern values had sprung) and to provide a telling contrast to the degeneracy and self-seeking futility of the modern age. For the antiquary and Gothicist John Carter, Neath Abbey in Glamorgan epitomised the challenge that modern commercial progress posed to the nation's Gothic fabric and the spiritual values of society. Within its ruins he found the copper-smelting furnaces of Sir Humphrey Mackworth, polluting the once-hallowed buildings with sacrilegious industry. 'How Horrid, how infernal, was all before me! Deep in the very centre of its sacred walls were set the furnaces wherein the poisonous ore becomes a prey to fusion' (Carter 1804: 430). This awareness of a rupture with the past was only heightened as news of the destruction consequent upon the French Revolution reached Great Britain during the 1790s, events which tended to reinforce the conservative values associated with the meaning of ruins and antiquities. Ruins in France were a modern creation, the product of radicalism, irreligion and constitutional breakdown. The ruins of Britain, by contrast, had been created by events long since past, historical occurrences which had laid the foundations for the stability and domestic peace currently enjoyed thanks to the political and religious settlement of 1688. Castles, asserted the picturesque theorist Uvedale Price, 'are the pride and boast of this island; we may well be proud of them, not merely in a picturesque point of view – we may glory that the abodes of tyranny and superstition are in ruin' (Price 1810: vol. 2, 264).

Recording and Preserving

Not all antiquaries, however, trod the primrose path of popularisation and romantic fancy. There were always the self-styled 'sour headed' antiquaries (Gough 1772), who preferred to maintain a rigidly 'scientific' and factual approach to their work, and whose publications found correspondingly less favour with the wider public. Their mission was to record, to analyse and to preserve, and in doing so, they laid the foundations of the modern preservation movement. They sought to trace the progress of architecture through accurate observation of the extant physical structures, and through this they developed a taxonomy of style that distinguished the different phases of architecture from 'debased Roman' or Saxon (our Romanesque and Norman) through to the early English, the decorated and the perpendicular. Terminology was not standardised until the nineteenth century, but long before Thomas Rickman's *An Attempt to Discriminate the Styles of English Architecture* (1817) codified the styles in an accessible format, antiquaries were looking at medieval buildings (including ruins) with a more discriminating eye. Key publications such as Thomas Warton's *Observations on the Fairy Queen of Spenser* (1762) or James Bentham's *History and Antiquities of the Conventual Church of Ely* (1771) concentrated on the evidence of ecclesiastical architecture. But castles, which were variously symbols of bygone feudal power and hospitality, scenes of knightly chivalry, reminders of domestic upheaval and instability, and imbued with Walpolian 'gloomth' following the rise of the Gothic novel, were also being studied more analytically. As Edward King demonstrated in a series of articles published in *Archaeologia*, and in his magnum opus *Munimenta antiqua* (1799), they were a mode of building that could be reduced to architectural types, categorised chronologically and analysed according to their defensive capacities. 'The Antiquary', he wrote, 'must undergo the laborious drudgery, of taking many accurate measures; [...] in order to form, as accurately as possible, exact plans, – instead of resting satisfied with mere picturesque views' (King 1799: vol. 1, vii). Close comparison of castellated remains and the careful study of issues such as floor plans, water supply and heating arrangements were of greater concern for King than their picturesque properties or romantic associations.

While these antiquarian books and articles were often regarded as dry and unappealing to the general reader, they provided the basis for more popular works such as Grose's *The Antiquities of England and Wales* or Thomas Hearne's *The Antiquities of Great Britain* (1786). Similarly, periodicals such as *The Gentleman's Magazine* or the shorter-lived *The Antiquarian Repertory* provided a steady stream of informative articles, which enabled autodidacts to teach themselves the principles of Gothic

Malmesbury Abbey. From Thomas Hearne, The Antiquities of Great Britain, Illustrated in Views of Monasteries, Castles and Churches, *London, 1786*

style. Francis Grose promised his readers that he would point out the principal characteristics of Gothic and Saxon architecture and explain technical terms and allusions, together with a history of castles, abbeys and other monastic foundations (Grose 1772–6: vol. 1, ii). This he did in the introduction, but thereafter further detail on architecture, rather than proprietors, was sketchy to say the least. *The Antiquities of Great Britain* followed a similar pattern of perfunctory comment with the occasional excursion into architectural analysis, so that of the ruins of Furness Abbey, for example, the prospective tourist was told (chiefly courtesy of Thomas Warton) that:

> The foundation of this religious house was laid whilst the Norman taste in building prevailed; and as it was carrying on (probably under the direction of different architects) the manner of its original design appears to have gradually deviated into that, which is distinguished by the appellation of Gothic. The progression from one style to the other is evident in this View, where the Door is in the former manner, whilst the large Window over it, with that at the south end of the Transept, and those of the Choir, approach towards the latter. (Hearne 1786: n.p.)

These sudden lurches in register – when a minimalist list of proprietors is suddenly followed by a detailed description or a didactic survey of historical style – were the consequence of the cut-and-paste methods of the antiquarian publishers. Rather than commissioning new work, they simply relied on piecing together snippets in the public domain or which were sent to them by correspondents. Such measures did, however, facilitate the dissemination of such information to a wider readership. Analysis of style informed appreciation of the skill in design and construction; it engendered a more discriminating awareness of buildings as the product of cumulative accretions rather than instant production; and it led the way to greater detail in description.

The education of the public in the principles of Gothic architecture was taken a stage further in the successful series edited by John Britton and Edward Brayley, *The Beauties of England and Wales* (1801–15), a county-by-county survey of the nation's antiquities. Britton, an autodidact enthusiast for the picturesque in general and antiquities in particular, went to some lengths to ensure that the letterpress was of a quality to match the engravings (for which many of the leading topographical artists and engravers of the day, including J. M. W. Turner, were engaged). More significantly, the introductory volume included a table of the different types of architecture displayed by the various parochial churches, cathedrals and monastic ruins across the country. This was the logical conclusion of the eighteenth-century urge to classify the natural and created world. Ruins were starting to be categorised according to their architectural style and date of construction: an approach that was the very antithesis of the romantic and imaginative response favoured by so many domestic tourists.

The question of how ruins should be preserved was, by the nineteenth century, one of increasing importance. Initially antiquaries had sought to 'preserve' ruins simply by recording details of their appearance and commissioning engravings; as early as the 1720s William Stukeley was inveighing against the ignorant destruction of the nation's built heritage. At Malmesbury he berated the local inhabitants who had pillaged the vaults of the monastic Great Hall to build 'a sorry house, contributing to the ruin of the sacred fabric, and to their own'. They did not, he claimed, 'discern the benefit accruing to the town from the great concourse of strangers purposely to see this abbey, which is now the greatest trade of it'. Not only did their actions show a wanton degree of disrespect for the venerable qualities of the ruin, but they betrayed a lamentable disregard for their own self-interest (Stukeley 1724: 145). Even by the 1720s, excursions to view the ruins of abbeys and castles had become sufficiently popular as to be a source of financial profit for those who lived in the vicinity.

Arguments for the preservation of ruins had to confront head-on the rights of landowners to do as they wished with their own property. Another of Stukeley's targets had been Sir Michael Bruce, 'the stone killer', who had pulled down the ruins of Arthur's O'on, a Roman structure in the Borders, in order to reuse the stones in a mill dam. Such penny-pinching destruction prompted Stukeley to suggest:

> in order to make his name execrable to all posterity, that he should have an iron collar put about his neck like a yoke. At each extremity a stone of Arthur's Oon to be suspended by the lewis in the hole of them. Thus accoutred let him wander on the banks of Styx,

perpetually agitated by angry daemons with ox goads, 'Sir Michael Bruce' wrote on his back in large letters of burning phosphorous. (Stukeley 1885: 242)

Stukeley published a print ridiculing the stone killer, but beyond a narrow circle of antiquarian friends, his outburst had no discernible impact on contemporary opinion.

Stukeley is important, however, for at least two reasons. First, he saw antiquities as part of a national heritage to be preserved in the national interest, claiming that their value as historical artefacts was more important than any potential monetary value that might be realised through their destruction. He had no patience with the argument that the property rights of the landowner on whose land such antiquities stood allowed them to do with them what they liked. Secondly, he exploited the medium of print to raise awareness of such antiquities and to argue the case for their preservation. Stukeley's mantle was taken up by antiquaries of the later eighteenth century, including Richard Gough, who shared Stukeley's concern at the neglect and despoliation of the nation's antiquities and who repeatedly made the case for the better preservation of the nation's ruins. To substantiate these criticisms, increasing recourse was made to the language of 'national antiquities' and public interest to counter the assumed right of proprietors to alter or damage monuments of 'national' importance. Landowners who, like the Duke of Beaufort, had taken pains to maintain a ruin such as Tintern Abbey in good condition were praised by the editors of *The Antiquarian Repertory* for their efforts to preserve this and other monuments 'which may be considered as national ornaments' (Grose and Astle 1775: 129). A convenient linguistic sleight of hand thus allowed a ruin like Tintern, held as private property, to be described as part of the national heritage, allowing in turn the proprietors – generally members of the ruling elite – to present themselves as the disinterested custodians of the nation's past.

As urban and agricultural improvement proceeded, however, so more and more ancient buildings and ruins fell into danger. John Carter, draughtsman to the Society of Antiquaries and close colleague of Richard Gough, pursued a journalistic campaign in *The Gentleman's Magazine* against 'architectural innovations' and the ignorant destruction of antiquities in the name of modernisation. The medieval walls encircling York, he claimed, were being deliberately neglected and despoiled in order that the Corporation might demolish them for private profit: they were 'absolute ruins; not that sort of ruin which Time with "stealing steps" brings on, but that sort of ruin caused by wanton and premeditated despoliation' (Carter 1806: 818). Even the appreciation of ruins fostered by the picturesque movement was a mixed blessing, and highlighted a growing gap between the picturesque or Romantic observer and the antiquary with a more scientific interest in observation and preservation. Aficionados of William Gilpin liked to see walls covered with ivy, in a suitably mouldering state of decay, with cattle grazing beneath. At Dartmouth Castle, John Swete, vicar, antiquary and amateur artist, noted how its outer walls were much dilapidated, 'a circumstance never regretted by the Painter, in whose eye the most Gorgeous Palace decorated with all the Orders of modern Architecture and kept in the highest preservation, possesseth not the tenth part of the attraction, as the ramified window, or the ruinated Arch of an Abbey' (Hunt 1984: 95). In 1826, Richard Warner, a clergyman with both antiquarian and picturesque pretensions, expressed his outrage that the draughtsman of the Society of Antiquaries had cut back the ivy from ruins at Glastonbury, destroying thereby much of their meditative potential: 'Nothing could be more *out of taste* than such a proceeding. To ruins of every description, and more especially to ecclesiastical ones, the accompaniment of *ivy* is essential' (Warner 1826: xliv).

The problem with ivy, however, was that it obscured the physical form of the building and its architectural detail: 'I approve of ivy when it hides deformities, not when it conceals beauties', remarked Sir Richard Colt Hoare at Llanthony Abbey (Thompson 1983: 98). More importantly, and as antiquaries were well aware, ivy, saplings and cattle were inimical to the long-term stability and security of the building. Unlike Gilpin, Swete and Warner, they were alarmed by suggestions that ruins might be rendered more picturesque if allowed to fall into a more complete state of disrepair. 'It is a pity', observed William Bray of the ruins of Kirstall Abbey, at that point being used as a cowshed, that:

> the noble owner (the Duke of *Montague*) should not pay so much regard to this structure, and the purposes for which it was originally designed, as to prevent this abuse of it. One sees, with veneration, these mouldering remains of the piety of our ancestors; and, if it

were only for the picturesque scenes which they exhibit in their present condition, one cannot but regret that they should want the little care which would preserve them very long from farther destruction. (Bray 1778: 137)

Antiquaries' concern at the neglect of ruins that were allowed to fall into ever greater disrepair while proprietors destroyed or plundered them led to early calls for intervention by the state and demands for legislation to protect the nation's heritage of ruins. In 1776 an anonymous pamphlet was presented to the Society of Antiquaries of London. Claiming to speak for the ruined abbeys of North Britain, it decried the decay and neglect into which the nation's ruins had been allowed to fall and demanded that the Society of Antiquaries take measures to bring a bill before Parliament:

> The
> GROANS
> Of the Abbays, Cathedrals, Palaces and other ancient buildings of
> North Britain.
> Illustrious Society, Can you tamely look on, and suffer our bodies
> To be basely torn, barbarously mangled, and layed [sic] in ruins by a
> selfish race of unfeeling Goths:
> Can you tamely look on, we say, and not punish these rude
> offenders?
> Many of us are entirely leveled! [sic]
> Some of us falling down with Gothic irons!
> Some of us tumbling down with old age!
> Pity our forlorn situation, and procure us necessary aid, by an Act of
> Parliament:
> Or Soon! Too soon alas! None of us will be left to Groan.
> (quoted in Evans 1956: 156)

Nothing was achieved in the eighteenth century, and Parliament certainly took no action. But by the 1820s and 1830s antiquaries were making more concerted efforts to secure legislative protection for 'ancient monuments', following the example of France where a General Inspector of Historical Monuments had been appointed in 1830 and the Commission des monuments historiques created in 1837 (Swenson 2013:

25–65). Moreover, by this point, antiquaries were no longer satisfied with simply leaving a ruin to romantic decay: they sought active steps for its preservation and even restoration. John Britton addressed a rallying cry to the readers of *The Gentleman's Magazine* in 1832, proposing an organisation to be known as the 'Guardian of Antiquities' which would have government sanction to prevent buildings from falling into ruin and to restore those that had. 'The zealous and high-minded antiquary', he claimed, was 'continually annoyed' by the 'entire extinction of many fine buildings and monuments' and the 'merciless and tasteless disfiguration of others'. He cited the example of Crosby Hall in Bishopsgate, a building of fifteenth-century origins boasting significant historical associations with leading merchants and nobility, William Shakespeare and Richard III, and which, having fallen into ruin, was preserved, restored and brought into functional use again by a successful preservation campaign (Britton 1832: 104).

Campaigns to rescue ruins such as Crosby Hall or the city walls of York betokened a new attitude to ruins: rather than being allowed to moulder into picturesque decay, active steps, it was argued, should be taken to preserve and even restore them, for however evocative a ruin might be, its ruinous state endangered the historic and evidential value that it represented. The question of how far to restore a ruinous building, and in what manner, started to be debated in the later eighteenth century, and is, of course, still a matter of contention today. Should a ruin simply be consolidated in its ruined state, or should it be restored to something approximating a status quo ante? There was no agreement even among the antiquarian world, as some favoured full-scale restoration while others, like John Carter, called simply for stabilisation of what had survived to the present. But the very fact that there was any kind of debate at all reflects the advances made in antiquaries' understanding of ruins: their architectural observations meant that it was possible accurately to date a building and to reconstruct what its original form might once have been, generating new knowledge in the process. Similarly, a ruin in the nineteenth century was analysed in its component parts and from a historicist perspective; thus later additions and modern restorations could be correctly identified – and found offensive. A modern addition or restoration was now anomalous in a way that had never been evident in earlier generations. The divergence between the picturesque antiquary such as Richard

Warner and the architectural antiquary such as Robert Willis, whose focus was upon the ruin as a 'complex spatial and structural system' (Buchanan 2013: 29), was growing increasingly wide. The ruin was no longer simply a memorial of earlier generations or a signifier of past events; it was an archaeological artefact in its own right.

In the 1830s and 1840s we find gathering momentum behind the study of the nation's antiquities and archaeology, evident in the establishment of bodies such as the British Archaeological Association and the Royal Archaeological Institute, as well as numerous provincial associations. Members of these societies, who tended increasingly to call themselves architects or archaeologists rather than simply antiquaries, continued to devote considerable energy to documenting the nation's ruinous buildings and to pass judgement upon those who did nothing to check the progress of dilapidation and decay. This emphasis upon the preservation of ruins as a national responsibility and a proper cause for public action differentiates the antiquaries of the nineteenth century from those of the eighteenth. Thomas Wright was one of the founder members of the British Archaeological Association and an antiquary who wrote for both a specialist and a popular audience. In the *Archaeological Album* (1845), he urged the public to combine together to purchase ruinous structures in London – such as Crosby Hall – that might be restored and put to good use for the benefit of the public. He continued with his theme, drawing attention to the fate of the ruins of Jewry Wall in Leicester, 'one of the most remarkable Roman monuments in our island'. The wall had become disfigured and damaged by the number of buildings that had been allowed to be erected against it and he called upon his readers to support the efforts of the local vicar to have them removed, arguing that 'it must be carried in mind that it is necessary not only to preserve national antiquities but to make them accessible to the eye of the public' (Wright 1845: 57). But the calls of Britton, Wright and their peers for a national society charged with preservation fell flat: although there were a number of other attempts to persuade Parliament to take action in the following decades, Parliamentary legislation for the protection of 'ruins' and ancient monuments more generally was not forthcoming until the Ancient Monuments Protection Act of 1882.

The rhetoric of the public good was accompanied by an increasingly democratic undertone in the proliferation of cheap literature aimed at the lower-middle and even working classes from the 1820s onwards, facilitated by the introduction of steam printing and steel press engraving (Anderson 1991). Thus the *Penny Magazine*, which retailed at 2d per issue, represented the ruinous Crosby Hall not as the private property of a single wealthy landowner, but as part of the 'public inheritance' of the population at large and as evidence of the 'diversified wealth with which we find the land we live in covered by the labours of the successive generations who have tenanted it before us' (1832: 385). At the same time, falling transport costs, especially after the advent of the railway, increased the market for railway guides and tourist literature that would provide the reading public with 'historical and topographical notices' of their destinations. Antiquaries contributed little directly to this genre, but the compilers of Measom's and Bradshaw's railway guides drew heavily on their publications, as did the authors of articles in the periodical press such as the 'Rambles from Railways' in the *Penny Magazine*. The lists of landowners and office-holders that had been the staple of antiquarian research were of little relevance to these readers: rather, ruins were presented as part of an overarching narrative of the nation's history, as evidence of the onward march of civilisation and the progress of liberal ideals. Instead of dewy-eyed nostalgia for a medieval Golden Age of monastic charity and feudal paternalism, such as that espoused in A. W. N. Pugin's *Contrasts* (1836), this literature tended towards a more robust celebration of Britain's commercial and manufacturing progress (Mandler 1997).

By 1850, antiquarianism as a pursuit and a mode of study was increasingly ceding place to the more specialised disciplines of archaeology, architectural history, art history and philology. The market for antiquarian publications had diversified considerably and ruins had been reinterpreted for an increasingly broad readership. The essential memorial function of ruins, however, had remained unchanged; while some observers were more enthused by picturesque decay and others by visions of knightly chivalry, the common ground was that ruins were a visible symbol of the events of the nation's history, a portal to the past, and a fundamental part of the identity of the British nation.

Further Reading

Myrone, Martin and Lucy Peltz (eds). 1999. *Producing the Past: Aspects of Antiquarian Culture and Practice, 1700-1850* (Aldershot: Ashgate).

Pearce, Susan (ed.). *Visions of Antiquity: The Society of Antiquaries of London, 1707-2007* (London: Society of Antiquaries of London).

Piggott, Stuart. 1976. *Ruins in a Landscape: Essays in Antiquarianism* (Edinburgh: Edinburgh University Press).

References

Addison, Joseph. 1726. *Dialogues Upon the Usefulness of Ancient Medals. Especially in Relation to the Latin and Greek Poets* (London).

Anderson, Patricia. 1991. *The Printed Image and the Transformation of Popular Culture, 1790-1860* (Oxford: Clarendon Press).

Aston, Margaret. 1973. 'English Ruins and English History: The Dissolution and the Sense of the Past', *Journal of the Warburg and Courtauld Institutes* 36: 231–55.

Bentham, James. 1771. *History and Antiquities of the Conventual Church of Ely*, 2 vols (Cambridge: Printed at the University Press by J. Bentham).

Boswell, Henry. 1786. *Historical Descriptions of New and Elegant Picturesque View* [*sic*] *of the Antiquities of England and Wales* (London: Alexander Hogg).

Bray, Sir William. 1778. *A Sketch of a Tour into Derbyshire and Yorkshire* (London: Printed for B. White).

Britton, John. 1832. 'Letter', *The Gentleman's Magazine* 102 (August): 104.

Britton, John and Edward Brayley (eds). 1801–15. *The Beauties of England and Wales*, 18 vols (London).

Buchanan, Alexandrina. 2013. *Robert Willis and the Foundation of Architectural History* (Woodbridge: Boydell & Brewer).

Buck, Samuel and Nathaniel Buck. 1737. *Proposals for Publishing by Subscription, Twenty-Four Perspective Views of the Present State of the Most Noted Abbies, Religious Foundations, Castles, and Other Remains of Antiquity, in Norfolk, Suffolk, and Essex* (London).

Burgess, Thomas. 1781. *An Essay on the Study of Antiquities* (Oxford).

Camden, William. 1610. *Britain; or, A Chorographicall Description of the most Flourishing Kingdomes, England, Scotland, and Ireland* (London: F. Kingston, R. Young and I. Legatt for George Latham).

Carter, John. 1804. 'The Pursuits of Architectural Innovation, no. LXXI', *The Gentleman's Magazine* (May): 429–31.

Carter, John [writing as Timothy Touch]. 1806. 'Walls and Gates of York', *The Gentleman's Magazine* 76, part 2 (September): 817–18.

Casaubon, Meric. 1638. *A Treatise of Use and Custome* (London: John Legat).

Colt Hoare, Sir Richard (ed.). 1806. *The Itinerary of Archbishop Baldwin through Wales, A.D. MCLXXXVIII by Giraldus de Barri*, 2 vols (London: Printed for William Miller by W. Bulmer).

Defoe, Daniel. 1971. *A Tour through the Whole Island of Great Britain*, edited by Pat Rogers (London: Penguin).

Dugdale, Sir William. 1656. *The Antiquities of Warwickshire Illustrated: From Records, Leiger-Books, Manuscripts, Charters, Evidences, Tombes, and Armes: Beautified with Maps, Prospects and Portraictures* (London: Printed by Thomas Warren).

Evans, Joan. 1956. *A History of the Society of Antiquaries* (Oxford: Oxford University Press).

Farmer, John. 1735. *The History of the Ancient Town, and Once Famous Abbey, of Waltham, in the County of Essex, from the Foundation to the Present Time* (London: Printed for the Author).

Farrant, John H. 1995. 'The Travels and Travails of Francis Grose FSA', *Antiquaries Journal* 75: 365–80.

Forsyth, Joseph. 1816. *Remarks on Antiquities, Arts and Letters, During an Excursion in Italy, in the Years 1802 and 1803*, 2nd edn (London: Printed for J. Murray).

Gilpin, William. 1792. *Three Essays: On Picturesque Beauty; On Picturesque Travel; and on Sketching Landscape: To Which is Added a Poem, on Landscape Painting* (London: Printed for R. Blamire).

Gough, Richard. 1772. British Library, BL Add. MS 29944, f. 324 (letter from Richard Gough to Foote Gower, 26 February 1772).

Gough, Richard. 1780. *British Topography*, 2 vols (London: Printed for T. Payne and Son, and J. Nichols).

Grose, Francis. 1772–6. *The Antiquities of England and Wales*, 4 vols (London: Printed for S. Hooper).

Grose, Francis. 1789–91. *The Antiquities of Scotland*, 2 vols (London: Printed for Hooper and Wigstead).

Grose, Francis. 1791–5. *The Antiquities of Ireland*, 2 vols (London: Printed for Hooper and Wigstead).

Grose, Francis and Thomas Astle. 1775. *The Antiquarian Repertory* (London).

Haistwell, Edward. 1765. Bodleian Library, Oxford University, MS Gen. Top. 41, f. 178 (letter to Richard Gough, 24 June 1765).

Hearne, Thomas. 1786. *The Antiquities of Great Britain* (London: Printed for J. Phillips and published by T. Hearne and W. Byrne).

Hunt, Peter (ed.). 1984. *Devon's Age of Elegance: Described by the Diaries of the Reverend John Swete, Lady Patterson and Miss Mary Cornish* (Exeter: Devon Books).

Hurd, Richard. 1762. *Letters on Chivalry and Romance* (Cambridge: Printed for A. Millar and W. Thurlboum and J. Woodyer).

King, Edward. 1799. *Munimenta antiqua: or Observations on Antient Castles, Including Remarks on the Whole Progress of Architecture in Great Britain*, 3 vols (London: Printed by W. Bulmer and Co. for G. Nicol).

Lyttelton, Charles. 1749. British Library, BL Add MS 3212 (letter to Jeremiah Milles, 12 August 1749).

Mandler, Peter. 1997. '"In the olden time": Romantic History and English National Identity', in *A Union of Multiple Identities: The British Isles, c. 1750–1850*, edited by Laurence Brockliss and David Eastwood (Manchester:

Manchester University Press), 78–92.

Penny Magazine. 1832. 'Crosby Hall' (December 1832).

Price, Uvedale. 1810. *Essays on the Picturesque, as Compared with the Sublime and the Beautiful*, 2 vols (London: Printed for J. Mawman).

Rawlinson, Richard. 1722. *History and Antiquities of Glastonbury* (Oxford: Printed at the Theatre).

Rickman, Thomas. 1817. *An Attempt to Discriminate the Styles of English Architecture* (London: Longman, Hurst, Rees, Orme and Brown).

Russell, Peter (ed.). 1769. *England Displayed: Being a New, Complete and Accurate Survey of the Kingdom of England and Principality of Wales. By A Society of Gentlemen* (London: Adlard and Browne).

Shaw, Stebbings and Sir Egerton Brydges (eds). 1790. *The Topographer: Containing a Variety of Original Articles, Illustrative of the Local History, and Antiquities of this Kingdom, Vol. II* (London: Printed for Robson and Clarke).

Slezer, John. 1718. *Theatrum Scotiae* (London: D. Browne, J. Senex et al.).

Stukeley, William. 1724. *Itinerarium curiosum: or, An Account of the Antiquitys [sic] and Remarkable Curiositys [sic] in Nature or Art, Observ'd in Travels Through Great Britain* (London: Printed for the Author).

Stukeley, William. 1770a. 'The sanctuary at Westminster', *Archaeologia* 1: 43–8.

Stukeley, William. 1770b. 'Account of Lesnes Abbey', *Archaeologia* 1: 49–53.

Stukeley, William. 1776. *Itinerarium curiosum: or, An Account of the Antiquities, and Remarkable Curiosities in Nature or Art, Observed in Travels Through Great Britain*, 2nd edn, 2 vols (London: Printed for Messrs Baker and Leigh).

Stukeley, William. 1885. 'The Family Memoirs of the Rev. William Stukeley, M.D. and the Antiquarian and Other Correspondence of William Stukeley, Roger & Samuel Gale, etc.', *Surtees Society* vol. 80.

Sweet, Rosemary. 2004. *Antiquaries: The Discovery of the Past in Eighteenth-Century Britain* (London: Hambledon and London).

Swenson, Astrid. 2013. *The Rise of Heritage: Preserving the Past in France, Germany and England, 1789-1914* (Cambridge: Cambridge University Press).

Thompson, M. W. (ed.). 1983. *The Journeys of Sir Richard Colt Hoare through Wales and England, 1793-1800* (Gloucestershire: A. Sutton).

Walpole, Horace. 1765-71. *Anecdotes of Painting in England*, 4 vols (London: Printed by Thomas Kirgate at Strawberry Hill).

Warner, Richard. 1826. *An History of the Abbey of Glaston; and of the Town of Glastonbury* (Bath: Printed by Richard Cruttwell).

Warton, Thomas. 1762. *Observations on the Fairy Queen of Spenser*, 2 vols (London: Printed for R. and J. Dodsley).

Willis, Browne. 1718-19. *An History of the Mitred Parliamentary Abbies, and Conventual Churches*, 2 vols (London: Printed by W. Bowyer for R. Gosling).

Wright, Thomas. 1845. *The Archaeological Album* (London: Chapman and Hall).

CROYLAND ABBEY

Rosemary Sweet

> O VENERABLE pile! whose shatter'd form
> From abject Croyland's melancholy site
> Looks proudly o'er this wide extended plain.
> Much of thy ancient grandeur and high name
> Old annals tell; much of fierce elfin shapes,
> And fiery forms, amid thy lonely fens
> Strange sojourners, who never dared invade
> Thy hallow'd precincts, but around them lurk'd
> To harm the holy pilgrim wandering nigh. (Herbert 1804: 58)

Croyland (or 'Crowland') Abbey, Lincolnshire, does not enjoy great fame today as a ruin. Originally founded in AD 716 by Ethelbald, King of Mercia, the abbey grew to enjoy considerable wealth and fame until the Dissolution of the Monasteries. During the Civil Wars, when

Croyland Abbey. From A New Display of the Beauties of England: Or, A Description of the Most Elegant or Magnificent Public Edifices, Royal Palaces, Noblemen's and Gentlemen's Seats, and Other Curiosities, Natural or Artificial [...], *1773-4*

it was used as a garrison by the King and besieged by Cromwell, it suffered serious damage and by 1700 much of the original complex had disappeared. All that remains today are the north aisle of the nave (used as a parish church), the west front and the tower. It has never been part of an established tourist itinerary, but in the eighteenth century it was far better known and assumed a particular significance for two of the century's leading antiquaries and campaigners for the better preservation of ruins: William Stukeley and Richard Gough.

Croyland attracted attention as much for the historical personages with whom it was associated as for its physical appearance, notably its abbot, Ingulphus, whose chronicle was highly valued as an authority for monastic history and the medieval past more generally. In his 'Dedicatory Epistle' to *Ivanhoe* (1820), Walter Scott, in the guise of the antiquary Laurence Templeton, invoked him as 'my honest and neglected friend' (Scott 1996: 21), and numerous historical novelists either drew on Ingulphus as a source, or, as in *Croyland Abbey*, a novel serialised in the *Ladies Magazine*, made the abbey the setting for their romance. Early accounts of Croyland, such as that by Browne Willis, relied heavily on Ingulphus: his description provided chapter and verse on charters and privileges and the abbey's wealth at the time of Dissolution, but said very little about the ruins that had survived, except to regret the passing of former ecclesiastic splendour. Browne Willis, inspired by high church sentiments of the beauty of holiness, saw the ruins 'miserably defaced for the lucre of lead' as symbols of past glories and noble piety (Willis 1718-19: vol. 1, 71-4); for others, Croyland was rather symbolic of the overweening wealth and worldliness of Benedictine monasticism that had given cause for the Reformation in the first instance. 'Where, CROWLAND, are thy domes, thy stately tow'rs? / The rust of time thy priestly pride devours' asked the 'Fen Parson' in a poem, written to inspire his fellow men to their religious duties: here the 'ancient grandeur' of Croyland was represented as chiefly redolent of the 'pampered Abbot' who had rioted on the fatness of the land (Fen Parson 1771: 12). In similar vein, the 'sins and subtleties' of the ecclesiastics at Croyland Abbey aroused the disgust of the hero of *Kilverstone Castle; or, the Heir Restored* (Anon. 1799: 23).

While the beauty of the ruined abbeys of Tintern or Rievaulx was inseparable from their location within the wider picturesque landscape, Croyland lay in the midst of the Lincolnshire fens, 'a horrid silence of bogs and thorns' as Stukeley put it, and even after the fen drainage of the seventeenth century it was hard of access (Stukeley 1776: vol. 1, 33). It was, however, not too far distant from the University of Cambridge, from whence Stukeley and Gough made the journey through the fens to view the ruins of Croyland and the extraordinary triangular bridge (the 'greatest curiosity in Britain or Europe' according to Gough) that stood nearby. In later life Stukeley recalled how 'When I was a youth, and began to have an inclination to the studies of Antiquity, I visited CROWLAND Abbey, and now once at least in the year, my affairs calling me that way, I visit it with as much pleasure as *Petrus Blesensis* formerly looked upon it' (quoted in Gough 1783: v). In *Itinerarium curiosum* (1776) he celebrated the 'majestic' ruin and berated the local population who plundered what remained of the 'holy shipwreck' for use in their own homes so that 'most of the houses in the town are become religious' (Stukeley 1776: vol. 1, 33). While he deplored the ruination of the building and the loss of the painted glass, his loudest lament was for the destruction of the tombs of 'illustrious persons' that had been dispersed 'to the irreparable damage of English history' (Stukeley 1776: vol. 1, 33).

Richard Gough, the most influential antiquary of the later eighteenth century, visited Croyland for the first time in 1756. He later recast it as a kind of antiquarian epiphany, when 'my career of antiquarian pursuits literally began' (Gough 1783: v). For Gough, Croyland was totemic as the monastery associated with Ingulphus, a text that was central to antiquarian research. But it also represented the site of his own antiquarian awakening and was a point of connection with his predecessor Stukeley, himself the most famous antiquary of the earlier part of the century. Both antiquaries sought out the testimony of living memory to record the changes that had taken place in their lifetimes, for Croyland was very much a ruin in the making: the roof had fallen in in 1720; the south wall was taken down in 1744 – when Stukeley helped himself to a wooden cherubim that had supported the roof (Stukeley 1880: 309); and the west front seemed in danger of imminent collapse throughout the period. Aware of this fragility, Gough sent the antiquarian draughtsman John Carter, who braved the fenland ague to make a series of drawings that were published in *Bibliotheca Topographica Britannica* along with a text that was rich in antiquarian research and architectural detail. Gough's description detailed the carving of the Norman arches, the tracery of the windows on the west front and the series of bas-relief carvings (Gough 1783: 80–94). Yet he did little to capture the *genius loci*, or prevailing spirit of the place. Gough was no romantic: his concern was to record and preserve. But Croyland's ravaged appearance and bleak isolation were captured in watercolours by Girtin and Cotman, and in a sonnet by John Clare. Clare visited the ruins in the 1820s, when he gazed upon 'the shattered pile / Of this old Abbey, struggling still with Time'. The sonnet is not Clare's finest, and he struggles to rise above the Gothic clichés of hooting owls and crumbling battlements, but in it we find echoes of Stukeley's holy shipwreck in the 'wrecks of ornamented stones' and the 'rank weeds, battening over human bones' (Clare 1835: 123).

References

Anon. 1799. *Kilverstone Castle; or, the Heir Restored: An English Gothic Story, Founded on a Fact which Happened on the Dawn of the Reformation* (London: Printed for Ann Lemoine).

Clare, John. 1835. *The Rural Muse: Poems by John Clare* (London: Whittaker and Co.).

Fen Parson. 1771. *The Inundation: Or, the Life of a Fen-Man, a Poem* (Lynn: Printed by W. Whittingham).

Gough, Richard. 1783. *Bibliotheca Topographica Britannica, Vol. VI: The History and Antiquities of Croyland-Abbey in the County of Lincoln* (London: Printed by and for J. Nichols).

Herbert, William. 1804. *Miscellaneous Poetry*, vol. I (London: Printed for T. Reynolds by I. Gold).

Scott, Walter. 1996. *Ivanhoe*, edited by Ian Duncan (Oxford: Oxford University Press).

Stukeley, William. 1776. *Itinerarium curiosum: or, An Account of the Antiquities, and Remarkable Curiosities in Nature or Art, Observed in Travels Through Great Britain*, 2nd edn, 2 vols (London: Printed for Messrs Baker and Leigh).

Stukeley, William. 1880. 'The Family Memoirs of the Rev. William Stukeley, M.D. and the Antiquarian and Other Correspondence of William Stukeley, Roger & Samuel Gale, etc.', *Surtees Society*, vol. 73.

Willis, Browne. 1718-19. *An History of the Mitred Parliamentary Abbies, and Conventual Churches*, 2 vols (London: Printed by W. Bowyer for R. Gosling).

RUINS IN FOCUS

The Antiquities at Stonehenge

Kelsey Jackson Williams

> O come, and wrapt o'er fleeting time, disclose
> How, and from whom, th' unperished dome arose.
> Place the rough heroes round their lasting fane,
> Whose date the antique sage hath sought in vain;
> Which braves the wreck of time and swift decay,
> That sweeps the labour'd domes of man away. (Anon. 1792: 2–3)

The ruins at Stonehenge, Wiltshire, have piqued the curiosity of Britons ever since, and no doubt long before, the twelfth-century historian Geoffrey of Monmouth attributed their construction to African giants under the foremanship of no less a figure than Merlin. William Camden included a brief description of the site in his landmark *Britannia* (1586), a survey of antiquities across the British Isles, and the Elizabethan poet Samuel Daniel ruminated in his poem 'Musophilus' (1599) on 'the

Stonehenge. From William Stukeley, Stonehenge: A Temple Restor'd to the British Druids, *1740 (plate xviii)*

misery of dark forgetfulness' as he gazed on 'that huge dumb heap, that cannot tell us how, / nor what, nor whence it is' (Daniel 1599: n.p.). By the seventeenth century this trickle of observations had become a flood, as scholars and architects waded into a decades-long argument over the megaliths' origins. Were they Roman? Danish? Saxon? Something else? It was not until 1666 that the antiquary John Aubrey proposed a new solution, one which was to have a tenacious afterlife: Stonehenge and circles like it were temples of the ancient Druids.

One avid reader of Aubrey's theories was William Stukeley. Stukeley was fascinated, almost obsessed, with Stonehenge and the nearby circle at Avebury, measuring, sketching and pondering over them for decades. His studies came to fruition in a lavish folio volume, *Stonehenge: A Temple Restor'd to the British Druids* (1740). In it he developed Aubrey's theory, arguing not only that Stonehenge was a Druidic temple, but that the Druids themselves were the remnants of an ancient prehistoric religion common to all humanity. He was also the first scholar to identify the astronomical alignment of the stones and, with his friend Edmond Halley, he attempted to date Stonehenge on the assumption that it had originally been aligned with magnetic north. The date he arrived at was 460 BC, but Halley, at least, believed that this was far too recent and had, according to one contemporary, 'a strange, odd notion that Stonehenge is as old, at least almost as old, as Noah's Floud' (Hearne 1906–21: vol. 7, 350).

Stukeley was mocked for his fanciful ideas of a global ancient religion, but the twin shibboleths of Druids and astronomy became essential tenets of megalithic interpretation in the generations that followed. John Wood, the architect of Bath, designed the famous Circus there based on his measurements of Stonehenge, and in his *Choir-Gaure, Vulgarly Called Stonehenge* (1747) elaborated Stukeley's ideas by attributing the stones' erection to Prince Bladud, the legendary founder of Bath itself. In 1771 John Smith, a physician, published his own *Choir Gaur; the Grand Orrery of the Ancient Druids, Commonly Called Stonehenge*, a study that, as its subtitle claimed, 'Astronomically explained, and Mathematically proved' the site to be an ancient observatory. Meanwhile, the handful of learned visitors from previous generations had become a horde of tourists, with one local man setting up shop within the circle itself and renting out measuring equipment for the satisfaction of visitors. Topographical poets of the period tirelessly speculated on its mysteries, while William Wordsworth would figure Stonehenge as an unfathomable site of human sacrifice in the series of poems that would eventually be published as *Guilt and Sorrow; or Incidents Upon Salisbury Plain* in 1842. By the end of the eighteenth century Stonehenge was already a locus for scholarly speculation, a fertile source for alternative histories, a tourist attraction, and an architectural wonder – just as it is today.

References

Anon. 1792. *Stone Henge: A Poem, Inscribed to Edward Jerningham, Esq.* (Norwich: Printed by J. Crouse and W. Stevenson for J. Robson).

Daniel, Samuel. 1599. *The Poeticall Essayes of Sam. Danyel. Newly Corrected and Augmented* (London: Printed for P. Short for Simon Waterson).

Hearne, Thomas. 1906–21. *Remarks and Collections of Thomas Hearne*, edited by Charles Edward Doble, 11 vols (Oxford: Clarendon Press).

Glastonbury Abbey

Nick Groom

> Where is the Abbey's each once-stately Tow'r?
> > Oh! how defac'd the venerable Pile!
> Disfigur'd how! by Eld's all-conquering Pow'r!
> > The glory long of Avalonia's Isle! (Andrews 1793: 60)

Glastonbury Abbey, Somerset, was reputed to be the first Christian foundation in England, established by the missionary Joseph of Arimathea, and a mystical tradition developed in the nineteenth century that claimed that Jesus Himself had walked there. Notwithstanding this, however, the abbey had been sacked by the Danes in the ninth century and, as the most splendid of the English abbeys, was dissolved by Henry VIII in the sixteenth century (the last Abbot of Glastonbury, Richard Whiting, was notoriously hanged at Glastonbury Tor).

Glastonbury Abbey. From A New Display of the Beauties of England: Or, A Description of the Most Elegant or Magnificent Public Edifices, Royal Palaces, Noblemen's and Gentlemen's Seats, and Other Curiosities, Natural or Artificial *[...]*, 1773-4

A summary of this history is given by Joseph Cottle in *Alfred, An Epic Poem, in Twenty-Four Books* (1800). Between these ruinous calamities, Glastonbury had also been celebrated as the final resting-place of King Arthur and his Queen Guinevere, whose tombs were 'discovered' at the end of the twelfth century (Rawlinson 1722: 46). The account given by the topographer Richard Rawlinson in his 1722 *History and Antiquities of Glastonbury* recorded that, following the Battle of Camblanus (or Camlann) in AD 542, the mortally wounded Arthur had been taken to the Abbey of Avalon, or Glastonbury, for burial. The truth of Glastonbury for the nation, therefore, lay beneath its remains. Rawlinson prefaced his *History* with the comment, 'I Intitle this Treatise, *A little Monument*, because the History of the Abbey is, in a manner, buried in it's Ruines' (Rawlinson 1722: cxcix). Glastonbury was synonymous with ruin.

Glastonbury's Arthurian relics were also memorialised in poetry and song. Not only does Rawlinson's account of Arthur emphasise his literary legacy for the Saxons (typically characterised as 'extravagant Fictions mingled with real Truths' – what at the time was known as the 'Gothic' style) but the very discovery of his tomb was brought about through bardic memory (Rawlinson 1722: 145–60, 154–8). While travelling through Wales, Henry II had learned the location of Arthur's burial-place from a ballad sung to him in Pembroke. On his return he set to work to excavate the abbey. Arthur's bones were 'discovered' – gigantic and entombed in a tree trunk – while Guinevere's body beside him was perfectly preserved and her golden hair still dressed in plaits; such details would, Rawlinson (writing over 500 years later) hoped, 'be sufficient to convince my Reader, that there was such a Person as King Arthur' (Rawlinson 1722: 160). The details were collected by a number of antiquaries, including John Leland, John Stow and John Speed.

It was inevitable that this material would be taken up by later eighteenth- and nineteenth-century writers in forging their own 'Matter of Britain'. Monarchical legitimacy and the wiles of dynasties (such as the rumours of the Stuart 'warming-pan' baby) obsessed eighteenth-century politics and literature (particularly so in Gothic novels), and Arthur's legitimacy was itself in doubt: he was the illegitimate son of Igerna (or Ygraine), the wife of the Duke of Cornwall, and Uther Pendragon. Through the sorcery of Merlin, Pendragon had come to Igerna in the guise of her husband, whereupon she conceived his child, Arthur.

In addition to this weighty mytho-politico significance, Glastonbury Abbey was also a fashionable health resort. 'A Physician', for example, published two editions of a treatise in 1751, combining legendary history with a lengthy disquisition on the efficacy of Glastonbury mineral water as a chic medical cure-all ('A Physician' 1751: 49–81). The treatise is a delicate balance of superstition and science, and the Physician's chemical analysis of the Chalice Well and other spring waters includes the pointed comment that 'so important a Subject as the *Health* of Mankind, highly deserves the serious Attention of our *Literati*, that *Gothic Ignorance* may no more prevail among us' ('A Physician' 1751: 52).

Both the dead – Arthur and Guinevere – and the living – the waters and well-being of life – accordingly formed the subterranean imaginative topography of Glastonbury Abbey. This is what inspired the Poet Laureate Thomas Warton's poem 'The Grave of King Arthur' (1777). Warton's preface to the poem notes that the twelfth-century excavation of the grave was literally 'the ground-work of the following Ode' (Warton 1777: 62). He describes the death and secret interment of Arthur:

> And deep intomb'd in holy ground,
> Before the altar's solemn bound.
> Around no dusky banners wave,
> No mouldering trophies mark the grave—

before recreating Henry II's rediscovery of the underground sepulchre:

> There shalt thou find the monarch laid,
> All in warrior-weeds array'd;
> Wearing in death his helmet-crown,
> And weapons huge of old renown.

It is thus King Henry, a remote historical figure himself, who first attempts to reanimate the heroic age in an act of national commemoration:

> To poise the monarch's massy blade,
> Of magic-temper'd metal made;
> And drag to day the dinted shield
> That felt the storm of Camlan's field.
> (Warton 1777: 72)

In writing of bygone memories of legendary tombs discovered below antique English ruins, Warton makes the fragments of Glastonbury Abbey a means of reflecting, and a way of reflecting upon, the deep political past, like the mirrors of succession that haunt Macbeth to the last syllable of recorded time.

References

'A Physician'. 1751. *A Compleat and Authentick History of the Town and Abbey of Glastonbury*, 2nd edn (London: Printed for R. Goadby).

Andrews, William. 1793. 'Glastonbury Abbey: An Elegy', in *The First Volume of the Poetical Works of William Andrews* (Southampton: Printed for the Author by A. Cunningham), 45–66.

Rawlinson, Richard. 1722. *The History and Antiquities of Glastonbury* (Oxford).

Warton, Thomas. 1777. *Poems: A New Edition* (London: Printed for T. Becket).

Chapter 2:
The Aesthetics of Ruin

Dale Townshend

More than ever before or since, ruins in eighteenth- and early nineteenth-century Britain were charged with the extraordinary ability to induce in those who viewed them vivid trains of imaginative reverie and reflection. Even as learned antiquaries of the period approached the nation's ruins through the quasi-scientific methodologies of measurement, illustration and historical description, so architectural aestheticians, theorists of the picturesque, writers on landscape gardening and countless topographical poets, novelists and essayists celebrated the same structures for their aesthetic potential, often jettisoning what was taken to be the 'dryness' of the antiquarian method in favour of a richer and more imaginative approach. In an important essay on ruins that he published in 1793, the English physician and writer John Aikin sought rationally to determine the grounds for 'the extraordinary passion for ruins of every kind which at present prevails', a 'predominant fashion' in contemporary taste, he claimed, that 'goes beyond all bounds of sober judgment' (Aikin 1793: 262). According to Aikin's 'anatomy', the passion for ruins resides in three principles: first, the visual or picturesque qualities that are intrinsic to ruins themselves; secondly, their ability to call forth in the perceiver imaginative, sentimental or associative responses; and thirdly, their status as objects of scholarly or antiquarian interest. It is this last aspect of ruin-appreciation that the sceptical Aikin finds the least convincing, for the antiquarian interest in ruins, he argues, is based on the questionable assumption that 'what would be of no sort of consequence if modern, acquires importance merely from its antiquity' (Aikin 1793: 270). Having retrieved an obscure architectural relic, Aikin satirically continues, the antiquary 'felicitates himself as the discoverer of a fact of high moment, and passes, among his brethren, as a most able and ingenious elucidator of the early history of Britain' (Aikin 1793: 272). Aikin refuses to discuss the antiquarian interest in ruins in any detail, and the bulk of his essay is given over to an exploration of the first two elements, the primary components of the eighteenth-century interest in ruins that I wish to explore further in this chapter. Central to the eighteenth-century aestheticisation of ruin was the discourse of architectural association, a strain of empiricist philosophy that celebrated the power of architecture to form ideas and ignite 'chains of associations' in the mind of the perceiver. While associationism constituted the philosophical basis of much ruin aesthetics in the period, it was in theories of landscape gardening, and the prominence that these accorded to both real and sham ruins in a landscape, that this aesthetic received its most practical application. In turn, theories of the sublime and the picturesque advanced by some of the century's most prominent essayists and thinkers adopted associationism as their point of departure, though frequently qualifying this underlying aesthetic with a number of careful modifications. Together, architectural associationism, landscape-gardening theory and accounts of the picturesque, the sublime and the beautiful combined in the work of topographical literature, the poetry and fiction of actual place and space that characteristically adopted the ruined piles to be seen across the British landscape as their primary point of inspiration. What resulted, this chapter demonstrates, was an extraordinarily consistent aesthetic discourse on ruin in Britain in the period 1700–1850, an established language, diction or set of literary conventions that writers would variously draw upon, perpetuate or modify in their task of 'writing' and responding to the nation's ruined abbeys and monasteries, forts and castles.

The Associationist Paradigm

It was the seventeenth-century philosopher John Locke who, in the fourth edition of *An Essay Concerning Humane* [sic] *Understanding* (1700; original edition 1690), coined the phrase 'the association of ideas' in his attempt at accounting for the links and connections formed between an object in the external world, the human perception of it and the ideas that it generated within the perceiving consciousness (Locke 1700: 221). As Locke's argument goes, there remains no necessary, innate or natural connection between an object and the mental ideas that it conjures up; rather, the link between them is often 'unnatural' insofar as it is learned, acquired or set in place through experience across time. The example to which he makes recourse is particularly telling, and one that would be crucial to aesthetic accounts of the imaginative potential of architectural ruins throughout the eighteenth century. Though there is no natural or obvious connection between the dark and a young child's fear-inducing 'Ideas of Goblines and Sprights [sic]', Locke argues, the associations between them, once set in place by the terrifying tales of a 'foolish Maid', are likely to endure well into adult life, the individual in all likelihood never 'able to separate them again so long as he lives' (Locke 1700: 223). As this suggests, Locke adopts a position of scepticism towards the association of ideas throughout the *Essay*, for while he countenances certain 'natural' links between objects and the ideas that they inspire as the sign of a healthy and functional faculty of reason, he consistently dismisses such learned or acquired associations as a child's irrational fear of the dark as 'madness' or 'wanton Phancies' (Locke 1700: 223).

Though he was neither a philosopher nor a theorist of architecture, it was the English politician and man of letters Joseph Addison who voiced an early and influential critique of Locke's theory of association, and one that served to relocate Locke's views firmly within the contemporary theory and practice of architecture. Commencing in the summer of 1712, Addison published eleven essays on 'The Pleasures of the Imagination' in *The Spectator*, the short-lived daily journal that he and Richard Steele established, and which ran between March 1711 and December 1712. In the celebrated essay No. 110 of Friday 6 July 1711, Addison described a night-time visit to a ruined and overgrown Gothic abbey in the vicinity of the house of his fictional friend, Sir Roger de Coverley, in the county of Worcestershire. Though warned by Sir Roger's servants of all manner of strange and supernatural occurrences at the abbey, Addison is initially undaunted, and, daring to visit the ruin, he provides in the essay a vivid description of the sensory impressions that he experiences within it:

> The Ruins of the Abby are scattered up and down on every Side, and half covered with Ivy and Elder-Bushes, the Harbours of several solitary Birds which seldom make their Appearance till the Dusk of Evening. The Place was formerly a Church-yard, and has still several Marks in it of Graves and Burying-Places. There is such an Eccho among the old Ruins and Vaults, that if you stamp but a little louder than ordinary, you hear the Sound repeated. At the same time the Walk of Elms, with the Croaking of the Ravens which from time to time are heard from the Tops of them, looks exceedingly solemn and venerable. (Morley 1888: 168)

No sooner has Addison described the ruin's effects upon his powers of perception, though, than he proceeds to outline the ideas or mental associations that these perceptions put in place: 'These Objects naturally raise Seriousness and Attention; and when Night heightens the Awfulness of the Place, and pours out her supernumerary Horrors upon every thing in it, I do not at all wonder that weak Minds fill it with Spectres and Apparitions' (Morley 1888: 168). If this seems like a bold riposte to Locke's dismissal of thoughts of ghosts and spirits as the stuff of childish and irrational fancy, Addison's subsequent musings on Locke's account of associationism make his critical intentions clearer: 'I think a Person who is thus terrify'd with the Imagination of Ghosts and Spectres', he argues, 'much more reasonable than the one who, contrary to the Reports of all Historians sacred and prophane, ancient and modern, and to the Traditions of all Nations, thinks the Apearance of Spirits fabulous and groundless' (Morley 1888: 169). Challenging Locke's scepticism, Addison thus places associationist aesthetics at the heart of the experience of ruined Gothic architectural space: arguing that he himself 'could not but fancy it one of the most proper Scenes in the World for a Ghost to appear' (Morley 1888: 168), his essay charges the ruin with the legitimate power and potential to provoke in the perceiver imaginative reveries that, with hindsight, seem indistinguishable from the conventions of later Gothic romance.

This is not to suggest that Addison was a champion of the native Gothic architectural style, and a number of his other publications, including the influential travelogue *Remarks on Several Parts of Italy* (1705), demonstrate an almost routine privileging of European Classicism over British Gothic architecture. Both his Classical predilections and his awareness of the ability of architectural form to conjure up imaginative trains become particularly clear in the essay on the imaginative pleasures of architecture that he published in *The Spectator* on 26 June 1712. Architecture built on a grand scale, he here claims, is capable of opening 'the Mind to vast Conceptions, and fit it to converse with the Divinity of the Place. For every thing that is Majestick imprints an Awfulness and Reverence on the Mind of the Beholder, and strikes in with the Natural Greatness of the Soul' (Morley 1888: 599). This nascent sense of the sublimity of architectural form, its ability to open up the mind of the beholder to 'vast Conceptions', is best illustrated for Addison by Classical structures: unlike the entrance to the Pantheon in Rome, which 'fills' the imagination 'with something Great and Amazing', the inside of a 'Gothick Cathedral, tho' it be five times larger than the other', leaves the viewer relatively unmoved (Morley 1888: 599).

Intended largely as a celebration of European Classicism though they were, Addison's essays on 'The Pleasure of the Imagination' nonetheless played an important role in the development of the aesthetics of architectural associationism in eighteenth-century Britain. As John Archer has argued, however, their effects were slow to become established, since the early-eighteenth-century vogue for Palladianism required that imaginative responses to architectural form be suitably moderated, controlled and chastened (Archer 1983). In *An Essay on the Nature and Conduct of the Passions and Affections* (1728), Francis Hutcheson reiterated the Lockean position by maintaining an equally critical attitude towards the principles of associationist thought. By contrast, David Hume's claim in *A Treatise of Human Nature* (1739) that all human knowledge depended upon the principles of association did much to encourage their application to architectural theory and practice; Hume's influence can be traced in such subsequent publications as Mark Akenside's *The Pleasures of Imagination* (1744) and John Baillie's *Essay on the Sublime* (1747). With David Hartley's *Observations on Man, his Frame, his Duty, and his Expectations* (1749), association became the fundamental principle governing the human appreciation of beauty. Even so, the dominance of Locke proved difficult to resist, and even as he countenanced a limited amount of associationism in *A Philosophical Enquiry into the Origin of Our Ideas of the Sublime and Beautiful* (1757), Edmund Burke echoed Locke in rejecting the associationist paradigm on the basis of what he took to be its tendency to detract from an object's innately sublime or beautiful qualities.

It was only with the publication of Alexander Gerard's *An Essay on Taste* and William Chambers's *A Treatise on Civil Architecture* in 1759, then, that British associationist architectural aesthetics officially came into their own. But here, too, their applicability to the aesthetics of Gothic ruin was compromised by at least three factors. First, Gerard and Chambers, at least in their studies of architectural associationism, were resolutely Classicist, and in both theorists, the Gothic is consistently relegated to the category of bad, uneducated and somewhat immature taste. Secondly, the forms of associative response to architectural space for which both theorists attempt to account was circumscribed by a prevailing emphasis on order and decorum: the 'wildest flights of ungoverned fancy', Gerard claims, 'are admired by the vulgar', while good taste resides in that which is rational (Gerard 1759: 116–17). Thirdly, and perhaps most significantly, none of these theorists of architectural association, their sights set firmly on lofty Classical structures, had much to say about architectural ruin. Instead, it is to the theory and practice of landscape gardening in the eighteenth century that we must look for accounts of the power of ruined Gothic architecture to inspire associative chains and reveries in the minds of those who perceived it.

Ruins in a Landscaped Garden

Stephen Switzer was one of the first English landscape gardeners to promote the ornamental use of architectural ruin as a means of provoking and courting the viewer's imaginative associations. In *The Nobleman, Gentleman, and Gardener's Recreation* (1715), the product largely of the work that he had undertaken on the gardens at Castle Howard, Grimsthorpe and Blenheim, Switzer argued in favour of introducing a ruin into a landscape, for 'to Noble and Ingenuous Natures', he claimed, 'a Piece of Ruin is more entertaining than the most beautiful Edifice; and the sorrowful Reflections they draw from the Soul ascend the very Heav'ns' (Switzer 1715: 149). Outlining the precise thoughts and associations that such a sight might engender, Switzer gives voice to a sentiment that would lie at the heart of the aesthetics of ruin throughout the eighteenth and early nineteenth centuries:

King Alfred's Hall, a ruinous folly erected in the grounds of Lord Bathurst's estate at Cirencester

> There may be read the Instability of all sublunary Affairs, and will remind us of the Frailty of these our Earthly Tabernacles; for if those magnificent Piles, compos'd of the hardest and most durable Materials of Wood and Stone, are subject to such Casualties; how much easier is it for Providence to destroy this tottering Frame of Nature, compos'd only of Flesh and Blood. (Switzer 1715: 149–50)

Ruins, in other words, were deemed capable of fulfilling the melancholy functions of the memento mori: their stones marked by the implacable passage of time, they stood as potent reminders that the human perceiver, too, eventually must die. Drawing strongly on the associative paradigm, Thomas Whately made a similar point in *Observations on Modern Gardening* (1770):

> At the sight of a ruin, reflections on the change, the decay and the desolation before us, naturally occur; and they introduce a long succession of others, all tinctured with that melancholy which these have inspired: or if the monument revive the memory of former times, we do not stop at the simple fact which it records, but recollect many more coeval circumstances, which we see, not

perhaps as they were, but as they are come down to us, venerable with age, and magnified by fame. (Whately 1770: 155)

Capable of inducing in the perceiver thoughts on such subjects as mutability, the passage of time, and the transience of human existence, the ruins within the landscaped gardens of eighteenth-century Britain were charged with certain moral functions.

Another function of ruin in the eighteenth century was to court patriotic, sentimental associations with Britain's ancient national past. The landscaping principles that Switzer outlined in *The Nobleman, Gentleman, and Gardener's Recreation* would be put to important use in the gardens of Lord Bathurst's estate at Cirencester, Gloucester, where Bathurst erected the ruinous folly, King Alfred's Hall, so as to evoke rich imaginative associations with English history. When the poet Edward Stephens addressed Bathurst's Cirencester estate in *A Poem on the Park and Woods of the Right Honourable Allen Lord Bathurst* (1748), he described the Gothic folly as an oxymoronic coupling of modernity and antiquity, completion and ruin:

> A lowly Pile, with antient Order grac'd,
> Stands, half repair'd, and half by Time defac'd;
> Imbrown'd with Age, the crusted, mould'ring Wall
> Threats the Beholders with a sudden Fall;
> There fix'd aloft (as whilom us'd) we trace
> Imperfect Semblance of the savage Race.
> This Pile the Marks of rolling Cen'tries wears,
> Sunk to Decay—, and built scarce twenty Years. (Stephens 1748: 8-9)

As David Stewart has pointed out, such constructions were often ideologically charged. The Gothic follies that Sanderson Miller erected at his own estate, Radway Grange, Edgehill, Warwickshire (1767); at Hagley Hall, Worcestershire, for George Lyttelton (1749); and at Wimpole, Cambridgeshire, for Lord Harwicke (1753), were all Whiggish celebrations of the Hanoverian defeat of the Young Pretender and the Jacobite uprising of 1745 (Stewart 1996). Even so, the taste for fake ruins did not escape the attention of contemporary satirists: as Mr Sterling humorously comments in David Garrick and George Colman the Elder's popular comedy *The Clandestine Marriage* (1766), 'It has

'A View in Hagley Park, belonging to Sr. Thos Lyttleton bart, to whom this plate is inscrib'd by his most obed.t Servt T. Smith'. T. Smith Pin, F.Vivares Sculp, 1749

just cost me a hundred and fifty pounds to put my ruins in thorough repair' (Colman and Garrick 1766: 24).

The man-of-letters-turned-landscape-gardener William Shenstone argued ardently in favour of the imaginative power of Gothic ruins in his 'Unconnected Thoughts on Gardening', a brief but influential tract that was published posthumously in *The Works in Verse and Prose, of William Shenstone, Esq* in 1764. Shenstone's theory of 'picturesque gardening', a landscape that, in his words, 'should contain variety enough to form a picture upon canvas', makes considerable use of architectural ruin: though neither necessarily novel, majestic nor beautiful, ruins 'afford that pleasing melancholy which proceeds from a reflexion on decayed magnificence', a sentiment similar to that described by Switzer above (Shenstone 1764: vol. 2, 126). 'Ruinated structures', Shenstone continued, derive their power from their irregularity and the 'latitude they afford the imagination', the creative faculties of the perceiver often seeking to imagine the ruins in their original state, or pondering on any events and circumstances that might have led to their current condition (Shenstone 1764: vol. 2, 131). The precise layout of the ground, though, should determine the nature and style of the ruin selected, for while high hills and sudden descents are 'most suitable to castles', fertile valleys in proximity to woods and water are 'the most imitative of the usual situation for abbeys and religious houses' (Shenstone 1764: vol. 2, 132). Here, Shenstone was reiterating the advice on the rational placement of Classical sham ruins in a landscape that Alexander Pope had offered to Richard Boyle in *An Epistle to the Right Honorable Richard Earl of Burlington* (1731), a poem better known as the essay 'Of Taste' or 'Of the Use of Riches':

> To build, to plant, whatever you intend,
> To rear the Column, or the Arch to bend,
> To swell the Terras, or to sink the Grot;
> In all, let *Nature* never be forgot.
> Consult the *Genius* of the Place in all,
> That tells the Waters or to rise, or fall,
> Or helps th' ambitious Hill the Heav'ns to scale,
> Or scoops in circling Theatres the Vale,
> Calls in the Country, catches opening Glades,
> Joins willing Woods, and varies Shades from Shades,
> Now breaks, or now directs, th'intending Lines;
> *Paints*, as you plan, and as you work, *Designs*. (Pope 1731: 7)

View of The Leasowes and Priory. H. F. James Del; engraved by I. C. Stadler, 1795 or later

For Pope, the placement of ruins in a landscape ought to accord with the rules of nature, reason and the presiding spirit or *genius loci* of the place. It was seemingly this advice, together with his sense of a ruin's imaginative lure, that informed Shenstone's own use of ruined Gothic follies in the landscaping of his Worcestershire estate, The Leasowes, from 1744 onwards.

Like most aspects of architectural theory and practice in this period, the aesthetics of ruin in the eighteenth century were structured around a firm distinction between the Classical and the Gothic styles. From Addison onwards, in fact, architects and architectural enthusiasts debated which of these two architectural traditions was the most imaginatively rich. Henry Home, Lord Kames, a seminal exponent of associationist aesthetics, argued strongly for the imaginative superiority of Gothic over Classical ruins in his account of architecture and gardening in *Elements of Criticism* (1762). Guided by the principle that the primary function of both gardening and architecture was to 'entertain the mind' by raising in it 'certain agreeable emotions or feelings', Lord Kames held that a Gothic ruin suggested 'the triumph of time over strength', a melancholic though by no means 'unpleasant' association that was favourable to the gloomy 'triumph of barbarity over taste' conjured up by a Grecian ruin (Home 1762: vol. 3, 296, 313). Unsurprisingly, it was Horace Walpole, the mastermind behind the Gothic Revivalist house Strawberry Hill, Twickenham, who was one of the century's most ardent champions of the associative properties of the Gothic. As he put it in the first volume of his *Anecdotes of Painting in England* (1762), 'It is difficult for the noblest Grecian temple to convey half so many impressions to the mind, as a cathedral does of the best Gothic taste' (Walpole 1762: 107). The celebration of the imaginative power of Gothic ruins that we see throughout Walpole's correspondence, published works and manuscripts was summed up in an epigram included in his 'Detached Thoughts', a collection of pithy reflections that was posthumously published in the fourth volume of his *Works* in 1798: 'A Gothic cathedral strikes one like the enthusiasm of poetry; St Paul's, like the good sense of prose' (Walpole 1798: vol. 4, 368). In his poem *The English Garden* (1772–81), Walpole's friend and correspondent William Mason similarly celebrated the imaginative power of Gothic ruins over their antique Greek and Roman equivalents, arguing that it was the Gothic more than the Classical that was best suited to recalling the nation's political and ecclesiastical past. Seeking to differentiate the category of the picturesque from the sublime and the beautiful, Uvedale Price in *An Essay on the Picturesque* (1794) followed the principles of William Gilpin in arguing that while Grecian buildings in their complete state might be taken to exemplify the aesthetic of the beautiful, it was ruins, and Gothic ruins in particular, that best demonstrated the principle of the picturesque. Praising Gothic ruin for the 'romantic effects' it is capable of inspiring, Price describes his night-time approach upon a fifteenth-century castle through an avenue of imposing trees: 'The whole scene', he writes, 'most forcibly brought to my fancy the times of fairies and chivalry' (Price 1794: 195). In his poem *The Landscape* (1794), Richard Payne Knight, too, argued in favour of the picturesque and imaginative potential of ruined Gothic abbeys and castles:

> Bless'd is the man, in whose sequestr'd glade,
> Some ancient abbey's walls diffuse their shade;
> With mould'ring windows pierc'd, and turrets crown'd.
>
> And pinnacles with clinging ivy bound.
>   Bless'd too is he, also, 'midst his tufted trees,
> Some ruin'd castle's lofty towers sees;
> Imbosom'd high upon the mountain's brow,
> Or nodding o'er the stream that glides below.
> (Knight 1794: 35–6)

Irrespective of whether ruins in a landscape were Classical or Gothic in style, ancient or modern in provenance, Knight, like Pope and Shenstone before him, argued that they ought always to maintain an appearance of authenticity through their accordance with the prevailing spirit of the place. Writing of such modern garden follies in England as overly large replicas of the Grecian ruins at Paestum, he claims that 'Such buildings English nature must reject, / And claim from art th' appearance of neglect: / No decoration should we introduce, / That has not first been nat'raliz'd by use' (Knight 1794: 37). In eighteenth-century Britain, the tasteful use of both real and sham ruins was subject to a range of important aesthetic considerations. As Price's later *On the Picturesque* (1842) reminds us, though, the function of ruin was as much political as it was aesthetic: 'The ruins of these once magnificent edifices are the pride and boast of this island; we may be proud of them, not merely in a picturesque point of view – we may glory that the abodes of tyranny and superstition are in ruin' (Price 1842: 366). Freighted with patriotic and other important cultural and political meanings, the ruined abbeys and castles in the landscape served to remind eighteenth- and early-nineteenth-century Britons of the vanquishing of Catholic 'superstition' at the Reformation, the overthrowing of 'tyranny' during the English Civil Wars, and, more recently, the quelling of the forces of Jacobite insurrection.

William Gilpin's Picturesque Ruins

Although Shenstone, Price and Knight all regarded themselves as writing within a picturesque tradition of landscape gardening, their particular version of the picturesque was considerably different from that proposed by William Gilpin, undoubtedly the most influential exponent of this aesthetic in the late eighteenth and early nineteenth centuries. In his seminal *Observations on the River Wye, and Several Parts of South Wales, &c. Relative Chiefly to Picturesque Beauty* (1782), Gilpin proposed the picturesque appreciation of the British landscape as 'a new object of pursuit', one that approached the landscape not by

Tintern Abbey. From William Gilpin, Observations on the River Wye, and Several Parts of South Wales, &c., *1782*

merely describing it but by 'adapting' the description of scenery 'to the principles of artificial landscape' (Gilpin 1782: 1–2). The notion of artifice was central to Gilpin's theories, and the very cornerstone of his conceptualisation of the picturesque: while beauty, he would later argue, was to be found in a state closely resembling that of nature, the picturesque, that which was 'suited to the pencil', was the product of thoughtful curating, artful contrivance and careful manipulation (Gilpin 1792: 1). Proceeding in this fashion to define a picturesque scene as any that would 'appear to advantage on canvas', Gilpin promoted the practice of viewing the landscape as if it were a painting rendered in the style of the seventeenth-century French painter Claude (Gilpin 1782: 40). Though more concerned with natural scenery than with the visible signs of human culture and intervention on the landscape, Gilpin's version of the picturesque afforded considerable importance to architectural ruins: ruined Gothic castles and abbeys, he argued, 'give consequence to the scene', to the extent that the 'landscape-painter seldom thinks his view perfect, without characterizing it by some object of this kind' (Gilpin 1782: 14). Although claiming that 'the shattered arches of a Gothic ruin', quite independent of the composition, were 'beautiful in themselves', Gilpin was not averse to offering advice on how the picturesque potential of a ruin might be enhanced, notoriously observing of the all-too-regular gable ends of Tintern Abbey, Monmouthshire, that 'A mallet judiciously used (but who durst use it?) might be of service in fracturing some of them' (Gilpin 1782: 13, 33). While smoothness and regularity were characteristics of a Burkean conceptualisation of the beautiful, a requisite amount of roughness was central to the Gilpinian picturesque. 'In short', he would insist, 'a *smooth* building' in the Palladian style must be turned into a '*rough* ruin' through the use of the mallet in order to render it sufficiently picturesque (Gilpin 1792: 7). For this reason, Gilpin tended to celebrate the verdancy of Gothic ruin throughout his works, seeing the ivy, lichen and mosses that grew wildly and abundantly in and around them not only as a sign of the triumph of the natural order over the world of culture, but also as a means of bringing to the picturesque composition the requisite element of roughness. 'Ivy, in masses uncommonly large, has taken possession of many parts of the wall', he approvingly observed of Tintern Abbey, 'and gives a happy contrast to the grey-coloured stone, of which the building is composed. Nor is this undecorated. Mosses of various hues, with lychens, maiden-hair, penny-leaf, and other humble plants, over-spread the surface; or hang from every joint, and crevice' (Gilpin 1782: 33–4).

Though ruins thus feature prominently throughout the many illustrated studies of the picturesque landscapes of England, Wales and Scotland that Gilpin published between 1782 and 1809, their aesthetic uptake was deliberately and self-consciously far less imaginative than that proposed by many of his contemporaries. Indeed, eschewing the principles of architectural associationism that had informed the use of ruins in landscape gardening, Gilpin ostensibly stripped ruins of their ability to provoke in the observer romantic flights of fancy, figuring them instead as picturesque images or visual representations on a flat, two-dimensional surface: the picturesque, he trenchantly argued, was to be distinguished from a 'romantic' tendency to 'give a loose to the most pleasing riot of imagination' (Gilpin 1782: 40). Showing little or no interest in the past, moreover, Gilpin's published tours confronted the history of a ruin only when it was of significance to the picturesque prospect in the present: of Raglan Castle, Monmouthshire, for instance, he merely observed that the pile 'owes its present picturesque form to Cromwell; who laid his iron hands upon it; and shattered it into ruin' (1782: 49). An equally superficial approach to a ruin's complex political history characterises his description of Donnington Castle, Berkshire: the crucial role that the castle played in the clash between Royalists and Republicans during the English Civil Wars is all but elided in Gilpin's casual description of it as 'one of those scenes, where the unfortunate Charles reaped some glory' (Gilpin 1782: 96). His particular approach to ruin is clearly demonstrated in the description of a picturesque scene near the Vale of Usk, Wales, in *Observations on the River Wye*:

> Amidst the gloom arose the venerable remains of the abbey, tinged with a bright ray, which discovered a profusion of rich Gothic workmanship; and contrasted the grey stone, of which the ruins are composed, with a feathering foliage, that floated round them: but we had not time to examine, how all these beauteous parts were formed into a whole.—The imagination formed it, after the vision vanished. But though it might possibly create a *whole*, more agreeable to the rules of painting; yet it could scarce do justice to the beauty of the *parts*. (Gilpin 1782: 52)

Studiously ahistorical, and lacking in all traces of imaginative response, Gilpin's picturesque ruins are markedly different from the historicised ruins of eighteenth-century antiquarianism and landscape gardening.

Picturesque Tourism

As Gilpin argued in his essay 'On Picturesque Travel', the tourist in search of picturesque scenery across the country ought to be more concerned with 'searching after effects' than 'assigning causes' (Gilpin 1792: 41): what was of importance was not an historical account of how a ruin came to exist as such, but rather the ways in which it might most effectively be incorporated into a picturesque composition. As Malcolm Andrews has shown, Gilpin's influence upon the practice of domestic tourism in Britain in the latter part of the eighteenth century was considerable (Andrews 1989). Armed with pedometers, makeshift lenses made from pieces of tinted glass, drawing pads, notebooks, watercolour paints, pens, pencils and tour-books, tourists set out in quest of picturesque scenes across the country, often pausing to draw, paint and write about the ruins that they encountered in the process. The Claude Glass, a small and portable shaded convex mirror through which tourists viewed the picturesque landscape, was another requisite

From the first edition of The Tour of Dr Syntax in Search of the Picturesque, *1812. (Syntax loses his balance and falls into the lake.) Coloured plate by Rowlandson*

piece of equipment: a framing mechanism and lens that tended to idealise, abstract and reduce the scene it reflected to its most dominant shapes, shades and tones, the Claude Glass facilitated the presentation of the ruin and the landscape in which it featured to its best possible picturesque advantage (Andrews 1989: 69–70). Amateur picturesque sketches and watercolour paintings of Britain's ruins became a recognisable genre, many of them executed on the spot and a number preserved in the journals of domestic travellers. Inevitably, some sites of picturesque tourism – such as Netley Abbey and Tintern Abbey – were more popular than others, but by the early nineteenth century, there was barely a ruin in Britain that had escaped treatment at the hands of amateur picturesque sketchers. Other better-known artists of the period produced picturesque impressions of ruined abbeys and castles, too. Some of the best-known examples include the artists J. M. W. Turner's and Philippe-Jacques de Loutherbourg's respective views of Tintern Abbey.

Like the taste for sham ruins in the landscape gardens of the gentry, the practice of touring ruins so as to sketch and write about them soon became the object of light-hearted satire. In his poem *The Tour of Dr Syntax in Search of the Picturesque* (1812), William Combe has his eponymous protagonist at one point dismount his horse Grizzle so as to sketch a picturesque prospect of the towers of the colleges of Oxford, only to be chased up a tree by a charging bull. Later, Dr Syntax pauses before a ruined Gothic castle to celebrate, like Gilpin, the ruin's visual, picturesque qualities over any potential historical significance that it might bear:

> But now, alas! no more remains
> Than will award the painter's pains:
> The palace of the feudal victor
> Now serves for nought but a picture.
> (Combe 1812: 70)

When, having decided to sketch it, he attempts to get a better view of the pile, Syntax the picturesque tourist loses his balance and tumbles headlong down the bank into the muddy lake below.

The Poetry of Britain's Ruins

'Word-painting' was as popular a response to Britain's ruins as the literal painting of picturesque sketches and watercolours, to the extent that vernacular ruin poetry – topographical poems written in, about and to ruined Gothic piles across the British landscape – became a recognisable sub-genre in eighteenth-century verse. The origins of poems about specific 'real' landscapes, places or sites in Britain are frequently said to lie in John Denham's *Cooper's Hill* (1642), a poem in which the Anglo-Irish poet and eventual Surveyor of the King's Works set out to capture in verse descriptions of the Thames valley landscape surrounding his home at Egham, Surrey. The invocation to Denham's poem turns boldly away from the mountain of Parnassus, the purported home of the Muses in Greek mythology, towards the inspiration offered by the more everyday but no less poetic Cooper's Hill:

> Sure we have Poets, that did never dreame
> Upon Parnassus, nor did taste the streame
> Of Helicon, and therefore I suppose
> Those made not Poets, but the Poets those.
> And as Courts make not Kings, but Kings the Court,
> So where the Muses and their Troopes resort,
> Parnassus stands, if I can be to thee,
> A Poet, thou Parnassus art to mee. (Denham 1642: 1)

Poised on Cooper's Hill above the surrounding landscape, the persona surveys such sights as the City of London, St Paul's Cathedral, Windsor Castle and Chertsey Abbey, the latter a site of architectural ruin that prompts Denham's reflections on the tumultuous present of the English Civil Wars and, in a later edition of the poem, his ire on Henry VIII's Dissolution of the Monasteries. The influence of the poem was almost immediate, and from the early 1640s onwards, several minor poets in Britain set about apostrophising in Denham's manner the landscapes, scenes and Gothic ruins that they encountered around them: local and vernacular alternatives, perhaps, to the ruins of Classical Greece and Rome that they visited on the Grand Tour. In his essay on John Denham in *The Lives of the Most Eminent English Poets* (1779–81), Samuel Johnson termed the poetic tradition that *Cooper's*

Hill initiated 'local poetry', glossing its 'fundamental subject' as 'some particular landscape, to be poetically described, with the addition of such embellishment as may be supplied by historical retrospection, or incidental meditation' (Johnson 1783: vol. 1, 110–11). Later, when the American poet Henry Wadsworth Longfellow compiled a thirty-one-volume anthology of poems written about specific sites and landscapes in, among other countries, England, Scotland and Ireland, he tellingly called his collection *Poems of Places* (1876–9).

While it is tempting to regard the topographical poetry of ruin in eighteenth-century Britain as the celebration of the particularities of local and national place and space, it soon becomes apparent that much ruin poetry was the result of a shared way of looking at the landscape, the product of a common poetic language or literary register that, habitually and indiscriminately applied to several sites across the country, effectively stripped each ruin of its novelty and singularity. This is to say that much of the eighteenth-century poetry of ruin is highly intertextual in nature, often self-consciously situating itself, through subtle allusion or direct quotation, within a national poetic tradition that goes back to the early modern period. In their concerns with impermanence and the implacable march of time, for instance, these poems frequently rework Shakespeare's references to 'unswept stone besmeared with sluttish time' in Sonnet 55, 'Not marble nor the gilded monuments / Of Princes' (Shakespeare 2008: 1964). John Webster's dramatic depiction of a ruined Gothic abbey in Act V, scene iii of *The Duchess of Malfi* (1612–13) provides another source of inspiration, particularly the often-quoted lines of Antonio, 'I do love these ancient ruins, / We never tread upon them but we set / Our foot upon some reverend history' (Act V, scene iii, lines 9–11; Webster 1986: 93). Equally pervasive in poems about ruined abbeys are allusions to John Milton's 'Il Penseroso' (1645), a poem in which the pensive and melancholic persona celebrates, among other objects, the mournful yet pleasurable emotional effects of Gothic architectural space:

> But let my due feet never fail,
> To walk the studious cloister's pale,
> And love the high embossed roof,
> With antique pillars' massy roof,

And storied windows richly dight,
Casting a dim religious light. (Milton 1990: 146)

Poems of eighteenth-century provenance exert their influence over the poetry of ruin, too. Alexander Pope's poem of thwarted romantic love and sexual desire within a convent setting in 'Eloisa to Abelard' (1717) would be tirelessly reworked in poems written about, in and to ruined abbeys, the Protestant biases of the age often appropriating it and putting it to voraciously anti-Catholic use in ruin-inspired poetic musings on the dangers of monasticism, the deprivations of clerical celibacy and the 'glorious' vanquishing of Roman Catholicism during the Reformation and the Dissolution of the Monasteries. Pope's opening evocations of the gloomy, melancholic associations of the Gothic architectural style in the poem are strongly indebted to Milton's description of Gothic architecture in 'Il Penseroso':

In these deep solitudes and awful cells,
Where heav'nly-pensive, contemplation dwells,
And ever-musing melancholy reigns;
What means this tumult in a Vestal's veins? (Pope 1993: 319)

In particular, poems written about the ruins of Godstow Abbey, Oxfordshire, made frequent use of Pope's depiction of conventual life in 'Eloisa to Abelard', for it was here during the twelfth century that the tragic Rosamund Clifford lived as a nun before King Henry II became enamoured of her. The Elizabethan poet Samuel Daniel had related a version of the legend in *The Complaint of Rosamond* (1592). Certain versions of the story claimed that Rosamund retired again to Godstow after her disastrous affair with the King, while others held that she was poisoned by Henry's jealous wife, Queen Eleanor, in the labyrinthine bower that Henry had built for her at Woodstock Palace. The anonymous 'On the Ruins of Godstow Nunnery' (1764) approached the ruin through Pope's depiction of strict monastical existence in 'Eloisa to Abelard':

The midnight bell, at whose accustom'd sound,
With pine and fasting pale, with watchings worn,
Each maiden trac'd the lonely cloister round,
Oft wak'd the sleeping lark before 'twas morn. (Anon. 1764: 513)

Similar echoes of Pope recur in the Reverend William Cooke's 'Stanzas Written at Godstowe Nunnery Near Oxford' (1774), particularly when Rosamond, faced with Henry's unwelcome advances, is led to cry out:

> Spare me, and then for ever will I dwell
> Where Virgin Saints, by the pale Taper's Rays,
> Immur'd beneath the Cloyster's gloomy Cell,
> Offer to Heav'n the Incense of their Praise. (Cooke 1774: 16)

The anonymous 'Lines Written at Godstowe, January 1779', too, echoed Pope in its depiction of Rosamond's pious, cloistered existence within a convent:

> Hither, of yore, retir'd the beauteous maid,
> To royal lust a prey, to royal pride
> A hapless victim; and, with early feet,
> Brush'd from the bending stalk the glitt'ring dew,
> Observant in the sprightly matin call;
> Unconscious yet of ill; unstain'd her cheek
> With flushing guilt:—Too soon, alas! to see
> The sad reverse, to know nor joy nor peace! (Anon. 1802: 207)

As these and other poems written to and about Godstow Abbey in the eighteenth century indicate, the literature of ruin often exploited the lore and legend that circulated around a particular site, sometimes figuring the historical and mythological personages involved as ghostly, spectral presences that continued to haunt it.

The poets of the so-called 'Graveyard School', including Thomas Parnell, Thomas Warton, William Collins, James Beattie and Robert Blair, were especially influential on the topographical poetry of ruin, and as in Milton's 'Il Penseroso' and Pope's 'Eloisa to Abelard', often situated their lugubrious speakers within ruined abbeys and overgrown churchyards, ideal sites for the experience and articulation of what they held to be pleasurable melancholy. The pleasures of ruin-inspired melancholy were often articulated in the poetry, not least of all in the responses of the persona to the sight of Classical ruin in John Dyer's *The Ruins of Rome* (1740):

One of Richard Bentley's designs for Gray's Odes, 1753; this picture appeared at the beginning of An Elegy Written in a Country Church Yard

There is a kindly Mood of Melancholy,
That wings the Soul and points her to the Skies;
When Tribulation cloaths the child of Man,
When Age descends with sorrow to the grave,
'Tis sweetly-soothing Sympathy to Pain,
A gently-wak'ning Call to Health and Ease,
How musical! When all-devouring Time,
Here sitting on his Throne of Ruins hoar,
With Winds and Tempests sweeps his various Lyre,
How sweet thy Diapason, Melancholy!
(Dyer 1740: 18–19)

Of all of graveyard poems, it was undoubtedly Thomas Gray's *An Elegy Written in a Country Church Yard* (1751) that was the most influential, bequeathing to a range of now-forgotten poets of ruin such stock conventions as a preoccupation with visiting the ruin at the fall of evening, the persona's awareness of the sound of owls and other wild birds therein, ivy-clad towers and abbeys, and sombre thoughts amidst the graves and ruins on the futility of human endeavour and the inevitability of death: 'The Paths of Glory lead but to the Grave' (Gray 1751: 7). With its description of the pensive persona in an overgrown churchyard at the fall of evening, the celebrated opening of Gray's poem encapsulates the mood, tone and setting of countless poems about architectural ruin in the period:

The *Curfew* tolls the Knell of parting Day,
The lowing Herd winds slowly o'er the Lea,
The Plow-man homeward plods his weary Way,
And leaves the World to Darkness, and to me.
    Now fades the glimmering Landscape on the Sight,
And all the Air a solemn Stillness holds;
Save where the Beetle wheels his droning Flight,
Or drowsy Tinklings lull the distant folds.
    Save that from yonder Ivy-mantled Tow'r
The mopeing Owl does to the Moon complain
Of such as, wand'ring near her secret Bow'r,
Molest her ancient solitary Reign.
(Gray 1751: 4)

From Gray onwards, in fact, the elegy – the poetic form and register of death, longing, absence and mourning – would become the form that was most frequently employed in the literature of ruin, topographical poets often seeing in ruin the inevitable disappearance of a noble national history and, by implication, the death of the persona who views it in the present.

One of the most characteristic elements of the eighteenth-century poetic discourse on ruin is a mournful and melancholic response to the ruin as testament to a glorious yet faded historical past. John Langhorne's 'Written Amongst the Ruins of Pontefract Castle' (1756), for instance, describes the dilapidated ruin as a vestigial remainder of that which was 'once of fair renown':

> A pile stupendous, once of fair renown,
>   This mould'ring mass of shapeless ruin rose,
> Where nodding heights of fractur'd columns frown,
>   And birds obscene in ivy-bow'rs repose [...]
> (Langhorne 1766: vol. 1, 155)

Surveying this mass, the speaker muses in the fashion of an 'historic sage' that 'these awful scenes of decay' once 'a refuge form'd from hostile rage, / In Henry's and Edward's dubious day' (Langhorne 1766: vol. 1, 156). If the phrase 'dubious day' suggests certain reservations with the historical past to which this ruin attests, other poets of the period were often more inclined to figure the ruin's past as an age of unprecedented cultural greatness and splendour, the passing of which automatically necessitated recourse to the elegiac mode. In 'An Elegiac Poem on the Magnificent Ruins of the Abbey at Aberbrothock', a poem by one 'A. B.' that was published in *The Scots Magazine* in 1775, the speaker suggests that the 'mournful lyre' is the only possible means of addressing so poignant a scene of devastation as this, not only to mourn the loss of the magnificent pile itself, but also the lost age of religious piety for which it stood:

> Awake, my Muse! and strike the mournful lyre,
> Fraught with the notes romantic scenes inspire;
> That mould'ring fabric, beauteous in decay,
> Demands thy weak, tho' sympathetic lay;

> Whene'er I saunter near these shaggy tow'rs,
> To view the scene, and cheat the ling'ring hours,
> I melt in pity, while my bosom burns
> With admiration and with love by turns.
> Sad devastations of revolving years,
> Around this venerable spot appear.
> The huge cathedral, mingling with the ground,
> Displays a wild, confus'd, unequal mound,
> Where nauseous weeds along the surface creep,
> Thro' which the mould'ring stones are seen to peep.
> (A. B. 1775: 101)

In the anonymous 'On Minsden Chapel, A Ruin Near Hitchin, in Hertfordshire' (1825), the mere sight of the ruin is enough to provoke in the speaker a mournful yearning for the vanished past, the ivy that covers it thus taking on the semblance of widows' weeds or other accoutrements of mourning:

> The ivy o'er those mouldering walls
> In fair festoons of nature falls,
>   And mantles on their brow:
> It seems to weep for that lone aisle
> That broken arch, and desert pile,
>   In ruin sinking low.
> (Anon. 1825: 263)

The only consolation that the poet finds is in the thought that 'The deeds of heroes cannot die': though the ruin itself will fall into oblivion, the memory of the deeds of those who built and inhabited it will live on eternally, populating the scene like ghosts.

Despite often being peopled with the spectres of those who once lived or worshipped there, the ruined castles and abbeys of Britain are characteristically figured in topographical ruin poetry as sites of overwhelming vacancy in the present moment. The speaker in J. Glasse's 'An Ode, Written Among the Ruins of Barkhamstead Castle' (1757), for instance, is struck by the lack of auditory stimuli within the ruinous space:

> Here what an awful silence reigns,
>   Not a sound
>   Is heard around,
> Save the flocks upon the plains;
> That as they crop their flow'ry food,
> Bleating speak their gratitude.
> (Glasse 1759: 485)

William Hodges's poem 'Lines, Written at Midnight, Amongst the Ruins of Ludlow Castle' (1794) captures the lack and absence at the heart of ruin particularly well:

> No more these walls with minstrelsy resound,
>   The gaudy pageants of a distant day;
> But here the bat and moping owl are found,
>   And mould'ring turrets intercept the way.
> (Hodges 1794: xxiv)

Here, as elsewhere, the stillness and vacancy of the present is juxtaposed with imaginative reconstructions of the ruin's vibrant, busy and colourful past. But as Hodges's poem so clearly points out, it is precisely the absence that poets encounter in the scene of ruin that prompts and incites the workings of the poetic imagination:

> To rescue from oblivion's dreary page,
>   Heroes, who rose sublime among their peers;
> To sing the chieftains of a martial age,
>   To shed oe'er Kath'rine's urn a flood of tears.
> (Hodges 1794: xxiii)

Seeking to recover the ruin from oblivion as much as mourn the passing of the national heroes to which it once was home, Hodges, like Shakespeare in Sonnet 55 before him, turns to the powers of memorialisation enshrined in the writing of poetry itself.

As this chapter has argued, ruins called to mind visions of Britain's sometimes glorious, sometimes shameful political and religious past, and often provoked in those who visited, viewed and wrote about them a pleasurable melancholia or a profound yet pleasing sense of loss and mourning. Their manifold 'pleasures' were thus inherently political, for it was not possible to derive enjoyment from scenes of architectural destruction without becoming complicit in the vexed historical processes – the Dissolution of the Monasteries, the Civil Wars – that brought them into being. Alongside these patriotic and sentimental functions, though, ran an equally strong tendency to appropriate ruin as a vehicle for seemingly transcendental moral didacticism. Indeed, there is no clearer illustration of Stephen Switzer's claim of 1715 that the mere sight of ruin attested to 'the Instability of all sublunary Affairs' (Switzer 1715: 149) than in the many poems that extracted from architectural ruin sobering lessons concerning the passage of time and the inevitability of death, reading in the crumbling facades and battlements moral 'truths' concerning the transience of human life and the futility of human ambition. 'Look round this vast and venerable place', the anonymous 'On the Ruins of Pomfret Castle' (1760) urged its readers, view how 'Savage Time with cankering tooth' has devoured 'The Solid fabric of yon mould'ring tower, / That now in undistingish'd chaos lies' (Anon. 1788: 176). The implication, of course, is that if time is capable of wrecking so sturdy a structure as Pontefract Castle, it is also likely to destroy the observer who ponders over it in the present. Herein lay the often-observed sublimity of Gothic ruin, its ability to provoke in the perceiver thoughts concerning the finitude of human existence and the ubiquitous presence of death. Observations about time and certitude of death were stock features in the poetry of ruin, and there is barely a poem in this tradition that does not invoke it. In 'On the Ruins of M__ le Chapel in Hertfordshire', another anonymous poem about the ruins of Minsden that was published in *The Gentleman's Magazine* in 1759, the persona describes unexpectedly stumbling across the site while out on a walk in the country:

> A mould'ring structure then appear'd in view,
> Around whose top the creeping ivy grew:
> Once a fair church, adorn'd by curious art,
> In crumbling stones now drooping part from part.
> (Anon. 1759: 382)

As in so many other ruin poems, the speaker is struck by the contrast between the flurry and activity of the chapel's imagined past and the vacancy and desolation that he experiences in the present. Its overgrown and reptile-infested interior, though, soon inspires the work of moral reflection, the poem ending on a commonplace comparison between architectural ruin and an ageing human body:

> Just such is man when vig'rous youth is fled,
> And feeble age has silver'd o'er his head:
> Downward he bends deserted and forlorn,
> Of all he meets the pity or the scorn,
> None haunt his dwelling but the reptile race,
> Who hope his fortune, or expect his place,
> Yet shall he rise and mount the realms of day,
> Where youth immortal shall no more decay.
> (Anon. 1759: 382–3)

Like ruins, human beings, too, will age and die, the only form of consolation being a Christian conceptualisation of the afterlife. A poet identified only by the initials 'R. S.' made much the same point in 'An Evening Walk. Written Beside the Ruins of the Royal Palace at Linlithgow' (1760), implicitly including the future existence of the human perceiver in his or her heightened awareness of the devastations wrought by the passage of time:

> All-destroying Time!
> What can resist thy rage? The iron bar
> Melts down before thee; and the solid rock
> Moulders away. With every stormy blast
> The fragments from yon broken arches fly.
> The spacious windows, where erewhile appear'd
> Beauty and royalty, robb'd of their pride,
> Are desolate and void; and in the hall,
> Where once assembled senates awful sat,
> And all the pomp of majesty, there dwells
> Ruin and Desolation; there the owl,
> Sad favourite of Night! eludes the day;
> And now, forth-issuing from his dark abode,
> Tunes his nocturnal elegy of wo.
> (R. S. 1760: 42–3)

In a concluding theological turn, the persona reads in ruin evidence of the work of God the Great Architect, articulating through this a providentialist vision of the rise and decline of empires:

> Sov'reign Director of unnumber'd worlds!
> 'Tis thine to bid cities and empires rise,
> And at thy pleasure fall; to lay in dust
> The proudest glories of the sons of men;
> To make a desert on the fertile plain,
> And with thy beauty clothe the barren wild:
> All is thy work, and all thou dost is good.
> (R. S. 1760: 43)

Albeit in a much less explicitly theological register, the ruins of Craigmillar Castle, Edinburgh, inspired in the Scottish antiquary John Pinkerton intimations of the destruction of all earthly beings and possessions. 'Such fate awaits all sublunary things', his *Craigmillar Castle: An Elegy* (1776) notes, 'Save those that rest on VIRTUE'S firm support; / She aid alone 'gainst Time's fell ravage brings, / And smiles secure at fortune's cruel sport' (Pinkerton 1776: 8). As of old, ruins in eighteenth-century Britain fulfilled the functions of a memento mori; as one G. J. urged his or her readers in 'Spontaneous Thoughts, Written in the Ruins of Winchelsea Castle, Near Rye, in Sussex':

> Dear Youth, whose lonely feet those ruins tread,
> Whose down-cast eye lets fall the gen'rous tear,
> Regard not transient life, which soon is fled;
> Reflect on Heav'n and all the glories there.
> (G. J. 1776: 148)

The poems cited in this chapter are only a small example of what was a thriving poetic tradition in Britain during the eighteenth and early nineteenth centuries. The irony, of course, is that the anxieties concerning death, oblivion and the destruction wrought by the passage of time to which they all gave expression are no better attested to than in the cultural place that these poems and poets occupy today: overlooked, forgotten and consigned to the category of minor eighteenth-century verse, their fate has been far more obscure and ignominious than the ruins that they described and celebrated. Indeed, it is only in some of the better-known poems of the period, those memorialised in the canonisation of 'Romanticism' over the course of the nineteenth century, that we might catch fragmentary glimpses of their existence. For, when William Wordsworth penned what is probably his best-known poem, 'Lines Written a Few Miles from Tintern Abbey, on Revisiting the Banks of the Wye During a Tour, July 13, 1798', he was situating himself within the tradition of vernacular, topographical ruin poetry that gained ground in the early eighteenth, and reached a certain efflorescence at the turn of the nineteenth, century. While 'Tintern Abbey' has been enshrined as one of Romanticism's greatest poems, the tradition that informs it, and from which it derives, has been all but forgotten. The same might be said of other well-known poems of ruin from the period: in Wordsworth, the ruin of Furness Abbey in Book Second of *The Prelude* (1805), Peele Castle in 'Elegiac Stanzas, Suggested by a Picture of Peele Castle in a Storm, Painted by Sir George Beaumont' (1807), and the monastical ruins in *Ecclesiastical Sketches* (1822); Walter Scott's evocative description of Melrose Abbey in *The Lay of the Last Minstrel* (1805); Byron's paean to the ruins of Newstead Abbey in the Norman Cantos of *Don Juan* (1819–24); Percy Bysshe Shelley's fragmentary poem of antique ruin in 'Ozymandias' (1818); Mary Shelley's response to Wordsworth's reading of ruin in 'On Reading Wordsworth's Lines on Peele Castle' (1825); and much more besides. While these are just some of the poems of ruin from the period that are recited and anthologised, quoted, remembered and cherished today, it is important to remember that their foundations lay in the pleasing melancholy and imaginative transport that Britain's ruinous monuments invoked in many an earlier picturesque traveller.

Further Reading

Bermingham, Ann. 1987. *Landscape and Ideology: The English Rustic Tradition, 1740–1860* (London: Thames & Hudson).
Copley, Stephen and Peter Garside (eds). 1994. *The Politics of the Picturesque: Literature, Landscape and Aesthetics since 1770* (Cambridge: Cambridge University Press).
Macaulay, Rose. 1953. *Pleasure of Ruins* (London: Weidenfeld & Nicolson).

References

A. B. 1775. 'An Elegiac Poem on the Magnificent Ruins of the Abbey at Aberbrothock', *The Scots Magazine* (February): 101-2.

Aikin, John. 1793. 'Letter XXIV: On Ruins', in *Letters from a Father to his Son, on Various Topics, Relative to Literature and the Conduct of Life, Written in the Years 1792 and 1793* (London: Printed for J. Johnson), 262-73.

Andrews, Malcolm. 1989. *The Search for the Picturesque: Landscape Aesthetics and Tourism in Britain, 1760-1800* (Stanford: Stanford University Press).

Anon. 1759. 'On the Ruins of M__ le Chapel in Hertfordshire', *The Gentleman's Magazine* 29 (August): 382-3.

Anon. 1764. 'On the Ruins of Godstow Nunnery', *London Chronicle* (29 November): 513.

Anon. 1788. 'On the Ruins of Pomfret Castle' (1760), reprinted in *The New Foundling Hospital for Wit, Vol. VI* (London: Printed for J. Debrett), 175-9.

Anon. 1802. 'Lines Written at Godstowe, January 1779', *The London Review and Literary Journal* (March): 207-8.

Anon. 1825. 'On Minsden Chapel, A Ruin Near Hitchin, in Hertfordshire', *The Gentleman's Magazine* 96, part 2 (September): 263.

Archer, John. 1983. 'The Beginnings of Association in British Architectural Esthetics', *Eighteenth-Century Studies* 16, no. 3 (Spring): 241-64.

Colman, George and David Garrick. 1766. *The Clandestine Marriage, A Comedy, As it is Acted at the Theatre Royal, Drury Lane* (London: Printed for P. Becket and P. A. De Hondt; R. Baldwin; and T. Davies).

Combe, William. 1812. *The Tour of Dr Syntax in Search of the Picturesque: A Poem* (London: R. Ackermann's Repository of Arts).

Cooke, William. 1774. 'Stanzas Written at Godstowe Nunnery Near Oxford', in *Poetical Essays on Several Occasions* (London: Printed for S. Smith), 13-18.

Denham, John. 1642. *Cooper's Hill: A Poeme* (London: Printed for Thomas Walkley).

Dyer, John. 1740. *The Ruins of Rome: A Poem* (London: Printed for Lawton Gilliver).

G. J. 1776. 'Spontaneous Thoughts, Written in the Ruins of Winchelsea Castle, Near Rye, in Sussex', *Universal Magazine* 59 (September): 147-8.

Gerard, Alexander. 1759. *An Essay on Taste* (London: Printed for A. Millar; Edinburgh: A. Kincaid and J. Bell).

Gilpin, William. 1782. *Observations on the River Wye, and Several Parts of South Wales, &c. Relative Chiefly to Picturesque Beauty; Made in the Summer of the Year 1770* (London: Printed for R. Blamire).

Gilpin, William. 1792. *Three Essays: On Picturesque Beauty; On Picturesque Travel; And on Sketching Landscape: To Which is Added a Poem, on Landscape Painting* (London: Printed for R. Blamire).

Glasse, J. 1759. 'An Ode, Written Among the Ruins of Barkhamstead Castle' (1757), reprinted in *Miscellaneous Correspondence, Containing a Variety of Subjects, Relative to Natural and Civil History, Geography, Mathematics, Poetry, Memoirs of Monthly Occurrences, Catalogues of New Books, &c, Vol. II,*

For the Year 1757 and 1758, edited by Benjamin Martin (London: Printed and Sold by W. Owen), 485–6.

Gray, Thomas. 1751. *An Elegy Written in a Country Church Yard*, 3rd edn, (London: Printed for R. Dodsley).

Hodges, William. 1794. 'Lines, Written at Midnight, Amongst the Ruins of Ludlow Castle', in *An Historical Account of Ludlow Castle* (Ludlow: W. Felton), xxiii–xxiv.

Home, Henry, Lord Kames. 1762. *Elements of Criticism*, 3 vols (London: Printed for A. Millar; Edinburgh: Printed for J. Bell).

Johnson, Samuel. 1783. *The Lives of the Most Eminent English Poets; With Critical Observations on their Works*, 2nd edn, 4 vols (London: Printed for C. Bathurst *et al.*).

Knight, Richard Payne. 1794. *The Landscape, A Didactic Poem. In Three Books. Addressed to Uvedale Price, Esq.* (London: Printed by W. Bulmer and Co.).

Langhorne, John. 1766. *The Poetical Worlds of John Langhorne*, 2 vols (London: Printed for T. Beckett and P. A. De Hondt).

Locke, John. 1700. *An Essay Concerning Humane Understanding. In Four Books*, 4th edn (London: Printed for Awnsham and John Churchil; and Samuel Manship).

Milton, John. 1990. *Complete Shorter Poems*, edited by John Carey (Harlow: Longman).

Morley, Henry (ed.). 1888. *The Spectator: A New Edition* (London: George Routledge and Sons).

Pinkerton, John. 1776. *Craigmillar Castle: An Elegy* (Edinburgh: Printed for the Author).

Pope, Alexander. 1731. *An Epistle to the Right Honourable Richard Earl of Burlington. Occasion'd by his Publishing Palladio's Designs of the Baths, Arches, Theatres, &c. of Ancient Rome* (London: Printed for L. Gilliver).

Pope, Alexander. 1993. *The Rape of the Lock and Other Poems*, edited by Geoffrey Tillotson. The Twickenham Edition of the Poems of Alexander Pope, vol. 2 (London and New York: Routledge).

Price, Uvedale. 1794. *An Essay on the Picturesque, as Compared with the Sublime and the Beautiful* (London: Printed for J. Robson).

Price, Uvedale. 1842. *On the Picturesque: With an Essay on the Origin of Taste, and Much Original Matter*, by Sir Thomas Dick Lauder, Bart. (Edinburgh: Caldwell, Lloyd and Co.)

R. S. 1760. 'An Evening Walk. Written Beside the Ruins of the Royal Palace at Linlithgow', in *A Collection of Original Poems. By the Rev. Mr Blacklock, and other Scotch Gentlemen* (Edinburgh: Printed for A. Donaldson), 40-44.

Shakespeare, William. 2008. *The Norton Shakespeare, Based on the Oxford Edition*, 2nd edn, edited by Stephen Greenblatt, Walter Cohen, Jean E. Howard and Katharine Eisaman Maus (New York and London: W. W. Norton & Co.).

Shenstone, William. 1764. *The Works in Verse and Prose, of William Shenstone, Esq.*, 2 vols (London: Printed for R. and J. Dodsley).

Stephens, Edward. 1748. *A Poem on the Park and Woods of the Right Honourable Allen Lord Bathurst*, 2nd edn (Cirencester: Printed for the Author).

Stewart, David. 1996. 'Political Ruins: Gothic Sham Ruins and the "45"', *Journal of the Society of Architectural Historians* 55, no. 4 (December): 400–11.

Switzer, Stephen. 1715. *The Nobleman, Gentleman, and Gardener's Recreation; or, An Introduction to Gardening, Planting, Agriculture, and the Other Business and Pleasures of a Country Life* (London: Printed for B. Barker and C. King).

Walpole, Horace. 1762. *Anecdotes of Painting in England; With Some Account of the Principal Artists; And Incidental Notes on Other Arts; Collected by the Late Mr. George Vertue; and Now Digested and Published from His Original MSS, Vol. 1* (Strawberry Hill: Printed by Thomas Farmer).

Walpole, Horace. 1798. *The Works of Horatio Walpole, Earl of Orford*, 5 vols (London: Printed for G. G. and J. Robinson, and J. Edwards).

Webster, John. 1986. *The Duchess of Malfi*, edited by Elizabeth M. Brennan (New York: W. W. Norton & Co.).

Whately, Thomas. 1770. *Observations on Modern Gardening, Illustrated by Descriptions* (London: Printed for T. Payne).

Byron and the 'Ruins' of Newstead Abbey

Holly Hirst

> Whatever may be its future fate, Newstead Abbey must henceforth be a memorable abode. Time may shed its wild flowers on the walls, and let the fox in upon the court-yard and the chambers; it may even pass into the hands of unlettered pride, or plebeian opulence; but it has been the mansion of a mighty poet. Its name is associated with glories that cannot perish, and will go down to posterity in one of the proudest pages of our annals. (Lake 1824: 25)

Strictly speaking, Newstead Abbey, Nottinghamshire, was never truly a ruin. The original religious site was Newstead Priory, an Augustinian establishment that, as tradition holds, was founded by Henry II in c. 1170 as penance for the bloody and sacrilegious murder of Thomas Becket. This was a romantic and dramatic origin for the building

Newstead Priory. From A New Display of the Beauties of England: Or, A Description of the Most Elegant or Magnificent Public Edifices, Royal Palaces, Noblemen's and Gentlemen's Seats, and Other Curiosities, Natural or Artificial *[...], 1773-4*

that the poet Lord Byron, its most famous resident, both relished and propagated, writing in his 'Elegy on Newstead Abbey' (1807) that the Priory was 'Religion's shrine! repentant HENRY's pride!' (Byron 1807a: 137). Any more prosaic a beginning is unthinkable for the ancestral pile of the great Romantic poet. Byron's dramatisation of his inheritance did not rest with his image of its origins, but spread to his depiction of its melancholy ruin, too, as we see in the poem 'On Leaving Newstead Abbey' (1803):

Through thy battlements, Newstead, the hollow wind whistles;
Thou the hall of my Fathers art gone to decay;
In thy once smiling garden, the hemlock and thistle
Have choked up the rose which late bloom'd in thy way.
(Byron 1807b: 1)

However, Byron's figuring of Newstead as a broken and decaying holy ruin here is somewhat misleading. When 'royal sacrilege their doom decreed' and Henry VIII dissolved it and dispersed the canons 'To roam a dreary world, in deep despair, / No friend, no home, no refuge, but their God' ('Elegy on Newstead Abbey'), the priory and all its lands were bought by Sir John Byron in 1541. By 1545, it was the main Byron family residence, for he had 'converted the saintly edifice into a castellated dwelling' (Irving 1835: 125) by demolishing the church and repurposing and renovating the rest of the priory's buildings, creating an imposing country house. The west front of the church remained standing, with an echoing space behind it. This is the closest to a ruin that the abbey provides, and it represents more a careful act of preservation than what Byron presents as the defiant 'remaining' of an architectural relic.

There is thus certainly an element of exaggeration at work in Byron's declaration in the poem 'Newstead Abbey' that 'ruin is fixed on my tower and wall' (Byron 1834: 118). And yet, this is not simply the fruit of the poet's invention, nor his deliberate echoing of the tradition of eighteenth-century topographical ruin poetry. He inherited Newstead Abbey from his great-uncle, the 5th Lord Byron, who was widely known as 'The Wicked Lord Byron', in 1798. According to the American author Washington Irving, writing on a three-week visit to Newstead Abbey after Byron's death:

> Being displeased at the marriage of his son and heir, he displayed an inveterate malignancy towards him. Not being able to cut off his succession to the Abbey estates, which descended to him by entail, he endeavoured to injure it as much as possible, so that it might come a mere wreck into his hands. For this purpose he suffered the Abbey to fall out of repair and every thing to go to waste about it.
> (Irving 1835: 129)

Whether through deliberate malignancy or simple profligacy, the 5th Lord Byron had reduced the abbey to an advanced state of disrepair by the time that Byron took possession of it. The rapidity of this descent into 'ruin' is evident if we compare the account in *A New Display of the Beauties of England* (1774) of the abbey's 'noble and majestic appearance, 'uncommon and picturesque' gardens and enviable collections of art and literature (Anon. 1774: 91) with Byron's friend Charles Skinner Matthews's claim in 1809 that 'every part of the house displays neglect and decay' (Matthews 1830: 172). But despite these signs of neglect and decay, Newstead Abbey did not moulder into ruin. The repurposed abode remained structurally intact, inhabited and inhabitable, with many rooms luxuriously 'fitted up' (Matthews 1830: 172) by Byron himself. Byron did not have the money for full-scale repairs, and so fitted up only a small proportion of the rooms and left many unused; others were famously re-employed for the practice of sports and pistol shooting.

Though neither a ruin nor an abbey, Newstead's depiction as such is a fitting shorthand for the fact that for both Byron and the literary pilgrims who flocked to his former home, the 'imagining' of the site was always more important than its everyday 'reality'. In his early poems dedicated to the abbey, including 'On Leaving Newstead Abbey', 'Elegy on Newstead Abbey' and 'Newstead Abbey', Byron 'imagines' the abbey not so much as a building but as a repository of history, and more particularly, his family's history. 'On Leaving' offers a succinct history of the past 'glories' of the Byron family, bemoaning plaintively:

> Of the mail-cover'd Barons, who, proudly to battle,
> Led their vassals from Europe to Palestine's plain
> The escutcheon, and shield, which with every blast rattle,
> Are the only sad vestiges now that remain.
> (Byron 1807b: 2)

Likewise, in 'Elegy', Byron reads the abbey through the lives once lived in it, whether a 'monarch's friend', 'The Monk [who] abjur'd a world, he ne'er could view' or the 'chief's retainers, an immortal band' (Byron 1807a). It remains peopled with 'pensive shades', the ghostly trace of whom is inextricable from the house's physical reality. The history that they have lived becomes the site's 'essence': irrespective of whether it is 'proudly majestic' or the locale of 'sable Horror', the past has entered Newstead's very stones. The history of the house offered in the 'Elegy' is divided, albeit unequally, between the ecclesiastical and the familial, the early 'sanctity' and isolation of the site being as important as its history as the home of the loyal, the courageous and the extravagant. It is equally split between the tragic ('From thee, poor pile! to lawless plunder given, / While dying groans their painful requiem sound') and the glorious ('The heralds of a warrior's haughty reign, / High crested banners, wave thy walls within'). The ignominy only arrives, for Byron, with the 5th lord, for then 'what saddening change of scene is thine!' (Byron 1807a).

Unlike the Bastille or the ever-present castle of Gothic fiction, Newstead Abbey was not a symbol of an oppressive past but a monument to the best of what had been: a monument to Lord Byron's familial past of excellence. Walpole's Gothic villa, Strawberry Hill, Twickenham, was also driven by this desire to celebrate ancestry. Medieval architecture's positive associations are similarly evident in Byron's 'Elegy' and 'On Leaving', where the 'ruin' of the abbey is not a cause for shame or even regret, but rather offers the promise of resilience, ancient worth and intimations of a better future:

> Yet are his tears, no emblem of regret,
> Cherish'd affection only bids them flow;
> Pride, Hope, and Love, forbid him to forget,
> But warm his bosom, with impassion'd glow.
>
> Yet he prefers thee, to the gilded domes,
> Or gewgaw grottos, of the vainly great;
> Yet, lingers 'mid thy damp and mossy tombs,
> Nor breathes a murmur 'gainst the will of fate.
>
> Haply thy sun, emerging, yet, may shine,

Thee to irradiate, with meridian ray;
Fortune may smile, upon a future line,
And heaven restore an ever cloudless day.
(Byron 1807a: 146–7)

As 'the last and youngest of a noble line' ('Elegy'), Byron envisioned himself as both the successor to the house's legacy and its hope, 'house' here meaning both the physical building and the family lineage, legacy and name. As he wrote in a letter to his mother in 1809, 'Newstead and I stand or fall together' (Byron 1836: vol. 1, 133). Unfortunately, it was the fate of both to fall. By 1811, when he wrote 'Newstead Abbey', and a year before his first attempts to sell 'the last vestige' of the 'inheritance' which he had earlier vowed 'no pressure, present or future' could induce him to part with (Byron 1836: vol. 1, 133), his optimism had faded. If he had before seen himself as the successor of the 'true' spirit of the house and family, he now comes to realise that he is really the successor to the Wicked Lord and the ruin that he had wrought:

And vain was each effort to raise and recall
The brightness of old to illumine our hall;
And vain was the hope to avert our decline—
And the fate of my fathers had faded to mine.

And ruin is fixed on my tower and wall,
Too hoary to fade, and too massy to fall:
It tells not of Time's or the tempest's decay,
But the wreck of the line that held it in sway.
(Byron 1834: 118)

'The wreck of the line' that began with the 5th Lord Byron did not stop there but rather continues with Byron the poet himself. Unable to pay for its repairs, running up ever-increasing debts as well as heaping upon himself scandal after scandal, Byron sold his home and fled the country. This sense of self-recrimination and despoiled majesty is also evident in the view of the abbey found in Canto I, stanza 2 of *Childe Harold's Pilgrimage* (1812), where it becomes the model for the eponymous hero's childhood home:

> The Childe departed from his father's hall;
> It was a vast and venerable pile;
> So old, it seemed only not to fall,
> Yet strength was pillar'd in each massy aisle.
> Monastic dome! Condemn'd to uses vile!
> (Byron 1829: 13)

He also tells us that Harold departed 'His house, his home, his heritage, his land' 'without a sigh' (Canto I, stanza 11). This admission on the part of what is often regarded as his fictional alter-ego is, perhaps, another example of the illusions falling like the proverbial scales from Byron's eyes. After all, for all his protestations of devotion to Newstead Abbey, he never regularly resided there and paid little more attention to the estate than his great-uncle had done.

'The Hours, splendid as the past' that Byron in 'Elegy' predicted for the abbey, and which he had so hopefully allied to himself, only came with his absence. He sold it in 1818 to his friend Thomas Wildman, and 'under his judicious eye and munificent hand, the venerable and romantic pile has arisen from its ruins in all its old monastic and baronial splendour, and additions have been made in perfect conformity of style' (Irving 1835: 138). After this decisive moment, Byron's use of Newstead in his poetry abandons the dreams of familial regeneration and architectural restoration. Instead, poems such as *Don Juan* (1819–24) and the 'Epistle to Augusta' (1818) look back with nostalgia on Byron's personal experience of Newstead. The 'Epistle to Augusta', a letter in verse to his half-sister who had resided with him at the abbey for a period of time, looks back to it as if it were a place of irrecoverable happiness:

> I did remind thee of our own dear Lake,
> By the old Hall which may be mine no more.
> Leman's is fair; but think not I forsake
> The sweet remembrance of a dearer shore:
> Sad havoc Time must with my memory make
> Ere *that* or *thou* can fade these eyes before;
> Though, like all things which I have loved, they are
> Resign'd for ever, or divided far.
> (Byron 1837a: 310)

Newstead has become, for Byron, the page on which his own history is written. The depiction of Newstead in *Don Juan,* where, in the so-called Norman Cantos, it is the model for the country seat of Lord Amundeville, follows a similar pattern. Recollections of the abbey in acute physical detail – from the statue of the Virgin in the west front, the formal gardens and the 'Gothic fountain' in the court to the succession of 'huge halls, long galleries, spacious chambers' – are mixed with a sense of longing for 'this grey ruin, with a voice to charm' (Byron 1837b: 748). It is simultaneously more 'realistic' and more romantic in its depiction, but this romanticism has a different target from Byron's earlier work. Tones of familiar nostalgia and the inevitability of architectural and generational decay remain – the west face's 'gothic arch' 'kindled feelings in the roughest heart, / Which mourn'd the power of time's or tempest's march' – but Byron no longer purely reads the abbey in terms of its history or its relation to his familial past (Byron 1837b: 747). Instead, it has become the architectural chronicle of the poet's own history, ruined hopes and personal disappointments.

This then became the fate of Newstead Abbey. In both Byron's works and in the minds of his admirers, Newstead was a 'memorable abode' (Lake 1824: 25) because it had been the residence of one of the nineteenth century's greatest poetic talents, 'the mansion of a mighty poet' (Lake 1824: 25) and 'hallowed by the genius of an immortal bard' (Fisher 1836: 196). In 1807, Byron had written optimistically of the house that 'Haply thy sun, emerging, yet may shine, / Thee to irradiate, with meridian ray' (Byron 1807a: 147). The sun did arise, but only upon the physical removal of the poet from the site and the replacement of the 'pensive shades' of his ancestors that he so highly valued with his own legend.

We see this clearly in the work of Sophie Hyatt, the 'second poet of Newstead' (Herbert 2009: 158), or the 'little white lady' that 'haunted' its grounds. Deaf, dumb and socially isolated, Hyatt left her home at the death of her parents to live as close to Newstead Abbey as possible. She often wandered its grounds during Wildman's occupation, finding there solace in a 'spiritual proximity' to the still-living Byron and composing a whole body of poetry dedicated to the same. Nor was she exceptional in this intense association of house and poet. The admirers of Byron who flocked to the site after his death, including the American writers Nathaniel Hawthorne and Washington Irving, came expressly to see 'Byron's' Abbey with all its Byronic artefacts, including, most notably, the 'Gothic fountain' mentioned in *Don Juan*, the skull cup immortalised in his 'Lines Inscribed Upon a Cup Formed from a Skull', and the memorial to his beloved dog Boatswain.

For nineteenth-century and modern visitors alike, the abbey remains as much a building of the imagination as an architectural reality: each visitor reads into the building the Byron they want to exist, and the house remains, today, the poet's most legible epitaph. Byron himself was impatient of the 'unmeaning flattery' so often 'inscribed over human ashes', writing in the 'Epitaph to a Dog' that is found on Boatswain's monument at Newstead that 'When all is done, upon the Tomb is seen, / Not what he was, but what he should have been' (Byron 1808). If we read Newstead Abbey as Byron's epitaph, this was the poet's own fate, too. Upon buying the abbey, Wildman both commemorated Byron and removed from it all traces of what he 'shouldn't have been'. Byron's genius, his noble lineage and his sporting prowess were commemorated by Wildman's collections of Byronic memorabilia. The bullet-holes from Byron's pistol practice in the Great Hall, by contrast, were panelled over, and where once raucous parties had taken place, baronial splendour was renewed. The old chapter house of the priory – converted by Byron into a menagerie for, among other things, his tame bear and wolf-dog – and the Slype (or plunge bath) that he had built over monastic remains were repurposed by Wildman into a chapel. The profanity, ungodliness and wildness implied by their very existence was thus carefully erased from the house that held Byron's memory. Even so, it is impossible to visit the 'ruins' of Newstead Abbey today and not meet Byron at every turn. The modern visitor will find in Newstead Abbey their own Byron, just as generations of literary pilgrims did before them, and as did Byron himself as he explored both his inheritance and his connection to it through his works. Byron and Newstead Abbey remain inextricably intertwined, but the reading of one through the other will always be, as it always has been, a question of the imagination.

References

Anon. 1774. *A New Display of the Beauties of England: Or, A Description of the Most Elegant or Magnificent Public Edifices, Royal Palaces, Noblemen's and Gentlemen's Seats, and other Curiosities, Natural or Artificial, in Different Parts of the Kingdom, Vol. II* (London: R. Goadby).

Byron, Lord George Gordon. 1807a. 'Elegy on Newstead Abbey', in *Hours of*

Idleness. A Series of Poems, Original and Translated (Newark: S. and J. Ridge), 137–47.

Byron, Lord George Gordon. 1807b. 'On Leaving Newstead Abbey', in *Hours of Idleness. A Series of Poems, Original and Translated* (Newark: S. and J. Ridge), 1–3.

Byron, Lord George Gordon. 1808. 'Epitaph to a Dog', transcribed from Boatswain's monument at Newstead Abbey.

Byron, Lord George Gordon. 1829. 'Childe Harold's Pilgrimage', in *The Works of Lord Byron*, vol. I (London: John Murray).

Byron, Lord George Gordon. 1834. 'Newstead Abbey', in *My Daughter's Book, Containing a Selection of Approved Readings in Literature, Science, and Art* (London: Baldwin and Cradock), 118.

Byron, Lord George Gordon. 1836. 'Letter to Mrs Byron, March 6 1809', in *The Works: With His Letters and Journals, and His Life*, edited by Thomas Moore, 6 vols (New York: George Dearborn), vol. I: 133–4.

Byron, Lord George Gordon. 1837a. 'Epistle to Augusta', in *The Complete Works of Lord Byron, Reprinted from the Last London Edition in one Volume* (Paris: A. and W. Galignani), 309–11.

Byron, Lord George Gordon. 1837b. 'Don Juan' in *The Complete Works of Lord Byron, Reprinted from the Last London Edition in one Volume* (Paris: A. and W. Galignani), 580–779.

Fisher, Richard Trott. 1836. *Eleusinia* (London: William Pickering).

Herbert, David. 2009. 'Sophia Hyatt: "The White Lady of Newstead"', in *The Gothic Byron*, edited by Peter Cochran (Newcastle: Cambridge Scholars Publishing), 158–64.

Irving, Washington. 1835. *Abbotsford, and Newstead Abbey* (London: John Murray, 1835).

Lake, J. W. 1824. 'A Sketch of His Life', in *The Works of Lord Byron, Comprehending the Suppressed Poems, Embellished with a Portrait, and a Sketch of his Life* (Paris: A. and W. Galignani).

Matthews, Charles Skinner. 1830. 'Letter from Charles Skinner Matthews, Esq. To Miss I. M.', in *Letters and Journals of Lord Byron with Notices of His Life*, vol. X (London: John Murray), 172–4.

The Gothic Folly at Wimpole, Cambridgeshire

Peter N. Lindfield

Wimpole Hall's Gothic folly, poised on Johnson's Hill in the parkland facing the house's garden facade, evolved over the course of twenty years. In 1749, initial designs were sought by Lord Chancellor Hardwicke of Wimpole from Sanderson Miller, a gentleman architect who had already begun fabricating a ruined folly to commemorate the battle of Edgehill (1642) on his own Radway estate in Warwickshire. Through Sir George Lyttelton, one of Miller's clients for whom he had created a ruined Gothic tower at Hagley Hall in Worcestershire, Chancellor Hardwicke outlined his thoughts on the erection of a new dilapidated castle. There should be, Lyttelton writes, 'no House or even room in it, but mearly [sic] the Walls and Semblance of an Old Castle to make an object from his House. At most he only desires to have a staircase carried up one of the Towers, and a leaded gallery half round it to stand in, and view the Prospect' (Warwick 1749). Miller's proposals were duly accepted and approved of; Chancellor Hardwicke, however, was in no hurry to realise

The Gothic temple at Wimpole. Engraving, 1777

the structure: 'As the building requires no great haste, I think there will be no great harm if it remains in the air a few months longer' (Warwick 1750). Indeed, the folly was not begun until the 2nd Earl of Hardwicke and his wife, Marchioness Grey, arrived at Wimpole in the late 1760s. Miller was, by this time, ill and not able to take responsibility for the fabric, and the structure was instead entrusted to Lancelot 'Capability' Brown, the famous Georgian landscape artist and folly-builder, and James Essex, a respected and scholarly Cambridge-based antiquary and architect. Chancellor Hardwicke's preference for a ruined structure that was reminiscent of antiquity and illustrative of the ravages of time, however spurious, was also favoured by the 2nd Earl: a ruined structure would explicitly suggest the estate's and family's lineage and prestige by association. Lady Grey criticised Brown's efforts in 1772 precisely because his work was too perfect: 'The Tower is better for being raised', she writes, but continues to note that 'the additions Mr. Brown has quite changed from our plan [...] that is, he has "Unpicturesqued" it by making it a mere continuous solid object, instead of a Broken one' (see Adshead 1998: 81). Nevertheless, Wimpole's Gothic folly was an admirable and important monument in Romantic landscape architecture. The ability of such ruined structures, even newly built ones, to convey thoughts and associations connected to the historical past was considerable, and is illustrated by the anonymous four-stanza poem inscribed beneath a 1777 engraving of the Gothic temple at Wimpole:

When Henry stemmd Iernes stormy Flood,
And bow'd to Britains yoke her savage brood;
When by true courage and false zeal impell'd
Richard encamp'd on Salems palmy field
On Towers like these Earl, Baron, Vavasor,
Hung high their Banners, floating in the air.

Free, hardy, proud, they brav'd their feudal Lord
And try'd their rights by ordeal of the Sword.
Now full board with Christmas plenty crown'd
Now ravag'd and oppress'd the country round.
Yet Freedoms cause once rais'd the civil broil,
And Magna Charta clos'd the glorious toil.

Spruce modern Villas different Scenes afford;
The Patriot Baronet, the courtier Lord,
Gently amus'd, now waste the Summers day
In Book-room, Print-room, or in Ferme ornée
While Wit, Champain, and Pines and Poetry,
Virtu and Ice the genial Feast supply.

But hence the Poor are cherish'd, artists fed,
And Vanity relieves in Bountys stead.
Oh might our age in happy concert join
The manly Virtues of the Norman Line,
With the true Science and just Taste which raise
High in each useful Art these Modern Days.

References

Adshead, David. 1998. 'The Design and Building of the Gothic Folly at Wimpole, Cambridgeshire', *The Burlington Magazine* 140, no. 1139: 76–84.

Warwick. 1749. Warwickshire Record Office, Manuscript CR125B/348 (1 June 1749).

Warwick. 1750. Warwickshire Record Office, Manuscript CR125B/788 (15 March 1750).

Cardiff Castle

David Punter

> Yon stately pile, whose ramparts frown
> 	O'er Taff's impetuous wave,
> Whose Keep, to ruin'd grandeur grown,
> All ivy-robed around, looks down
> On Ratostabius' ancient town,
> 	Like guardian sternly grave,
> And, high on central mound, appears
> Moulder'd beneath the tread of years,
> Recalls, with warning voice, to mind
> The transient might of humankind.
> (Williams 1827: 12)

Cardiff Castle, referred to in, for example, William Frederick Williams's Gothic fiction *The Witcheries of Craig Isaf* (1805), now sits rather demurely within the city of Cardiff, and is probably at least as well known for its extraordinary role in the Second World War, when tunnels

'The South Gate of Cardiff Castle'. Paul Sandby, aquatint, 1776

within its walls were developed to serve as air-raid shelters for up to 1,800 people, as for its relevance to the Gothic. However, what is significant about it in Gothic terms is twofold: first, there is the history of the castle itself, and, second, there are the remarkable Gothic Revival interiors laid out by the man known as 'the richest baby in Britain', the 3rd Marquess of Bute.

The castle has Roman origins, or at least antecedents, but these were only discovered for the modern age when Bute began his work and uncovered parts of Roman walls, which he subsequently rebuilt – the tunnels that ran through them were originally added, it is said, so that Bute could take his daily exercise even in bad weather. The Normans founded their castle in 1081, building an artificial motte and raising a keep, the slightly later, twelve-sided stone version of which is still in evidence today, although a number of eighteenth-century paintings show it entirely ruined.

We know that gradually during the sixteenth century the castle was changed into a mansion, replete with intricate decoration; but it was only with the arrival of the Butes that it was transformed, with the architect Henry Holland and the landscape gardener Lancelot 'Capability' Brown employed to undertake a major overhaul. New Gothic Georgian wings were then added to the house, which came to resemble in significant ways a larger version of Horace Walpole's Strawberry Hill, Twickenham; but most of all the 3rd Marquess, working with William Burges, created at the castle a medievalist fantasy of painted murals, stained glass, gilding and sculpture.

This is Burges's most memorable work. We have, for example, the glorious orientalism of the Arab Room, commissioned shortly before his death in 1881, made of wood and covered with pure gold leaf. We have the roof garden at the top of the Bute Tower, which was inspired by Pompeii but is further ornamented with a host of animal motifs that also run through other areas of the house. The library chimneypiece is a work of genius in itself, referring as it does to a variety of ancient languages. The Clock Tower, seen as sensational at its time of completion, dominates the house and displays a remarkable confectionery of motifs that appear to draw more inspiration from elsewhere in Europe than from anything previously seen in Britain. The library, one of the house's many masterpieces, resembles a fantasised version of the library at Tyntesfield, North Somerset, but the decoration is far more ornate, and the wild colours of the Reformed Gothic decoration even spread to the children's bedrooms, replete with friezes and tiles representing key figures from children's literature; all in all, Cardiff Castle became and remains, in both its interiors and its exteriors, a singular icon of modern Gothic architecture.

Reference

Williams, Taliesin. 1827. *Cardiff Castle: A Poem* (Merthyr Tydfil: Printed and Sold for the Author).

Chapter 3:
Exploring Britain's Ruins

Emma McEvoy

In 1809, a gentleman sets out on a tour of England. He has evidently toured before, for the guide who shows him round the spar manufactory at Derby remembers 'how I was affected last year by the fetid smell of the black marble' (Anon. 1809: 17a). With his companions, Miss Wegg and Nancy, the gentleman makes his way from the Home Counties to the Lake District. In many respects, his is a typical tour. He travels in the summer months (1 July to 30 September); he has the money to stay in a succession of inns, and the social cachet to gain entrance to a range of cultural attractions. As he goes, he records his impressions and opinions, as well as details of expenditure, distances covered and the like, in a journal: in this case, a small and narrow book bound in brown calfskin and fastened with a metal clasp. The gentleman, whose name, because he did not enter it in his diary, is now unknown, visits ruins – including Kenilworth Castle, Warwickshire, and Furness Abbey, in what was then Lancashire – in the course of his journey. They form part of a varied itinerary. He, Miss Wegg and Nancy also travel to notable towns, visiting their main historic monuments and new building developments; they call in to inspect thriving new industries, such as button-, pin- and whip-manufacturing in Birmingham; they tour country houses and comment on their artworks; they make their way to, and sit in aesthetic judgement upon, celebrated landscapes; they explore the geological marvels of the Peak District; and they are keen to visit gardens everywhere. As they travel, there is evidence of a service industry ready to accommodate them and others like them, an infrastructure that comprises accommodation, stabling, food provision, guides, equipment hire, travel facilities and more. The anonymous gentleman soon moves into what is already a recognisable 'tourist mode'. Some days in, he starts recommending viewpoints.

As it happens, the anonymous gentleman has left little record of his behaviour at the ruins he visited, apart from the fact that he evidently did some 'halloo-ing' at Furness Abbey, where he experienced 'one of the most distinct & articulate Echoes I ever heard' (Anon. 1809: 45a). Fortunately, other visitors to ruins in the period left fuller accounts of their experiences, and it is the task of this essay to consider some of them. I will be drawing upon a variety of sources: unpublished journals and published travel writing, guidebooks and letters, as well as contemporary images, both published and unpublished. The texts are, for the most part, taken from the 1780s to the late 1830s, a period which, in many ways, was the heyday of domestic tourism in Britain. British domestic tourism only really took off in the 1770s. Its first half-century is characterised by exploration, experimentation, a high sense of dramatic possibility, emotional and philosophical engagement and aesthetic delight; it set in place patterns of tourist behaviour, especially in and around ruins, that were to endure for a long time to come. In what follows, I consider travellers' behaviour at ruins, discussing how they felt, what they thought about and the language in which they talked about their experiences. I look at some of the issues on which they ruminated – whether the work of Time, the business of preservation, or aesthetics – and consider some of the literary contexts through which they experienced ruins. This chapter also identifies some of the creative activities that ruins inspired in the fields of literature, art and music in the eighteenth and early nineteenth centuries. Tourists in this period developed a special kind of vision when it came to ruins. They saw and felt them not as isolated phenomena, but as an integral part of the landscapes in which they were situated. Indeed, as many antiquarian-inclined travellers knew, much of the British landscape was itself a ruin. The presence of a ruin could affect a traveller's sense of everything around it, living people included, as testimonies from Wales, in particular, show. In the final section, I consider the tourist industry itself, thinking about the ruin as a place of consumption, one that was often characterised by some interesting cross-class encounters.

'An Effect, Which Was Rarely to Be Met With'

An 1814 aquatint of Netley Abbey, Southampton, shows some of the forms of behaviour that might be encountered at a popular tourist site in the early nineteenth century. There is the obligatory sketcher, himself a representative figure of the activity of the recording artist, positioned in such a way that the two trees in front of him will frame his picture, and allow the picturesque, ivy-covered window that provides a view of the surrounding landscape to become its focal point. As well as this more sedate figure, there is the active figure in red, gesturing with his stick. Eighteenth-century prints of ruins frequently show such men with their sticks, pointing at, measuring or prodding the structure. Above him is a figure in blue whose activity is of a more adventurous sort: he is exploring the fabric and has clambered up to the triforium, from where he is calling down to his friend, also gesturing with his stick.

An 1812 watercolour of Tintern Abbey, Monmouthshire (*see frontispiece*), shows tourist activity in a different mode. The focus here is on ladies and gentlemen visiting, by moonlight, what was perhaps the most celebrated ruin in Britain. The scene is designed to appeal to the most romantic of sentiments. The image brings out both the sense of benign calm, with the full moon floating in beautifully illuminated

Netley Abbey. J. B. Harraden, aquatint, 1814

clouds, and the drama of the building below, where local men hold flaming torches. There is a nice interplay here of shadow and glare. Men are pointing their sticks, and the women (and some of the men) are holding up their arms in gestures of wonder and delight. At the edges of the image, couples and small groups are entering and leaving inner spaces. The couple in the foreground, who convey the kind of authority associated with the most cultured and wealthy tourists, are illuminated, as if in a spotlight, by the moon and by not just one torch, but two; they hold hands, looking upwards, exuding a sense of both wonder and contentment. High above them are the more adventurous gentlemen, and attention is drawn to their precarious position by the exaggerated posture of the local guide. The whole scene has a sense of drama, even pageantry, about it. This is not merely the conceit of one particular watercolourist, but an aspect of the tourist experience itself. The image depicts a staged visit: a designedly dramatic event that plays to its visitors' sense of the romance of the medieval ruin and caters to their desire for a sublime and moving experience.

A third image, with its associated text, gives us another insight into tourism of ruins in the Romantic period. It is a watercolour from the Reverend John Swete's journal, recording his 1790 tour of Yorkshire. The woman standing in the doorway is Swete's wife, Charlotte. The image, made during a visit to Roche Abbey, Yorkshire, has to be read in conjunction with the description of their visit. Swete's account is

Roche Abbey. Watercolour from the Reverend John Swete's journal, recording a tour of Yorkshire in 1790

characterised by a sense of excitement and adventure: 'As soon as the Carriage stopt we hurried away to the Abbey, to which We had to descend over a Cliff'. The experience, as the cheerful Swete makes clear, meets all expectations: 'In short, even to the very walls of Roche Abbey, there was no intermissing [sic] of pleasing Objects'. He and his wife are 'conducted to the Ruins' by a local guide, about whom he gives no details, and although access to the Abbey is by a 'rude path', Swete is 'agreably disappointed in discovering [... Roche] to be clear of all those entanglements: so that we had it in our Power without inconvenience to survey all their beauties as well as those of the sequester'd Valley' (Swete c. 1790: 11). Swete and his wife are 'enchanted', so much so that they decide to visit the abbey again on their way back south. For their return visit, they decide to treat themselves to a 'fete champêtre' or picnic:

> Having given orders to the Servants that a table and chairs should be procured from the neighboring Farm House, and that the provisions which had been brought from the Inn at Doncaster should be convey'd to some pleasant spot near the Ruins We began our stroll through this little Scene of Enchantment. (Swete, c. 1790: 59)

He and his wife eat, drink and take in the scene, and Swete makes a series of sketches, including a last 'from the spot, where we had luxuriously enjoyed our "fete champêtre"'. By all accounts, the whole affair was a tourist experience of the highest calibre: Swete writes of 'an Effect, which was rarely to be met with, and that never could be exceeded' (Swete c. 1790: 57).

Swete's accounts of Roche Abbey illustrate how a ruin could elicit many different responses, even within the same visit. As well as demanding exploration, aesthetic appreciation and commemoration (in a series of sketches, in this case), the ruin could also be a place of indulgence, a site where tourists could picnic and be waited on, savouring a sense of luxury that existed in exciting contrast not just to everyday life but also to the idea of monastic privation that the building elicited. Consumption of food and drink near or next to ruins was not just something that Swete dreamed up as an extravagance: numerous contemporary accounts have references to the practice. As a guidebook to Tintern Abbey comments:

Nothing can be more agreeable in the summer season, when the tide accords with the hour of the day, than for parties, who descend the Wye in a boat, to have the table cloth spread on the floor of the Abbey, and within the cool shade of its walls to enjoy the repast of Dinner. (Heath 1828: n.p.)

John Byng gives us an idea of what might have been eaten on such occasions when he notes that 'The way to enjoy Tintern Abbey properly, and at leisure, is to bring wines, cold meat, with corn for the horses; (bread, beer, cyder, and commonly salmon, may be had at the Beaufort Arms)' (Byng 1934–8: vol. 1, 24). At the beginning of the period, some dining would have taken place in summer houses, built by private individuals on their estates. Such summer houses are sometimes the subject of complaints by tourists, who consider themselves to be more discriminating, and who disapprove of the juxtaposition of old and new, of monastic solemnity and modern gaiety. Byng, for instance, in a tour of North Wales in 1784, writes of 'a green and white summer house, at the end of a spruce fishing canal' built by Sir Watkyns Williams-Winn, near to the east front of Valle Crucis Abbey in Llangollen, noting scornfully that 'from this well-fancy'd retreat, the abbey is conceal'd by the apple trees in a cabbage garden' (Byng 1934–8: vol. 1, 178). Byng's response to the perceived incongruity and insensitivity of the building is heavily sarcastic. He compares the taste of the wealthy landowner, who was also a well-known patron of the arts, with that of Londoners of the middling classes, alluding to the kinds of places they might frequent on their Sunday jaunts into the suburbs: 'What charming elegance! How worthy of Clapham or Hackney!!' (Byng 1934–8: vol. 1, 178).

'That Solemn Stillness Which Has a Tendency to Lead on the Mind to Meditation'

Byng himself visited Roche Abbey in 1789. Characteristically, he reacts with annoyance to unsympathetic modern developments, carping that 'certainly there shou'd not have been a modern lodge built close to this picturesque old gateway of entrance [...] and to suffer the abbey to be made a lodgement for carts, rollers, &c, &c, is most intolerable!!!' (Byng, 1934–8: vol. 2, 19–20). In general, however, he is charmed by the place, stressing its serenity: 'for fishing there cannot be a better situation; or for love or for contemplation' (Byng 1934–8: vol. 2, 19). In contrast to the dramatic night-time scene at Tintern Abbey discussed above, many visits to ruins were characterised by a sense of contemplative quietness. Indeed, the visit to the ruin was often a welcome relief from the exertions of other kinds of tourist activity. Charlotte Malkin's journal of a tour of Scotland made in 1814, for example, contains a striking instance of the physical discomfort likely to be experienced when tourists ventured into sublime scenery: Malkin walks miles across the Highlands in soaking-wet clothes, after the pony that she has hired decides to lie down in the middle of a ford. A visit to a ruin might well be free from such 'irascible pleasures'. Numerous watercolours and sketches show visitors to ruins relaxing. One image of Kirkstall Abbey in Yorkshire, by Swete, features men very much at leisure – dozing by the stream and perhaps, like Byng, thinking about a spot of fishing.

Contemporary images depict people seated on rocks or leaning on sticks, cattle grazing and horses with reins dropped; this last image conveying a sense of normal business suspended, and the previous one perhaps hinting at the tourists' ruminations. Musing on the state of Kirkstall Abbey that has been 'defiled by vagrant Herds', Swete compares it to Tintern Abbey, already well known for being overly

Swete with a friend reclining lazily outside Kirkstall Abbey. Pencil sketch by the Reverend John Swete

tidied-up. Here, he claims, there is 'not a scratching bramble for the prying Antiquary, nor a stumbling stone for the Man of Contemplation [...] to be met with' (Swete c. 1790: 31). The 'Man of Contemplation' is a figure frequently to be met with at ruins. It is not so much that ruins attract men and women of contemplation, though of course they do, but that ruins themselves have the power to *render* men and women contemplative. Swete refers to this phenomenon when he remarks on: 'that Solemn Stillness which has a tendency to lead on the Mind to Meditation, and which is so peculiarly adapted to the notions we entertain of Monastic Retirement [which] must have been here met with, and experienced by the tenants of this Religious Structure in its fullest extent' (Swete c. 1790: 54).

Visiting the ruin could be a deeply meditative experience, but it was not always a happy one. For Charlotte Malkin, the sublimity in and around the aptly named Castle of Gloom (Castle Campbell) in central Scotland awakens what seems to be an underlying melancholy:

> The grandeur of the fall at the Linn, and the sublimity of the scenery which surrounds it, quite overcame my spirits; nor were these improved by our visiting afterwards the Castle of Gloom, now called Campbell's Castle, at Dollar. I rather wish I could visit scenes of this nature, without my sensibilities being so much awakened. Perhaps if I felt their sublime beauties less enthusiastically, I should behold them with a pleasure better adapted to the warmth [...] and the useful purposes of society. (Malkin 1814: n.p.)

Tourists 'philosophised' at ruins, and often recorded their musings in their journals. Unsurprisingly, they were frequently struck by the ruin as an emblem of mortality and a reminder of the ravages wrought by time. As Swete puts it, 'these [broken pillars] the rent arches and the dilapidated roof offer to the Eye a picture of desolation and raise in the mind a reflexion on the vicissitudes of things!' (Swete c. 1790: 28). Visitors regarded the ruin not only as the remains of the past but also as representative of that vanished history. They imagined its past life and thought about it in relation to some of the leading figures from history. Often they attempted a mental reconstruction of the ruin, too. Lord Grenville, for instance, notes at Caerphilly Castle, South Wales, that 'Enough still remains to enable the imagination to supply the ruined parts, and to trace the outlines of the impregnable fortress, and the Royal Palace' (Grenville 1801: 23). Swete at Karnbre (or Carn Brea) Castle, Cornwall, even executes a drawing that restores the ruin to what, with the help of an engraving from Borlase, he imagines its former condition to have been (Swete 1788–98: 4). Very frequently, visitors give standard reactions when visiting castles or abbeys, and muse upon what the antiquarian topographer Richard Warner, writing of Dunster Castle, Somerset, calls the 'rude times of feudal insolence' (Warner 1800: 80), a bygone era of darkness, savagery and violence that he implicitly juxtaposes with the modern, enlightened present. Sometimes, however, the ruin summons up in visitors thoughts of a less complacent nature. Although William Gilpin blithely comments on the 'picturesque genius' of Thomas Cromwell and Henry VIII in terms that could be said to aestheticise and excuse the horrors of the Dissolution of the Monasteries and the English Civil Wars (Gilpin 1792: vol. 2, 122), other tourists are more critical of the violence endemic to British history. For instance, the remains of Pontefract Castle, Yorkshire, stir Swete to invective against Cromwell and his 'Hypocrisy', finding it unimaginable that Cromwell could have set in motion such desecration 'had he profess'd any real sense of Religion' (Swete c. 1790: 32). It is important to remember that the monastic ruin could inspire real religious feeling and sometimes even a measure of sympathy towards Roman Catholicism and the monastic life. As Swete writes of his visit to Kirkstall Abbey, Yorkshire, 'I cannot but conceive that He may be more immediately there, where, in Edifices constructed for his service by the Piety of his Creatures, his praises are, or have been offered in the hymn of gratitude and adoration' (Swete c. 1790: 32).

Tourists of 'Genius & Sensibility' at the Ruin

Making a ten-day tour down the Wye in 1807, the poet Robert Bloomfield gives an account of the activities that he and his friends engaged in during a daytime visit to Tintern Abbey. They all 'took sketches of the interior', but Bloomfield punningly tells us that 'I found it above my reach' (Bloomfield 1807: 28). He settles instead on another form of activity, and gives 'vent to my feelings by singing, for their amusement and my own, the 104th psalm. And though no "fretted vault" remains to harmonize the sound, it sooth'd me into that state of mind which is most to be desired' (Bloomfield 1807: 28). Bloomfield's response is both a religious and a musical one. While it is an expression of worship akin to Swete's, in that the 104th Psalm praises God and His creation, it is also a performance, one undertaken not merely for self but for friends, too. Singing solo, unaccompanied, is of course a highly suitable act in such a place: Bloomfield's response summons up a medieval musical tradition.

Beyond this localised example, ruins in the eighteenth century often elicited both vocal and musical responses. The most frequently heard instrument was probably the flute, a popular and highly portable instrument. Samuel Taylor Coleridge writes amusingly to Robert Southey of a flute-playing incident in the ruins of Denbigh Castle, Denbighshire, that occurred when he was touring Wales with his friend Joseph Hucks in 1794. His account manages to convey a nice sense of a certain kind of tourist mode – the 'comparative rating' involved, the emotional responses elicited and the language in which they might be relayed. Coleridge starts by building up a sense of atmosphere, describing how Denbigh Castle 'surpasses everything I could have conceived – I wandered there an hour and a half last evening', and then writes of his anticipation when one of two 'well drest young men' suggests to the other, 'Come [...] I'll play my flute – 'twill be romantic!' (Coleridge 2000: vol. 1, 89). The incident climaxes in bathos when, instead of some plaintive and solemn air, the young man plays a popular tune of the day: 'Bless thee for the thought, Man of Genius & Sensibility! I exclaimed – and pre-attuned my heartstring to tremulous emotion. He sat adown (the moon just peering) amid the most awful part of the Ruins – and – romantic Youth! struck up the affecting Tune of *Mrs. Casey*! – 'Tis fact upon my Honour!' (Coleridge 2000: vol. 1, 89–90).

When Bloomfield sings the 104th Psalm in Tintern Abbey, his response is not only musical and religious, but literary, too. Bloomfield's experience of Tintern is framed and informed by his reading of Thomas Gray. The language in which he describes the incident is reminiscent of that poet's language, and he borrows the phrase 'fretted vault' from Gray's *Elegy Written in a Country Church Yard* (1751). As Tim Fulford has pointed out, this tourist act, as Bloomfield well knows, 'is overdetermined: he sees the abbey and imagines his Psalm-singing in relation to Gray's portrait of the country church as a place where the act of commemoration acquires value' (Fulford 2010: 241).

It was not merely published poets such as Bloomfield who experienced the ruins that they visited through literary texts. A visit to a ruin was, for many, an intensely literary experience. John Taylor Coleridge's itinerary for his eight days' tour of 1813 seems to have been much influenced by his knowledge of his celebrated uncle's earlier life and work (Coleridge 1813). Malkin's visit to Rosslyn (or Roslin) Castle, Midlothian, on 12 July 1814 was made in the company of James Hogg and his friend James Gray, also a writer, with whom she met up in Edinburgh expressly for the purpose; it is tempting to think that keeping company with Hogg might have had something to do with her sense of desolation at Campbell Castle two days afterwards. However, the majority of tourists travelled with their favoured authors committed to their memories rather than physically present at their side. Theirs was a literary culture in which poetry was often recited and known by heart, and when they arrived at ruins, visitors and tourists quoted from these with gusto. It is tempting to think of the literary quotations with which tourists respond to ruins as 'tags', a label that not only runs the risk of underestimating the validity or depth of the experience, but also of ignoring the fact that often the quotations were highly appropriate to the ruins in which they were cited. Such quotations give us an insight into the imaginative worlds summoned up by ruins. What is most surprising, particularly at the beginning of the period, is the extent to which so many of those who have left accounts of their visits tended to perceive British Gothic ruins through the works of Classical Roman and Greek authors. In Swete's earlier journals, for instance, Classical quotations predominate. He quotes Lucan when he visits medieval English castles. Visiting the possible site of a stannary court – a medieval regional legislative and legal institution – on Dartmoor in 1797, his immediate recourse is to Cicero: 'But if these rude rocks have ever been rendered memorable by the British Cato's and Cethegi – by the rites of the Druids or the decrees of the Judge how sad is the change!' (Swete 1797: 9). It is difficult to overestimate how central the Classical imagination was to the experience of British ruins for many in the late eighteenth century. Partly, of course, this is due to the fact that a great number of those touring – and an even greater proportion of those whose records of their tours have survived – were university men who had been schooled in the Classics. Latin was thus the language through which their experiences might be mediated and intellectually filtered.

There were, of course, other literary cultures on which visitors to ruins in the period could draw. Unsurprisingly, the influence of Shakespeare looms large, and Romantic-period writers often referred to the history plays when visiting castles, and cited 'Bare ruin'd choirs' and other lines from the sonnets when visiting ruined ecclesiastical buildings. Alexander Pope's 'Eloisa to Abelard' (1717) appears frequently in ruin musings, and John Milton is often called upon too. In *A Tour through the Northern Counties of England, and the Borders of Scotland* (1802), Richard Warner quotes the phrase 'bosomed high in tufted trees' from Milton's 'L'Allegro' (1645) in his account of Dudley Castle, West Midlands (Warner 1802: vol. 1, 98); he uses the phrase again in the second volume when writing of Kenilworth Castle (Warner 1802: vol. 2, 225). Milton's 'Il Penseroso' (1645) was an even more popular text on which to draw. There was also an extensive body of eighteenth-century literature devoted to ruin and ruins that tourists could mine. Much of the poetry of William Lisle Bowles, James Beattie and Thomas Gray, for example, is preoccupied with the response of the sensitive-minded observer to architectural ruin. These, together with texts by earlier English writers, became part of the furniture of the Romantic tourist's mind. Some of the poems with which Romantic-period tourists were well acquainted are not necessarily those that are familiar to the twenty-first-century reader. At Harewood Castle, Yorkshire, for instance, Warner quotes from William Crowe's *Lewesdon Hill* (1788), a topographical poem in the style of John Denham's *Cooper's Hill* (1642):

> It has no name, no honourable note.
> No chronicle of all thy warlike pride.
> To testify what once thou wert, how great,
> How glorious, and how fear'd.
> (quoted in Warner 1802: vol. 1, 244)

Tellingly, many such quotations stand without attribution, a detail that indicates that they had been so assimilated into eighteenth-century tourist practice that they served as a common discourse or language for the perception of ruins.

A 'polished-up' piece from a tour made by Edward Daniel Clarke in 1791 gives an insight into the literary worlds through which the ruin might be experienced. It also reminds us that poetry at ruins was not only heard internally, but audibly recited, too. Like Coleridge's account of the flute-playing at Denbigh Castle, Clarke's account has been deliberately heightened for the purposes of comedy, but it is no less useful for that. Indeed, the comedy could be said to make explicit the kinds of response that other writers do not feel the need to note. Clarke published his tour anonymously in 1793 as *A Tour through the South of England, Wales, and Part of Ireland, Made During the Summer of 1791*. For the most part the work is characterised by a quirky and whimsical tone, though a vein of rather heavy-handed humour in the form of comic portrayal of the lower classes runs throughout. The chief butt is Clarke's manservant Jeremy, whose habits among the ruins are at one point contrasted with those of his master: 'At length, to my unspeakable surprise, I discovered my supposed virtuoso giving ease to nature, in a snug corner among the ruins, and, with the most supercilious contempt for those venerable vestiges of antiquity, dedicating the ivy-mantled walls of Narbarth to the goddess Cloacina' (Clarke 1793: 221).

Into his primarily Sternean narrative, Clarke incorporates a Gothicised interlude dealing with his adventures at Cilgerran Castle in Pembrokeshire, a formidable thirteenth-century ruin set high above the river Teifi. Clarke introduces us to 'Cilgerron' through John and Anna Laetitia Aikin's Gothic fragment 'Sir Bertrand' (1773), noting that 'all that the imagination has suggested of Sir Bertrand, and the terrors of enchantment, seemed here verified' (Clarke 1793: 249). The 'verification' of Clarke's literary imagination continues throughout the piece. The Aikins's fragment informs not only the atmosphere, but the slender narrative elements, too, as well as heightening the sense of suspense and climax. Seeing the castle from below, Clarke depicts the local men, in their 'old-world' coracles, as wizard-like figures, supernaturally swift and prone suddenly to disappear: 'While we were gazing at the shattered walls of this gloomy fortress, a number of figures apparently in punch bowls, with each a wand in his hand, came suddenly floating round the foundation, and passing us like lightning, were hurried down the stream until we saw them no more' (Clarke 1793: 250).

The account continues with the motif of the ruin as a place of terrifying enchantment as Clarke is guided by a young Welsh-speaking boy, against whose advice he climbs a 'shattered staircase' to explore 'old apartments whose floors had given way by time and fallen in huge fragments below'. Both are seized by fear at the sound of a 'coarse convulsive hissing'; in a pointed allusion to the haunted battlements of Elsinore in Shakespeare's *Hamlet*, Clarke tells us that it makes his 'blood curdle in my veins'. At this point, Clarke turns the tables and finishes the anecdote in a manner that, at the expense of the uneducated local, vindicates the perception of the tourist. The boy is sure that 'there is sperrits about!', but Clarke, rejoicing in a superior education, eschews the idea of 'supernatural agency'. He discovers that the source of the sound is an owl and then proceeds to recite 'Beatties beautiful lines' (Clarke 1793: 254–5) about an 'owl on pinions grey' from James Beattie's poem 'Retirement' (1758). This is not just an off-the-shelf allusion but one that is strikingly fitting to the situation, not only because there is an owl present, but because the owl in the poem flies from a haunt in a cliff over a 'gloomy stream'. The passage then comes full circle. It began with Clarke perceiving the locals as wizards, but by the end he depicts himself as an object of fear, when, reciting loftily, he is taken for someone with occult tendencies: 'Whether my guide thought I was invoking Hecate, or saying the Lord's prayer backwards […he] took care to keep me at a distance' (Clarke 1793: 256).

Visiting ruins did not merely encourage acts of reading and recitation. The practice also inspired original acts of literary composition. Of the figures shown in contemporary images, not all of those figured musing amidst the ruins with a pencil in hand and a book open before them are sketchers of the picturesque. In the revealingly titled *Observations on a Tour Through Almost the Whole of England, and a Considerable Part of Scotland, in a Series of Letters, Addressed to a Large Number of Intelligent and Respectable Friends* (1801), the actor and song-writer Charles Dibdin complains of the number of recent authors that tourism has created, comparing them to 'adventurers on the stage' (Dibdin 1801–2: vol. 1, 67). Dibdin has in his sights not the writers of travel narratives, of which he is one, but of inferior poems and literary musings generated on the spot by tourists of the day, the subject of the previous chapter of this book. Meditations at ruins inspired many poetic rhapsodies. Ruin-inspired amateur writers tend to express themselves in short poetic forms such as the sonnet, or through medium-length verse written in iambics. Loco-descriptive poems that, taking their cue from Beattie and West, are steeped in elegiac sentiment and atmosphere predominate. This kind of poetic effusion needed no relation to an accepted body of work, or even to the title of poet, but could stand alone, a monument in itself. As such, many examples made their way into not only private manuscript journals and albums, but also print. Such works often feature in early guidebooks (such as those by Charles Heath of Monmouthshire).

Ruins, Landscape and Locals

A ruin for a Romantic-period tourist is not just a fixed site whose boundaries are its external walls. Rather, it is intimately connected to the landscape in which it lies. Writers of journals not only describe the ruin's interiors and exteriors, but the approach to the ruin and the way that it relates to the surrounding landscape, too. Artists, professionals and amateurs alike, picture the ruin from many different angles and vantage points. They also take a variety of sketches from the ruin itself, experimenting with different views, determined to convey different aspects of the landscape of which the ruin is a part. Romantic-period tourists are supremely aware of the relation between the ruin and the surrounding landscape. Sometimes they see the latter as a setting for the former. Often, however, they envisage a more integral relation between the two, seeing the ruin as an expression of place. Numerous sketchbooks and travel journals testify to this tendency. The unknown artist of a set of 1802 sketches shows a Welsh ruin that almost seems to have grown from the landscape. For some tourists, the relation between landscape and building was one of the defining characteristics of ancient architecture. Lord Grenville, on a tour of South Wales and the West Country in 1801, comments at Goodrich Castle, Herefordshire on 'the manner in which both the Rock and the Tower are adapted in every part of their varied shape to the basis of earth from which each appears to rise'. He concludes that it is this harmony between ground and building that makes ancient buildings more aesthetically pleasing than modern ones, with their 'straight lines' ill-adapted to the earth (Grenville 1801: 23).

The ruin was in more ways than one an unstable edifice. Its meanings, primarily its connotations of antiquity, spilled out of it and onto the surrounding landscape and people. The tendency was particularly marked in Wales, a country where, as Byng proudly points out, 'we tred castellated ground every day' (Byng, 1934–8: vol. 1, 172). English tourists in particular were inclined to see Wales as being disconnected from

View of Dinas Bran, or Crow Castle, from the road to Llangollen, 5 August 1802

modernity. For them, not only was Wales an ancient land, but its people were an ancient people, living embodiments of the Ancient Britons, too. The anonymous 1802 sketches include three Welsh women, not just because their costumes are 'picturesque' but because the artist thinks of them as being of a piece with the ruin. Hearing a Welsh harpist play was an experience without which a tour to Wales was incomplete. When Clarke mentions the occasion on which he and his companions 'had, for the first time since we entered Wales, the pleasure of hearing the music of the country, in its pure state, from a poor blind harper' (Clarke 1793: 257), he is assuming, like many others, that the music he hears is the original music of the British Isles. Listening to the music of the harpers was, in some ways, the apogee of the ruin experience, or at least its ultimate complement. Welsh harpers could conjure up the ancient world; they could *realise* the ruin. Byng encourages harpers 'to repeat the tunes of the greatest antiquity'. He writes semi-playfully of 'the best harper we have met with; (by name Erasmus, a sound bespeaking great learning and antiquity)' (Byng 1934–8: vol. 1, 161). In Dolgellau, Clarke is played to by a 'descendant of Cadwallader', a variant spelling of Cadwaladr, the name of the seventh-century king of Gwynedd (Clarke 1793: 277). The best of these performances revived the past for their audiences, having the power to bring the momentous events from ancient history back to life before the tourists' eyes. Writing of the soul-stirring performance of the female harper at the Talbot Inn in Aberystwyth, Clarke notes that her harp 'sung the fall of Llewellyn, and broke forth in a rapid tumultuous movement, expressive of the battles he had fought, and the laurels he had won' (Clarke 1793: 258–9). Earlier in the period, being played to by a Welsh harper usually took place away from the ruin, though Byng notes in 1781 that 'possibly a Welsh harper might be procured from Chepstow' to entertain those picnicking in Tintern Abbey (Byng 1934-8: vol. 1, 24). By the 1840s, harpers at some Welsh ruins had become more of a fixture: Emily Hall remarks on two harpers at the entrance to Raglan Castle, Monmouthshire, in 1847 (Freeman 2017).

The exploration of ruins involved both travellers and local people in some interesting cross-class contact. The Reverend John Skinner, who rode round southern England in a series of tours from the 1790s to the 1830s, is one of many antiquaries who made a habit of talking to locals, particularly the aged, in an attempt to capture disappeared or rapidly disappearing local history. Walking along part of the hilly road from Bridport to Dorchester, he takes up with an 'Old Veteran' (Skinner 1804, 1827, 1829: 304) whom he quizzes about the surrounding land, sometimes mentally correcting him when he considers him to be mistaken. Such conversations could prove highly productive for the travellers involved. Near Padstow in Cornwall, for instance, Richard Warner, 'having accidentally met with a very intelligent farmer', is lucky enough to come across a kistvaen (a box-like tomb or burial chamber) that even the 'indefatigable Borlase' (William Borlase, the Cornish antiquary) had not discovered (Warner 1809: 322). Swete, on Dartmoor, is much taken with an ancient yeoman (Swete 1797): 'Old Cator', for Swete, is not so much a source of information about the surrounding area as a representative of a simpler, truer past. Swete questions him about his way of life and notes his answers meticulously over several pages of his journal. Old Cator, a noble primitive of old for Swete, inspires him to quote Ovid, Horace, Virgil and Juvenal. He sketches the old man in front of his cottage and even writes a sonnet about him.

Tourists might encounter people working and even living in the ruins that they visited. Byng records such an encounter at Valle Crucis, Llangollen, hinting that he did not meet with the respect that he felt he deserved. He writes that south of the 'solemn ruin [...] is now the habitation of a farmer [...] the forward ground is now enclosed for a farm-yard, and every quarter disgrac'd by farming utensils and total neglect. The farmer is a fellow of most insolent manners' (Byng 1934–8: vol. 1, 178). Beggars were common at many of the better-known ruins across Britain. As Malcolm Andrews notes of Tintern Abbey, many poor people 'occupied ramshackle huts set up amongst the monastery ruins, and the tourist could only avoid them by exercising a little charity' (Andrews 1989: 102). Tourists also encountered local people working in a fast-developing service industry. One of the many pleasures to be had from reading Bloomfield's journal derives from the unusual amount of attention that he devotes to the people of all classes around him. Bloomfield chats with a boatman on the Wye about the price of cider, and at Tretower Castle, Powys, with the aid of an interpreter, converses with Jane Edwards, 'an upright woman, an hundred years old', who 'asked charity' (Bloomfield 1807: 48). Beside his sketches of Tretower Castle ruins and Jane Edwards, Bloomfield notes that she pronounces her name 'Etwarts' (Bloomfield 1807: 49).

The most direct and prolonged encounter with local people at ruins occurred in the business of guiding. Sometimes guides were those living in the ruins, some of them established nearby in humble dwellings by the owner. In many cases, guiding was closely linked to

Bloomfield's sketch of Jane Edwards and Tretower Castle. From his Journal of a ten days' tour from Uley in Gloucestershire by way of Ross [...], *August 1807*

begging. Often writers are relatively uninformative about their guides, giving little more information than their sex or age. Guiding seems to have been primarily a business for either the old or the young of both sexes. Sometimes, the guide is effectively written out of the account, as happens when Swete writes, in the passive mode, of being 'conducted to the Ruins' of Roche Abbey. In this instance, as in many others, the function of the guide may have extended to little beyond the most basic sense of the term. There are, however, anecdotes that tell us something about the way in which guides went about their business. Inevitably there are dismissive references to ill-educated, mentally feeble guides. Byng at Tintern, for example, writes of being 'accompany'd by a boy who knew nothing, and by a very old man who had forgotten every thing' (Byng 1934-8: vol. 1, 24). Other accounts suggest that guides operated with élan, not just leading tourists but imparting – and, conceivably, inventing – local lore. The boy who warned Clarke about the 'sperrits', for one, seems to have had a lively sense of drama, as does the 'country woman' encountered by Bloomfield at Raglan, who wavers effectively between scientific and supernatural explanations: 'when a light is carried in, it is soon extinguish'd, and that they say it is because of damps, but for her part she was inclined to believe with many of her neighbours, that the Devil was there' (Bloomfield 1807: 39).

With 'Utmost Ease and Convenience': The Development of the Tourist Industry

Byng, exploring Welsh ruins in 1784, finds much to complain about as regards the state in which he finds them. Sometimes they are filled with miscellaneous local businesses. The courtyard of Caernarfon Castle, complains Byng, is 'disgrac'd by a saw pit and a carpenter's yard' (Byng 1934-8: vol. 1, 163). Chepstow Castle was given over to an even greater variety of 'common purposes; such as a stable, dog-kennel malt-house, and not long ago a glass-house' (Heath 1826: n.p.). Sometimes, as at Llangollen, 'few remains of the castle are existing, as the country people throw down the stones; & have lately by these frolicks kill'd some sheep' (Byng, 1934-8: vol. 1, 177). On occasion, local landowners are presented as failing in their responsibilities to the buildings. Byng, as we saw, found fault with the inappropriate construction near Valle Crucis, Denbighshire. In 1791, Clarke notes that Margam Abbey, Wales, was protected by only 'a paltry covering of oiled paper' (Clarke 1793: 191). Sometimes it is treasure-hunters who are at fault: 'the idea of hidden treasure tempts the mischievous and idle, to dig about their foundations to the destruction of their ruins; and the misfortune is, that they often find enough to gratify (at least) their curiosity' (Byng 1934–8: vol. 1, 168–9). Some of these complaints would become less common as the years went on – or, at least they were not so regularly to be heard in those places in England and Wales where tourism established itself most firmly. The record is different for much Scottish tourism in the same period. Generally speaking, as tourism increased, so the tourist experience was refined and finessed, though many ruins continued to host local businesses.

Some ruins became hubs within dense tourist economies, places of consumption where visitors might be catered to by means of a complex network of local services. Local people might provide not only food and drink, but lighting, transport, porterage and items such as blankets, too. The Wye valley was one of the first areas to be set up with such a comprehensive tourist package. Bloomfield in his account of his Wye valley tour pays particular attention to this service industry. He writes about the pleasure boats and the conveyance of food and drink. His illustrations are filled with the ingenious contrivances set up for tourism. He records, for example, the complex arrangements for passenger transport on the river and determinedly juxtaposes, with a nice sense of ridiculousness, the fashionable ladies and gentlemen with the rural settings in which they find themselves.

Ruin tourism transformed local economies and created many different kinds of work. A note by a Mr Wyatt from the eighth edition of Charles Heath's *The Excursion down the Wye* (1826) alerts us to the fact that preparing 'Ragland' (now known as Raglan) Castle for tourism required the removal of rubbish, the chopping back of briars and the regular mowing of grass. As a result of these preparations, Wyatt tells us, the castle could now 'be surveyed with the utmost ease and convenience' (Heath 1826: n.p.). As well as manual labour, building work was often required too. By the late 1830s, Tintern Abbey had been provided with 'steps, rails, and planks [by the means of which] all travellers, even elderly ladies, may safely traverse the walls […] from summit to floor' (Matheson 2007). Wyatt notes that the porters' lodges of Raglan, having been 'divested' of 'stables, pigsties, and cider houses', were then modified: two rooms above had been 'rendered easy of access by a commodious staircase', for the purposes of rest or 'retreat from weather' (Heath 1826: n.p.). Such facilities demanded staff. Wyatt talks of the installing of resident caretakers at Raglan. One of the rooms in the porters' lodges was for a 'female [...] who has charge of the interiors'; a 'conductor to strangers' was also appointed there. From the same guidebook we learn that, at Goodrich, a 'Mr. Morgan, who has the care of the Castle, is in constant attendance, from morning till night, during the season' (Heath 1826: n.p.).

The local 'conductor to strangers', however, could only provide so much, and pleasure-seeking tourists inevitably wanted more. Byng, in his *Tour of South Wales* of 1787, gives a rather comprehensive account of the kinds of information, both learned and practical, that tourists wanted to be able to access when visiting the nation's ruins. Notably dismissive of guides throughout his travels, he is here equally dismissive of contemporary travel writing:

> Most modern tours are written (in my mind) too much in the stile of pompous history; not dwelling sufficiently upon the prices of provisions, recommendations of inns, statement of roads, &c. so that the following travellers reap little benefit from them.
>
> I have often thought that maps, merely for tourists might be made. And have wish'd that some intelligent traveller (for instance Mr Grose) wou'd mark on such touring maps, all the castles, Roman stations, views, canals, parks &c, &c. which accompanied by other common maps, wou'd lead the researching tourist to every proper point & object; and not subject him (as at present) to ask questions of ignorant innkeepers, or to hunt in books, for what is not to be found; for till lately we had no inquisitive travellers and but few views of remarkable places. (Byng 1934–8: vol. 1, 249)

From the last years of the eighteenth century a new kind of guidebook, one that well suited Byng's requirements, came into being. Some of the most engaging examples are those produced by Charles Heath, a printer based in Monmouthshire. Heath was well placed to take advantage of Wye valley tourism: he lived locally, had a good knowledge of the surrounding area and a good education. He was also particularly fortunate as regards his social status, having contacts from all across the class spectrum. Heath was friends with learned scholars both nearby and further afield, and he was assiduous when it came to collecting the reminiscences of elderly locals. As C. S. Matheson points out in an essay on Heath's guidebooks, 'Guide books attend to the mechanisms and institutions of travel (which they have a hand in constructing) even as they address and administer to the individual' (Matheson 2012: 51). Heath did all these things successfully. He gathered information, consolidated and codified typical practice, made useful suggestions, directed tourists to local services, pointed out the best view points, and accrued a selection of interesting anecdotes. When it came to the business of ruins, Heath ensured that, in Byng's phrase, 'inquisitive travellers' did not need to be 'researching' tourists, compelled to hunt in books or question 'ignorant innkeepers' for the information that they required.

The manuscript journals of the Rev. John Skinner, now held in the British Library, are testimony to both the amount of research and the communal effort that might lie behind an antiquary's successful tour. At Chichester, for example, where he savours the glories of the cathedral by moonlight and rummages among the ruins of the Roman wall in the bishop's garden, he also visits Brewer's Museum, browses through collections (including the Roman coin collection of his host at the inn), finds some 'coarse British pottery' in a friend's garden and procures an introduction to a scholar further along his route (Skinner 1821: 36). In various private houses Skinner gains access to artefacts that help to enrich his sense of the ruins that he visits – and, of course, he has the benefit of exchanging opinions with, and learning from, various learned friends. Even when undertaken alone, his journeys are in some ways a community event, made possible by what Rosemary Sweet calls a 'flourishing network of exchange and correspondence' (Sweet 2004: 61). Fellow antiquaries, as well as offering their own hospitality, provided letters of introduction to other scholars, amassed relevant texts, excavated sites and assimilated their findings.

Heath and others like him made sure that the requisite historical information was gathered together in one useful, purchasable and affordable book. His guidebook to Tintern, *Historical and Descriptive Accounts of the Ancient and Present State of Tintern Abbey*, points out in its subtitle that it is *Collected from Original Papers, and Unques-*

tionable Authorities. Heath's tone is particularly noteworthy. The guidebook is not written 'in the stile of pompous history', but in an entertaining and engaging manner. Significantly, Heath frequently provides the provenance of the information that he draws on, and by so doing, allows tourists themselves to feel that they are associates of the learned. His history is not just that of the distant past. He recounts local anecdotes to give the sort of information that might be gathered from the kind of innkeeper that Byng rarely seemed to run into. Heath tells his readers about the buildings' recent history, relating what aged locals had told him. A certain Charles Lewellyn, Heath informs us, told him that 'when he was a young man' Tintern Abbey had been used as 'the village fives court' and that 'the body of the church [had been used] for playing quoits', a knight's effigy used as a 'stop'. Heath manages to be both colloquial and gently coercive, getting the reader on side when, for example, he recounts examples of bad tourist behaviour, such as that of the 'plundering marauder' who removed a tile from Tintern (Heath 1828: n.p.).

Heath, of course, not only had much to impart to tourists in the Romantic period, but he also has much to tell the twenty-first-century reader about Romantic-period tourism: not least the fact that tourists, like Bloomfield, expected to buy guidebooks when they visited Britain's ruins. From Heath's guide to Tintern we learn that visitors to the abbey who had arrived by boat had only two hours maximum to inspect the ruins because of the times of the tides. We hear of the popularity of evening visits: 'the still hour of evening', he writes, 'has always been preferred for the most agreeable enjoyment of the scene' (Heath 1828: n.p.). Heath notes that his own favourite time to visit is during the harvest moon. We learn too that the cottages adjoining the abbey, 'so offensive to the eye of Mr Gilpin' in his account of Tintern's picturesque splendours, have now been removed (Heath 1828: n.p.). As Matheson comments, the eleven editions of Heath's Tintern Abbey guidebook provide 'a detailed and entertaining picture of the evolving tourist infrastructure of the region' (Matheson 2007).

It is interesting to compare Heath's guidebooks with those published twenty years later. Heath's still retain something of the quality of the private journal, with its poetic effusions by amateur writers and its attention to named people. The same, however, cannot be said of such works as Adam and Charles Black's *Picturesque Tourist and Road-Book of England and Wales* (1847) or John Murray's *Handbook for Travellers in North Wales* (1861). These are corporate, mass-produced guidebooks published for a larger metropolitan market. Murray's guide was one of a series and was published hundreds of miles away in London, while Black's was published in Edinburgh. This is tourism considered on a national scale. The studied individuality that characterises Heath's works has disappeared. Neither book relays the knowledge of a community of amateur scholars. Murray's guide imparts useful tourist information – geographical, geological, antiquarian and linguistic – but it is delivered in an encyclopaedic mode at the beginning of the work. The knowledge that it contains has no provenance, and the itineraries that it sketches out are, in keeping with the development of the railways, on a significantly larger scale. The guides give information about roads and railways and provide skeleton routes for the whole of Wales. Black's has a special section containing 'Hints to all railway travellers'.

These guidebooks clearly mark the emergence of a different tourist mode. They are aware of this, and even register regret for the passing of the older style of tourism. Noting the improved roads of North Wales, Murray's guide comments: 'The "horsepaths" have long since disappeared, and broad smooth roads have taken their place [...] Indeed, the great highways permeate the mountains too freely to please many an ardent lover of untamed nature, who would rather meet with more difficulties and more solitude' (Murray 1861: xxiv). Gone, then, is the sense of exploration to be found in such travellers as Skinner and Malkin. Timetabled, met and directed, these later tourists expected, and for the most part found, a range of services and conveniences at their disposal: Murray's guide even advises on how much constituted an acceptable tip. Their travel was smoother and their accommodation more reliable. Tourists might now stay in hotels with customised notepaper decorated with vignettes of the local ruins. There was much more for them to buy. Whereas earlier tourists to Wales could purchase local prints and knitted socks as souvenirs, later tourists had a range of themed objects to choose from: photographs, glass paperweights, crockery, silver thimbles and so on. Ruin tourism had become merely one expression of a much more commodified and commercialised world.

In 1860, Frederica Rouse Boughton left her home in Shropshire for a short holiday in Merionethshire, Wales. She visits many of the ruins frequented by earlier generations of tourists and, while there, she does many of the things that her predecessors did, including making aesthetic judgements, sketching and musing. In some respects, however, her experiences are markedly different from those of earlier tourists. Boughton and her party spend a day visiting Valle Crucis and Dinas Bran. Valle Crucis is no longer in the state of 'total neglect' in which Byng found it, and there do not seem to be any farmers with 'insolent manners' around. Boughton's account conveys the serenity of the experience, but it is most interesting in its suggestion that tourism is now an ignoble activity. Indeed, she conveys a self-consciousness about the business of being a tourist that finds no equivalent in the writing of Byng or Swete: 'The ruins are beautiful, quite so beautiful as to make one forget the fact of being a tourist' (Pitman 2009: 125–6). Boughton is very aware of the ironies inherent in this attitude, and she makes them the subject of her wit in the succeeding passage. From Valle Crucis, she and her party proceed to Dinas Bran with their Black's guide, as she is careful to point out. They make the thirsty climb up to Crow Castle but are doomed not to experience the sublime once there. The castle is no longer the deserted building recorded by the anonymous artist of 1802. To their horror they find 'a vulgar little shop established amongst the ruins for ginger beer' (Pitman 2009: 126). Boughton's reaction is bittersweet. Made of sterner stuff, her companions resolve that they will not patronise the establishment and decide to forgo the ginger beer. Boughton, however, humorously notes in her journal that actually she would have quite liked some.

Further Reading

Bloomfield, Robert. 2012. *The Banks of the Wye: A Romantic Circles Electronic Edition*, edited by Tim Fulford, https://www.rc.umd.edu/editions/wye/HTML/MSJournal.html [last accessed 29 May 2017].

Watson, Nicola. 2006. *The Literary Tourist: Readers and Places in Romantic and Victorian Britain* (Basingstoke: Palgrave Macmillan).

References

Andrews, Malcolm. 1989. *The Search for the Picturesque: Landscape, Aesthetics and Tourism in Britain, 1760–1800* (Aldershot: Scolar Press).

Anon. 1802. *Sketches in North Wales, chiefly cos. Merioneth and Denbigh; July–August 1802*, British Library, BL Add MS 24003.

Anon. 1809. *Travel Journal of an anonymous Englishman in the Lake District*, British Library, BL Add MS 59867.

Black, Adam and Charles Black. 1847. *Picturesque Tourist and Road-Book of England and Wales* (Edinburgh: Adam and Charles Black).

Bloomfield, Robert. 1807. *Journal of a ten days' tour from Uley in Gloucestershire by way of Ross, down the River Wye to Chepstow, Abergavenny, Brecon, Hereford, Malvern, &c., August 1807*, British Library, BL Add MS 28267.

Byng, John, Viscount Torrington. 1934-8. *The Torrington Diaries*, edited by C. Bruyn Andrews, 4 vols (London: Eyre and Spottiswoode).

Clarke, Edward Daniel. 1793. *A Tour through the South of England, Wales, and Part of Ireland, Made During the Summer of 1791* (London: Minerva Press).

Coleridge, John Taylor. 1813. *Journal of a tour in North Devon with his Father Col. James Coleridge, John Keble and Mr Gaussen*, British Library, BL Add MS 86007.

Coleridge, Samuel Taylor. 2000. *Collected Letters of Samuel Taylor Coleridge*, edited by Earl Leslie Griggs, 6 vols (Oxford: Clarendon Press).

Dibdin, Charles. 1801-2. *Observations on a Tour Through Almost the Whole of England, and a Considerable Part of Scotland, in a Series of Letters, Addressed to a Large Number of Intelligent and Respectable Friends* (London: G. Goulding).

Freeman, Michael. 2017. *Early Tourists in Wales; 18th- and 19th-century Tourists' comments about Wales*, https://sublimewales.wordpress.com [last accessed 20 May 2017].

Fulford, Tim. 2010. 'The Road Not Taken: Robert Bloomfield's Wye Valley and the Poetic Imagination', in *English Romantic Writers and the West Country*, edited by N. Roe (Basingstoke: Palgrave Macmillan), 237–54.

Gilpin, William. 1792. *Observations, Relative Chiefly to Picturesque Beauty, Made in the year 1772, On Several Parts of England; Particularly the Mountains and Lakes of Cumberland and Westmoreland*, 3rd edn (London: R. Blamire).

Grenville, William Wyndham. 1801. *Journal by Lord Grenville of a tour in South Wales and the West Country; August 1801*, British Library, BL Add MS 69158.

Heath, Charles. 1826. *The Excursion down the Wye from Ross to Monmouth; Comprehending, Historical Accounts of Wilton and Goodrich Castles and Memoirs of John Kyrle the Man of Ross*, 8th edn (Charles Heath: Monmouth).

Heath, Charles. 1828. *Historical and Descriptive Accounts of the Ancient and Present State of Tintern Abbey; […] Collected from Original Papers, and Unquestionable Authorities*, 11th edn (Monmouth and London: Charles Heath and Longman & Co).

Malkin, Charlotte. 1814. *Journal of a Tour of Scotland; July–August 1814*, British Library, BL Add MS 85321.

Matheson, C. S. 2007. *Enchanting Ruin: Tintern Abbey and Romantic Tourism in Wales*, https://www.lib.umich.edu/enchanting-ruin-tintern-abbey-romantic-tourism-wales/introduction.html [last accessed 29 May 2017].

Matheson, C. S. 2012. '"Ancient and Present": Charles Heath of Monmouth and the *Historical and Descriptive Accounts […] of Tintern Abbey*, 1793–1828', in *Travel Writing and Tourism in Britain and Ireland*, edited by Benjamin

Colbert (Basingstoke: Palgrave Macmillan), 50–67.

Murray, John. 1861. *Handbook for Travellers in North Wales. With a Travelling Map* (London: John Murray).

Pitman, Liz. 2009. *Pigsties and Paradise: Lady Diarists and the Tour of Wales, 1795-1860* (Llanrwst: Gwasg Carreg Gwalch).

Skinner, Rev. John. (1804, 1827, 1829). *Journal of the return from the Channel Islands through Southampton, Wimborne, and other places in co. Dorset; 1827. County of Dorset: Tours through, with views and drawings: 1804, 1827, 1829. Channel Islands: Tour to, with views.* British Library, BL Add MS 33700.

Skinner, Rev. John. 1821. *Journal of tour from Bath to Winchester, thence into Sussex; 1821. City of Winchester: Tour to, from Bath: 1821. County of Sussex: Tours through, with views and drawings,* British Library, BL Add MS 33670.

Sweet, Rosemary. 2004. *Antiquaries: The Discovery of the Past in Eighteenth-Century Britain* (London: Hambledon & London).

Swete, Rev. John. 1788-98. *Tour in Cornwall, Nottinghamshire, Yorkshire,* Devon Archives and Local Studies Service, ref. Z/19/2/19.

Swete, Rev. John. *c.* 1790. *Tour in Yorkshire,* Devon Archives and Local Studies Service, ref. Z/19/2/16.

Swete, Rev. John. 1797. *Devon Tour,* Devon Archives and Local Studies Service, ref. 564M/F14.

Warner, Richard. 1800. *A Walk through some of the Western Counties of England, and the Borders of Scotland* (Bath: Richard Cruttwell).

Warner, Richard. 1802. *A Tour through the Northern Counties of England, and the Borders of Scotland,* 2 vols (Bath: Richard Cruttwell).

Warner, Richard. 1809. *A Tour Through Cornwall, in the Autumn of 1808* (Bath: Richard Cruttwell).

RUINS IN FOCUS

Icolmkill: The Ruins of Iona

Sally Foster

> That man is little to be envied, whose patriotism would not gain force upon the plain of Marathon, or whose piety would not grow warmer among the ruins of *Iona*! (Chapman 1930: 135)

Iona, a small island off Scotland's west coast, was famed as a cradle of Christianity, a place of erudition and royal burials. The writings about its ruins between the years 1700 and 1850 fall between rare travellers' descriptions, notably the first visual record, and the earliest significant scholarly works (Campbell and Thomson 1963; Graham 1850). The 1770s marked a milestone in literature about the island, with published accounts of visits that opened up access, in all senses, to the Highland's *terra incognita* (Rackwitz 2007). The intrepid were inspired by Samuel Johnson's above-quoted eloquence about the place in *The Journal of a Tour to the Hebrides* (1785), but also his companion James Boswell's *The Journal of a Tour to the Hebrides* (1785), Thomas Pennant's *A Tour*

'*Reileag Orain.* Burial ground of St Oran'. From Henry Davenport Graham, Antiquities of Iona, 1850 (plate v)

in Scotland, and Voyage to the Hebrides (1774), and Sir Joseph Banks's 'discovery' of nearby Staffa in the early 1770s (Chapman 1930; Simmons 1998). As travellers and tourists started coming to Scotland in greater numbers, they could add to their itinerary Mull, Iona and – often the greater lure – Staffa's Fingal's Cave, 'of all worldly wonders the most wonderful' (Otter 1824). Beyond simply offering an experience of the Scottish picturesque, a boat journey could propel visitors to an awe-inspiring place romantically linked (with varying degrees of credulity) to the content of Ossianic poetry, and the ruins of the venerated isle (Durie 2003: 38–9). By 1800 Iona experienced regular tourist traffic. Notable artists, composers and writers left inspired, but the majority of the writings are accounts of early travellers and tourists, articles in antiquarian journals and magazines, personal correspondence, and, latterly, books for visitors about the island (RCAHMS 1982: 150–1).

The total impression or *'tout ensemble'* of the ruins of Iona needed to be appreciated (Leigh Richmond in a letter to his lady from Iona, 1819, quoted in MacLean 1833: 20). The schoolmaster, often the only islander speaking both Gaelic and English, regularly led the tours. These focused on a block of land embracing the abbey church and its associated monastic buildings, the enclosed burial ground and chapel at St Oran's, a stone causeway, the nunnery and the many carved stones. Detailed observations expressed concerns about the antiquities' condition: crumbling buildings, dung- and weed-covered ground obscuring interiors and sculptured monuments, badly behaving tourists, and damage caused by antiquarian digging. Visitors implored the dukes of Argyll to act, and some recommended courses of preservation (Logan 1832; Laing 1856). Most stayed only a matter of hours, but those who sojourned commented on the warmth of Hebridean hospitality amidst the island's challenging living standards. Today's pilgrim encounters tidy ruins, a reconstructed abbey, and a much-transformed landscape (MacArthur 2002).

Authors were often sceptical of the colourful stories of the 'insular antiquarian' (Garnett 1800: vol. 1, 243) – Samuel Johnson's disparaging term for local antiquarian authorities – that they heard on Iona, narratives that their visits both influenced and created the demand for. These stories wove in local superstitions, figuring a topography populated by scenes from the abbot of Iona Abbey Adomnán's seventh-century *Life of St Columba*, druidical activities and traditions about the burials of Scottish, Irish, Norwegian and French kings. Native culture on Iona was largely oral, but lost sources for Gaelic Columban stories do emerge from the account of an educated Gaelic-speaker who visited in 1771 (Sharpe 2012).

Visitors such as Boswell sought quiet contemplation on Iona (Pottle and Bennett 1963: 330–9). For some, though, the simple nature of the ruins, landscape, lifestyle and behaviour of the inhabitants was disappointing. Though the extraordinary geological features of Staffa were often compared favourably to 'the cathedrals or the places built by men' (Simmons 1998: 257), travellers avoided explicit comparison with the ruins of Iona. Instead, it was important to 'pay the tribute of a sigh to the departed glories of the consecrated island' (Botfield 1830: 270), still 'one of the greatest curiosities of the kind in the British Isles' when its history was taken into account (Garnett 1800: vol. 1, 264).

References

Botfield, Beriah. 1830. *Journal of a Tour through the Highlands of Scotland during the Summer of MDCCCXXIX* (Edinburgh: Privately Printed for the Author by J. Johnstone).

Campbell, John Lorne and Derick S. Thomson. 1963. *Edward Lhuyd in the Scottish Highlands 1699-1700* (Oxford: Clarendon Press).

Chapman, R. W. (ed.). 1930. *Johnson's Journey to the Western Islands of Scotland, and Boswell's Journal of a Tour to the Hebrides* (London: Oxford University Press).

Christian, Jessica and Charles Stiller. 2000. *Iona Portrayed: The Island Through Artists' Eyes, 1760-1960* (Inverness: The New Iona Press).

Durie, Alastair J. 2003. *Scotland for the Holidays: Tourism in Scotland c. 1780-1939* (East Linton: Tuckwell Press).

Garnett, Thomas. 1800. *Observations on a Tour through the Highlands and Part of the Western Isles of Scotland, Particularly Staffa and Icolmkill*, 2 vols (London: T. Cadell & W. Davies).

Graham, Henry Davenport. 1850. *Antiquities of Iona* (London: Day & Son).

Laing, David. 1856. 'On the present state of the ruins of Iona, and their preservation. In a letter to the Hon Lord Murray', *Proceedings of the Society of Antiquaries of Scotland* 2 (1855-6): 7-12.

Logan, J., 1832. [Letter to Editor]. *The Gentleman's Magazine* 102 (2): 497-8.

MacArthur, E. Mairi. 2002. *Iona. The Living Memory of a Crofting Community*, 2nd edn (Edinburgh: Edinburgh University Press).

MacLean, Lachlan. 1833. *A Historical Account of Iona, from the Earliest Period* (Edinburgh: Stirling & Kenney).

Otter, William. 1824. *The Life and Remains of the Rev. Edward Daniel Clarke, L.L.D. Professor of Mineralogy in the University of Cambridge* (London:

George Cowie and Co.).

Pottle, Frederick A. and Charles H. Bennett (eds). 1963. *Boswell's Journal of a Tour to the Hebrides with Samuel Johnson, L.L.D., 1773* (London: William Heinemann).

Rackwitz, Martin (ed.). 2007. *Travels to Terra Incognita. The Scottish Highlands and Hebrides in Early Modern Travellers' Accounts c. 1600-1800* (Münster, New York, Munich, Berlin: Waxmann).

RCAHMS. 1982. *Argyll: An Inventory of the Monuments, Volume 4: Iona* (Glasgow: HMSO).

Sharpe, Richard. 2012. 'Iona in 1771: Gaelic tradition and visitors' experience', *Innes Review* 63 (2): 161-259.

Simmons, Andrew (ed.). 1998. *A Tour in Scotland; and Voyage to the Hebrides; MDCCLXXII, by Thomas Pennant* (Edinburgh: Birlinn).

Dryburgh Abbey

James A. McKean

> There are fragments of ruins lying on the ground, and the whole air of the thing is as wild, and dreamlike, and picturesque as the poet's fanciful heart could have desired. (Stowe 1854: 68)

Dryburgh Abbey, on the banks of the river Tweed in the Scottish Borders, could be thought of as the cousin of Melrose Abbey, which lies three miles north of it. In his influential study of the ruins, the eighteenth-century antiquary Francis Grose highlighted the druidical Celtic or Gaelic etymology of the name 'Dryburgh', a word deriving from the '"*Darach-bruach*", or "*Darachbrugh*"', and meaning 'the bank of the sacred grove of oaks' (Grose 1797: vol. 1, 101). It could be argued, however, that to many since the nineteenth century, the most 'sacred' part of the abbey is the tomb of Sir Walter Scott, who was buried there in 1832.

The abbey was founded in around 1150 by Hugh de Morville, Lord of Lauderdale, and his wife Beatrix de Beauchamp. It was the victim of English attacks in the fourteenth and fifteenth centuries, the most devastating of which came from Edward II in 1323, which destroyed

A view of Dryburgh Abbey and the Elden Hills. Drawn by C. Catton Jr, engraved by F. Jukes, 20 March 1793

parts of the abbey that were never rebuilt. The fourteenth-century Scots poet John Barbour makes mention of this in his historical verse romance *The Brus* (or *The Bruce*) (c. 1375). Despite the abbey's turbulent history, Grose described it as being of the 'most beautiful colour and texture', the ruins defying 'the influence of the weather for more than six centuries'; 'nor is the sharpness of sculpture', he continued, 'in the least affected by the ravages of time' (Grose 1797: vol. 1, 108). This opinion is very much in keeping with that of other visitors, such as the American writer Harriet Beecher Stowe, who visited Scotland in the middle of the nineteenth century, and who was intoxicated by the landscape largely due to its connections with the life and work of Sir Walter Scott: 'almost every name we heard spoken along the railroad, every stream we passed, every point we looked at', Beecher Stowe wrote, 'recalled some line of Walter Scott's poetry, or some event of history' (Stowe 1854: 62).

Although struck by what she found to be the picturesque beauty and wonder of Dryburgh Abbey's ruins, Beecher Stowe could not bear to see Sir Walter Scott buried so harshly beneath the flagstones: 'It seemed to me', she wrote, 'that the flat stones of the pavement are a weight too heavy and too cold to be laid on the breast of a lover of nature and the beautiful' (Stowe 1854: 68). This soon turns to optimism, though, as she spies the springing flowers above his grave, a sight that provides her with hope that his mortal body will become immortal through his work. This sentiment was shared by the poet William Anderson, who wrote:

> A ruin is his resting place, – no vile
> Unconsecrated grave-yard is the soil –
> Few moulder there, but these, the loved, the good
> The honoured, and the famed – and sweet flowers smile.
> (quoted in Menzies 1855: 50)

In Felicia Hemans's 'The Funeral Day of Sir Walter Scott', the weeds that grow in the ruins, too, are said to be touched by his passing:

> – a place where leaf and flower,
> By that which dies not of the sovereign dead,
> Shall be made holy things, where every weed
> Shall have its portion of th' inspiring gift
> From buried glory breathed. (Hemans 1849: 585)

Perhaps Beecher Stowe and the others who saw the ruined abbey as the writer's ideal resting-place would have been upset to learn that Scott was initially not 'greatly impressed' at the prospect of being interred there, but was cajoled into it by the 11th Earl of Buchan (Hutchings 1889: 99). Nonetheless, Paul Westover has claimed that in his burial at Dryburgh, Sir Walter Scott unwittingly left behind him a fully fledged cultural heritage industry (Westover 2012: 47).

Stories surrounding the abbey, however, are not restricted to Sir Walter Scott. A strange female recluse is said to have sought shelter within the ruins of the abbey as a means of fulfilling her vow never to see the sun again until a man to whom she was attached returned from the Jacobite Rebellion of 1745. The legend tells of her leaving the vault only to seek provisions from a local house, returning by candlelight at midnight. The most unusual element of her stay at the abbey is the presence of a spirit whom she named Fatlips, and whom she described as a little fat man wearing iron shoes which he used to 'trample the clay floor of the vault to dispel the damps' (Anon. 1825: 172). This legend was included in nineteenth-century travel guides that claimed that Fatlips still haunted the vault of Dryburgh, describing it as a 'dreaded and haunted spot, which few of the neighbouring peasantry dare to enter' (Menzies 1850: 51). Her lover never did return, and her body is said to be buried in the abbey's graveyard (Hutchings 1889: 99).

References

Anon. 1825. 'Strange Recluse', *The Repository of Arts, Literature, Fashions, Manufacturers, &c.* 3rd series vol. 1, no. 33 (September): 172.

Grose, Francis. 1797. *The Antiquities of Scotland*, 2 vols (London: Printed for Hooper and Wigstead).

Hemans, Felicia. 1849. *Poems of Felicia Hemans* (Edinburgh and London: William Blackwood and Sons).

Hutchings, W. W. 1889. *The Rivers of Great Britain, Descriptive, Historical, Pictorial: Rivers of the East Coast* (London: Cassell and Co., 1889).

Menzies, John. 1855. *Menzies' Pocket Guide to Abbotsford, Melrose and the Scottish Border* (Edinburgh: John Menzies).

Stowe, Harriet Beecher. 1854. *Sunny Memories of Foreign Lands* (London: G. Routledge and Co.).

Westover, Paul. 2012. *Necromanticism: Traveling to Meet the Dead, 1750-1860* (New York: Palgrave Macmillan).

Rhuddlan Castle

David Punter

> Pious hermit! knowest thou not, from dusk eve until return of morn, that tortured spirits in yon castle rove? E'en now, the blood runs chill within my veins, while I do think on what I've seen. Such groans have met my ears! – such sights my eyes! – and screams and riotous laughs mingled with the winds that whistled through the broke arches of the courts! – e'en now, the sweat of terror dews my brow, and languid beats my heart. (Earle 1802: 4–5)

As a ruin and as an antiquity, Rhuddlan Castle, Denbighshire, has roots that take the visitor back to the battle of Rhuddlan Marsh in AD 796, when the English inflicted a defeat on the Welsh; later again, Gruffudd ap Llywelyn was driven from his base here by the English Earl Harold, before Harold lost the rather more decisive battle of Hastings. The castle itself was later moved, or rather reconstructed on a different site, which benefited from the partial draining of the marshes, giving it access to a canalised transport system. As with many other castles on Welsh soil, most of them of English manufacture, after its late medieval heyday it underwent a temporary renaissance during the Civil Wars,

South-east view of Rhuddlan Castle. Engraving by Samuel and Nathaniel Buck, 1742

after which (in 1648) it was deliberately reduced to ruin – or at least to a condition in which it would no longer be able to pose a threat to English rule. It now presents an appearance little different from its condition then.

There was also a Dominican friary at Rhuddlan, home to the 'Black Friars' beloved of Gothic writers, although this does not play an immediate part in William Earle's *Welsh Legends: A Collection of Popular Oral Tales* (1802), which instead focuses, in 'The Knight of Blood-red Plume', on a ghost story connected to the castle itself. The story the protagonist hears when he is forced to take shelter in the castle ruins concerns one Erica, daughter of Sir Rhyswick, lord of the castle. Promised in marriage to Morven, heir apparent of Wales, she instead falls under the spell of a Saxon stranger with demonic overtones. This stranger, Wertwrold, not only seduces her away from Morven but also tricks her into accidentally killing her own father. She has thus committed an act of double betrayal and is doomed to wander as a ghost within the castle walls, a potent symbol of the lost Welsh past and English deceit. The castle itself, as we now see it, is certainly a picturesque mouldering fabric rather than a sublime one: four-square, with towers which are squat and rotund rather than looming in deathly majesty, it looks down onto the marsh and the canalised river which once provided it with provisions in time of need.

An engraving by Samuel and Nathaniel Buck shows the castle to best advantage. Executed from a low angle beside the river Clwyd, the engraving shows off the towers and curtain walls well, with boats plying the river. Rhuddlan has had a complex history and, as with many other castles in Wales, the part it played during the Civil Wars proved to be defining: again as with others, it was taken for the Parliamentarians by Major-General Thomas Mytton, and the High Sheriff, Roger Hanmer, was charged, in what may now appear slightly contradictory terms, with its 'care and demolishment'. That 'demolishment' may have been militarily effective, but not aesthetically, as we can see from its condition both in 1742 and today; it forms a romantic ruin, replete with resident ghost and bloody political history, in all the requisite details.

Reference
Earle, William. 1802. *Welsh Legends: A Collection of Popular Oral Tales* (London: Printed for J. Badcock).

Chapter 4:
Writing the Ruined Abbeys of Netley, Tintern and Melrose

James Watt, Dale Townshend and Nicola J. Watson

Introduction

>Then from its tow'ring height with horrid sound
>Rush'd the proud abby. Then the vaulted roofs,
>Torn from their walls, disclos'd the wanton scene
>Of monkish chastity! Each angry friar
>Crawl'd from his bedded strumpet, mutt'ring low
>An ineffectual curse. The pervious nooks
>That, ages past, convey'd the guileful priest
>To play some image on the gaping crowd,
>Imbibe the novel day-light; and expose
>Obvious, the fraudful engin'ry of ROME.
>As tho' this op'ning earth to nether realms
>Shou'd flash meridian day, the hooded race
>Shudder abash'd to find their cheats display'd:
>And conscious of their guilt, and pleas'd to wave
>Its fearful meed, resign'd their fair domain. (Shenstone 1764: 319–20)

Thus wrote the English poet and landscape gardener William Shenstone of Henry VIII's Dissolution of the Monasteries in 'The Ruin'd Abbey: or, The Effects of Superstition' in 1743, a lengthy poem that was later published in *The Works in Verse and Prose, of William Shenstone, Esq.*

in 1764. Standing in for all Catholic monasteries, nunneries, convents and cathedrals that fell with Henry's suppression of the religious houses, the unidentified and unnamed ruin in Shenstone's poem occasions the poet's reflections on Britain's past, and charting a line of historical progress that runs from antiquity through to the present day, Shenstone celebrates the Reformation for its vanquishing of the powers of Roman Catholic darkness. As his references to lascivious monks, guileful priests and other nefarious clerics in this quoted extract indicate, Shenstone regarded the institutions of medieval Catholicism as little more than nurseries of superstition, lust, gluttony and crime; throughout the poem, in fact, Britain's abbeys and monasteries become the locale of 'perjur'd monks', 'infernal shrieks', 'Roman magic' and the 'pensive gloom which superstition loves' (Shenstone 1764: 311–12). Ecclesiastical ruin thus serves for Shenstone as the sign of national progress, the turning away from the gloom, ritual and magic of the Catholic past and the felicitous embrace of the modern, enlightened present; 'The Ruin'd Abbey' thus offers a way into recovering some of the political meanings that Shenstone courted in his placement of ruined Gothic follies on the landscape of his Worcestershire estate, The Leasowes, in the 1740s.

These sentiments, however, were by no means particular to Shenstone. Throughout the period, in fact, responses to the ruined abbeys and monasteries in the British landscape were marked by virulent anti-Catholicism, the mere glimpse of ecclesiastical ruin often enough to occasion discourses on such topics as the 'unfair' demands of clerical celibacy, the use of 'idolatry' in Catholic acts of worship, and 'superstitious' beliefs and practices of the Catholic faith in general. In a national context that, as Linda Colley has shown, self-consciously identified itself as Protestant, such expressions of anti-Catholicism were bound up in the work of nation-building: the very notion of 'Great Britain', a precarious formation that had been brought into existence with the Acts of Union of 1707, in some senses demanded and relied upon a shared sense of national Protestantism in order to constitute and define itself (Colley 2005). But Catholics who, in the tradition of the Renaissance humanist philosopher Erasmus, doubted the practice of monasticism could still put ecclesiastical ruins to similar purposes. Patently influenced by Shenstone's poem, the Catholic poet Edward Jerningham, too, regarded the Reformation as the glorious overcoming of monkish darkness and superstition in *An Elegy Written Among the Ruins of an Abbey* (1765):

> To Truth at length dissolv'd the mental Chain,
> And banish'd Error from th'enlighten'd Shore:
> So clos'd at length the busy-acted Scene,
> The Curtain drop'd, and Folly's Mask was o'er.
> (Jerningham 1765: 8)

In view of the anti-clericalism that Jerningham expressed in this and other poetic renditions of Catholic clerical existence, it is hardly surprising to learn that he became a convert to Anglicanism during the 1790s. In 'On Monastic Institutions', an important essay that she published in her and her brother John's collaborative collection *Miscellaneous Pieces, in Prose* (1773), the Dissenting poet Anna Laetitia Aikin (later Barbauld) described a walk to 'the venerable ruins of an old Abbey', an unnamed or even entirely imaginary pile situated somewhere in the English landscape (Aikin 1773: 88). The mental associations that somewhat impulsively crowd in upon her mind recall those of Shenstone, Jerningham and many others: at least initially, the ruin is a horrid reminder of a past of monkish indolence, depravity, debauchery and superstition. In the remainder of the essay, however, Aikin seeks to subject these commonplace mental associations to careful scrutiny, effectively looking beyond them so as to recuperate many of the positive roles and functions that the monastical institutions of the past played, including their encouragement of learning and artistic creativity, their provision of education, and their administering of hospitality and charity to those in need. Shenstone's 'The Ruin'd Abbey', by contrast, is more concerned with how the sight of a ruined abbey might serve the aesthetic ends of the modern, Protestant British present:

> While thro' the land the musing pilgrim sees
> A tract of brighter green, and in the midst
> Appears a mouldering wall, with ivy crown'd;
> Or gothic turret, pride of ancient days!
> Now but of use to grace a rural scene;
> To bound our vistas, and to glad the sons

Of George's reign, reserv'd for fairer times!
(Shenstone 1764: 321)

Having been emptied, even exorcised, of its Catholic past, the ivy-covered fragments of the ruin serve the ends of quiet contemplation and picturesque tourism; as the poem indicates, it is only the passage of time and the marks of decay itself that have made possible its recuperation as a reminder of the 'pride of ancient days'. Similar claims run throughout topographical ruin literature in the eighteenth and early nineteenth centuries, permeating poems, novels, essays and dramas set in both real and imagined ecclesiastical piles. The following three sections in this chapter explore further the legacy of ecclesiastical ruin in the period, focusing on three sites across England, Wales and Scotland that generated particularly large numbers of literary and visual responses: Netley, Tintern and Melrose. It is no coincidence that all three were Cistercian establishments, and part of their appeal doubtless lay in the fact that they were built, in accordance with the order's statutes, 'far from the concourse of men' (Norton 1986: 318). The beauty and appeal of the bucolic setting of Cistercian abbeys was recognised as long ago as the twelfth century. Walter Daniel, monk of Rievaulx and biographer of Aelred of Rievaulx, provided a description of the abbey that continues to resonate to this day: 'High hills surround the valley, encircling it like a crown. These are clothed in trees of various sorts and maintain in pleasant retreats the privacy of the vale, providing for the monks a kind of second paradise of wooded delight' (Powicke 1994: 98).

Netley Abbey

And there in Netley's mouldering cells
The solitary nightbird dwells;
There in each moss-grown stone we trace
The pious tenants of the place;
There in each lingering footstep tread
Upon the unmonumented dead.
Yes, image of Rome's fallen pow'r,
This, this is Netley's hallowed bower!
(Mitford 1827: 319)

'View of Part of the Ruins of Netley Abbey, near Southampton'

Horace Walpole visited the ruins of Netley Abbey, a Cistercian monastery near Southampton, in 1755, and he later wrote to his friend Richard Bentley that he found them 'not the ruins of Netley, but of Paradise. – Oh! the purple abbots, what a spot they had chosen to slumber in! The scene is so beautifully tranquil, yet so lovely, that they seem only to have *retired into* the world' (Walpole 1937–83: vol. 35, 249). Walpole's evocation of monastic indolence appears to draw upon a familiar anti-Catholic caricature, but his often-cited account of this picturesque locale also suggests that the abbots of Netley chose their place of retreat wisely. For Walpole here, the abbey is associated with a generalised 'atmosphere' rather than with a specific history, and later travel guides adopted a similar perspective in referring to how 'Time has [...] brought this venerable pile, as a piece of ruins, to its highest perfection' (Anon. 1790: vol. 1, 30).

In the late eighteenth century the ruins of Netley provided inspiration for at least ten poems. The first of these, George Keate's *Netley Abbey: An Elegy* (1769), challenges any idea of the 'perfection' of ruin by moving from its evocation of a spirit of place to lamenting the demise of an institution which once had an important social function: it records how Netley is now 'chang'd, alas! from that revered Abode, / Grac'd by proud Majesty in ancient Days, / When Monks recluse these sacred Pavements trod, / And taught th' unletter'd world its MAKER's Praise!' (Keate 1769: 20). Keate's poem names both Henry III, 'that sceptred Founder ... / Whose Virtues bade these friendly Walls ascend' (Keate 1769: 27), and Henry VIII, the 'royal Plund'rer' (Keate 1769, 26) who dissolved Netley Abbey during the first wave of the Dissolution of the Monasteries. It also alludes to the story of one Walter Taylor, the 'rude dismantler' (Keate 1769: 23) who, local tradition tells, tried to use the abbey's ruins as a quarry for stone, only to receive his comeuppance when he was crushed to death by the walls that he attempted to undermine. The story of Taylor is rehearsed in written accounts of Netley throughout this period, and for Keate, at least, Taylor's sacrilegious act made him a plebeian counterpart to Henry VIII.

Unlike Keate's elegy, however, the Netley poems written in this period generally do not present the abbey's ruins as emblematic of a world that has been lost. Edward Hamley's 'Reflections in Netley Abbey' (1789), for example, picks up on and extends Walpole's reference to slumbering abbots, while also sympathising with those 'finer souls', ahead of their time, who chafed against the tedium of abbey life: one such figure is a 'vot'ry sad of feeling heart' who the poet imagines to have wandered in the grounds of the abbey, consumed by thoughts of a 'tender maid he lov'd too well' (Hamley 1789: 38). Whereas Hamley's poem invites its readers to congratulate themselves on having left Catholic superstition behind, the high church clergyman William Lisle Bowles's 'Netley Abbey' (also 1789) considers the passing of time in apolitical terms, without making any reference to historical process or human agency. Beginning with an address to the abbey's ruins, 'Fallen pile! I ask not what has been thy fate', Bowles's sonnet evokes a space that is conducive to solitary and melancholic contemplation: 'When the weak winds, wafted from the main, / Through each lone arch, like spirits that complain, / Come mourning to my ear, I meditate / On this world's passing pageant, and on these / Who once, like thee, majestic and sublime / Have stood' (Bowles 1789: 29).

The title of the collection in which Bowles's poem appeared, *Sonnets, Written Chiefly on Picturesque Spots, During a Tour* (1789), reminds us that the encounter with abbeys and other ruins commonly took place in the context of a flourishing culture of domestic tourism; the war with Revolutionary France that began in 1793 all but closed off continental Europe and further stimulated travel within Britain. In his *Observa-*

tions on the Western Parts of England (1798), William Gilpin identified the 'picturesque' qualities of the 'great Church' at the heart of Netley's ruins, although he also stated that 'the whole body of the church is now so choked with ruin, and overgrown with thickets and ivy-bushes, that the greatest part of the building is invisible' (Gilpin 1798: 351). Gilpin complained of the difficulty of finding a position from which to 'take a view' at Netley, and artists often responded to this problem by using ivy and other foliage as a framing device. Like other ruined abbeys, Netley was painted 'by moonlight' (most famously by John Constable, c. 1833), and there is a rich tradition of visual representations of the abbey, from Samuel and Nathaniel Buck's hand-coloured print of 1733 to Constable's watercolour a century later, and beyond.

In many of the best-known and most culturally prestigious literary and visual representations of Netley, then, the ruins of the abbey are depicted as the object of serious attention of one kind or another; where (unlike, say, Constable's *Netley Abbey by Moonlight* [c. 1833]) images of the abbey do not feature a solitary visitor, they tend to be populated by people sketching or by gentlemen with antiquarian leanings. Netley was also available for less elevated kinds of tourist experience than this, however, as Thomas Gray acknowledged in 1755 when he observed that nearby Southampton was 'full of Bathers' – people drawn to the town because of its recently acquired reputation as a spa resort: 'here

Netley Abbey. Drawn by R. B. Harraden and engraved by J. B. Harraden, 1814

is no Coffeehouse, no Bookseller, no Pastry-Cook', he wrote, 'but here is the Duke of Chandos'. Gray noted that 'the walks all around [...] are delicious' (Gray 1764), and the first edition of *The Southampton Guide* (1768) described Netley's ruins as among those local sites likely to 'form Part of the Amusement of the Company during the Season' (Anon. 1768: 32); *The Antiquarian Repertory* (1775) subsequently referred to the numerous 'parties that come by water, from Southampton, to drink tea among these ruins', recommending this excursion 'to all persons of taste' (Anon. 1775: vol. 1, 246). It was around this time that the owner of the Netley estate, Thomas Dummer, moved the north transept of the abbey to the grounds of his estate at Cranbury Park near Winchester, Hampshire, thereby making him in some respects a 'despoiler' like Walter Taylor, but also emphasising that the site itself had its own contemporary history and did not simply represent a static 'perfection' of ruins.

Perhaps the most prolific late-eighteenth-century mediator of Netley to a wider public was the antiquary Richard Warner, who took up a curacy in Hampshire in the late 1780s, and wrote several local histories and tourist guidebooks which sought to exploit the popularity of domestic tourism for commercial gain. Warner also incorporated a 'pleasing and picturesque' Netley (Warner 1795: vol. 1, 132) into *Netley Abbey: A Gothic Story* (1795), an historical romance of the thirteenth century that culminates in its hero's marriage to the female captive whom he had discovered, after various supernatural promptings, in the abbey's imaginary subterranean apartments; a number of sections in the novel read as if they had been lifted from the tourist guides that Warner wrote. William Pearce's *Netley Abbey: An Operatic Farce* (1794) similarly makes Netley central to its plot, creatively reworking the traditional story of Walter Taylor in a morality tale about architectural improvement and proper respect for the past. The play was first performed on the London stage against the backdrop of a scene painted by John Inigo Richards of the Royal Academy, and described by Pearce as 'one of the most picturesque Portraits of a Gothic Ruin that the hand of Science ever produced' (Pearce 1794: advertisement).

The jovial Irishman M'Scrape in Pearce's play at one point declares that he loves 'a ramble' in the grounds of the abbey 'to watch the ships pass to and fro' (Pearce 1794: 31), and it is significant here that while he is at the abbey, he looks away from the ruins themselves in order to consider Netley's coastal situation. The play repeatedly alludes to the mobilisation of Britain's navy in response to the threat of invasion by Revolutionary France, saluting the nation's fleet as 'floating towers, [...] castles on the main' which ensure that 'ENGLAND, a WORLD WITHIN ITSELF shall reign' (Pearce 1794: 23). During an earlier invasion scare, after France had allied itself to Revolutionary America, the bluestocking author Elizabeth Carter accentuated the symbolic resonance of the Gothic in a rather different way, writing to Elizabeth Vesey in August 1779 that in the unlikely event of defeat, the appearance of a Britain reduced by its enemies could be compared to 'the condition of Netley Abbey' (Carter 1809: vol. 4, 229). A military hospital was built near the abbey in the aftermath of the Crimean war, and it remained in use until the end of the Second World War, demonstrating the extent to which, at particular times at least, the seemingly sequestered site celebrated by Walpole and others has been connected to geographically distant events.

The possible associations of Netley and its environs exceeded the domain of picturesque tourism, then, and as M'Scrape's ramble among the abbey's ruins suggests, the nature of visitor experience at Netley could itself be diverse. John Bullar, in his travel guide *A Companion in a Tour Round Southampton* (1799), implicitly acknowledged this by addressing an audience eager to distinguish themselves from 'the whole tribe of those who never think seriously on any subject; and who visit this place, as they do another, merely "to stare about them, and to eat"' (Bullar 1799: 178). A decade later, a French traveller complained of how, while he was 'employed in admiring and drawing' at the abbey, 'a large company arrived in two smart carriages, preceded by a convoy of provisions for a picturesque dinner; – masters and servants dispersed immediately among our ruins, and the solitary aisles resounded with loud and trite remarks' (Simond 1815: vol. 2, 246). While both of these writers stigmatise what they present as an uninformed and unthinking approach to Netley's ruins, however, it is interesting to consider the ways in which popular tourism at Netley may have had a creative dimension, involving an interactive relationship with the ruins rather than the inattentive, if noisy, consumption referred to here. Netley offered no formal viewing position of the kind that was built to overlook Rievaulx Abbey in North Yorkshire in the 1750s, and – the efforts of Richard Warner and others notwithstanding – it had no literary aura of the kind that was acquired by Melrose Abbey in the wake of Sir Walter Scott's poem *The Lay of the Last Minstrel* (1805). In the absence of any such 'proper' view of the ruins, visitors may have felt themselves more at liberty to roam and explore than at comparable sites. When M'Scrape says that he loves 'a ramble' at Netley he seemingly expresses both his freedom to move wherever he pleases and his ability to enjoy the abbey on his own terms rather than in the culturally prescribed language of aesthetic appreciation.

In his *Observations on the Western Parts of England*, Gilpin wryly remarked that despite the well-publicised fate of Walter Taylor, 'others [...] have been found, notwithstanding this example, who have pursued the design, for a mere fragment of the roof only now remains' (Gilpin 1798: 351). As well as chipping away souvenirs of the abbey to take home with them, visitors in this period also sometimes carved their name and the date of their visit, occasionally their place of residence and even their occupation, on its walls. In some cases this would have required much effort, and the use of a hammer and chisel – generating considerable noise – rather than, as with the graffiti tags of today, a spray-can or marker pen. Such visitors may have owned Claude Glasses that enabled them to admire Netley from a distance and within the requisite picturesque frame, but by leaving a permanent record of their presence in this way they also perhaps sought to defy both the conventions of polite spectatorship and the inexorable logic of that 'mutability' that ruins were so often called upon to illustrate. As elsewhere, a commercialised culture of Netley-related souvenirs began to develop in the late eighteenth century, and while pottery and porcelain decorated with images of the abbey would have been available for purchase to people who never visited Netley, they potentially offered their owners a portable memory of personal experience, as objects to which individual meanings of various kinds could be attached.

We can of course only speculate now about the diversity of the tourist experience at Netley Abbey. While it seems fair to suggest that Netley, because of its proximity to Southampton, hosted a greater number and a more socially diverse range of visitors than many comparable destinations, individual encounters with the abbey's ruins were still compatible with forms of collective self-understanding: M'Scrape celebrates his freedom to move on his own terms, but he also performs his loyalty to the British state. Alison Shell has argued that the institutional history of Netley was inescapable for many Gothic tourists, and that in the early nineteenth century, an era that was generally more sympathetic to Catholic devotion, engagements with the abbey's ruins were alert to 'reverberations of the sacred' (Shell 2007: 45), and therefore perhaps less insouciant than the previous responses of Walpole and others. The potential for Gothic tourism at Netley and elsewhere to be sociable, and even gregarious, rather than necessarily solitary and serious, nonetheless continues to be under-explored. If the Freudian concept of the uncanny remains enormously valuable, not least for thinking about the apprehension of the past in the present, it does not exhaust the variety of meanings that Britain's ruins afforded to Gothic tourists in this period. Visiting Netley today provides an interesting perspective on the possibility of experiencing its ruins as pleasingly familiar. Although Netley Abbey is administered by English Heritage, there is only a minimal tourist infrastructure – a small car park and some signage – at the site, and modern Gothic tourists are likely to find that they are outnumbered by local dogs and their walkers enjoying what remains, over two and a half centuries after Walpole's visit, a beautifully tranquil spot.

Tintern Abbey

> It is allowed by all those who have made observations on the Religious Houses in England, that there is no one so perfect remaining as that of *Tintern Abbey*. (Heath 1793: n.p.)

When Robert Southey reviewed *Lyrical Ballads, With a Few Other Poems*, Samuel Taylor Coleridge and William Wordsworth's collaborative collection of poetry that was first published in 1798, he singled out the last poem in the collection, Wordsworth's 'Lines Written a Few Miles from Tintern Abbey, on Revisiting the Banks of the Wye During a Tour, July 13, 1798', as the volume's finest achievement. 'In the whole range of English poetry we scarcely recollect any thing [sic] superior', Southey enthusiastically claimed, quoting some sixty-six lines of the poem as evidence of its excellence (Coleridge and Wordsworth 2008: 148). Ever since then, Wordsworth's 'Tintern Abbey' has consistently enjoyed both popular appeal and critical approbation. For many, the poem is said to epitomise the central preoccupations of British Romanticism,

'View of Tintern Abbey on the River Wye'. From an original drawing by E. Dayes, engraved by F. Jukes, 1 November 1799

including an emphasis upon the awe-inspiring yet consoling powers of the natural world, that 'sense sublime / Of something far more deeply interfused' evoked by the landscape; the 'still, sad music of humanity' to which the persona is particularly attuned; the importance of memory and a focus upon childhood and early formative experience; and insight into the human minds that 'half create' and half 'perceive' the world around them.

On the most superficial of levels, the poem describes Wordsworth's return to Tintern Abbey, the ruined Cistercian abbey on the banks of the river Wye in Monmouthshire, after an absence of five years. Unlike so many other poems written in, about and to imaginary monastic ruins in the period, Wordsworth's poem cultivates a sense of topographical accuracy by naming the poet's visit to a specific abbey (Tintern) at a specific point in time (13 July 1798). If Wordsworth's visit of 1798 is, as the title indicates, a 'return' to a scene that he had visited earlier in 1793, this is figured poetically in the repetition of the phrase 'once more' several times within the poem itself. The title also does much to situate Wordsworth's poem within the tradition of domestic picturesque tourism, a practice that, in the wake of the endeavours of writers such as William Gilpin, became a fashionable middle-class pursuit in the last three decades of the eighteenth century. Of the many picturesque destinations across Britain, Tintern was a particularly popular spot: in addition to Gilpin and the numerous other picturesque tourists who visited and drew it in the period, Thomas Gainsborough produced a sketch of the ruin in 1782 and J. M. W. Turner several drawings and watercolours of the abbey throughout the 1790s. In his influential *Observations on Modern Gardening* (1770), landscape designer Thomas Whateley argued that the follies and artificial ruins now fashionable among members of the landed classes ought to be modelled on the splendid ruins at Tintern; in the third volume of his *Antiquities of England and Wales* (c. 1784), antiquary Francis Grose provided a detailed and highly influential description of the pile, supplementing his measured assessment of its beauties with two striking plates by Samuel Hooper. The minor eighteenth-century poets Edmund Gardner and Edward Jerningham both wrote short poems about the abbey in 1796. Other, more prominent writers who recorded their impressions of Tintern in the period include Thomas Gray, in a letter to his friend Dr Thomas Wharton in 1771; the antiquary-turned-Gothic novelist Richard Warner, in *A Walk through Wales, in August 1797* (1799); John Thelwall, in an essay in *The Monthly Magazine* in 1798; Jane Austen, in *Mansfield Park* (1814); Mary Brunton, in her journal of 1815; and Dorothy Wordsworth, the poet's sister and the addressee of the final sections of Wordsworth's poem, in her 'Thoughts on my Sick-bed' (c. 1832).

Indeed, together with the ruins of Netley Abbey, Tintern Abbey was one of the most frequently drawn, engraved, painted and written-about Gothic ruins of the late eighteenth and early nineteenth centuries. As early as 1745, Sneyd Davies's poem 'A Voyage to Tinterne [sic] Abbey, in Monmouthshire, from Whitminster in Gloucestershire' had claimed that the beauty of the sight far exceeded any act of linguistic or pictorial inscription: 'These lines, my C – , read, and pity too / The shadowing Pencil to the Scene untrue: / See the bright Image of thy Thought decay'd, / And all it's [sic] Beauties in Description fade' (Whaley 1745: 188). When Robert Bloomfield visited the area in 1807, he responded by claiming that it was 'a place so often described by pen and by pencil' that his own descriptions were barely necessary (Bloomfield 1807: f. 28). Entering into this tradition of picturesque tourism, yet substituting the requisite pencil of the picturesque tourist for the pen of the poet, Wordsworth in 1798 set out to fashion a poem that, in the end, is more

'The Grand West Entrance of Tintern Abbey'. Frederick Calvert, 15 April 1815

about the poet's own subjectivity, his memories, his early engagement with the natural world and his important familial relations than it is about the ruined abbey itself.

These and other aspects of the poem have inspired a controversial but nonetheless persuasive reading by the critic Marjorie Levinson in her influential study, *Wordsworth's Great Period Poems* (1986). Here, Levinson argues that 'Tintern Abbey' is worryingly escapist and apolitical in ideological import, a tendency that she traces throughout several of the poem's details. First, Levinson argues, the aesthetic of the picturesque that Wordsworth is self-consciously drawing upon in the poem leads him to occlude the harsh political and economic realities that he would have encountered in and around Tintern Abbey in the late 1790s. By this time, the area had long been the site of intensive industrial activity: the Company of Mineral and Battery Works had set up wireworks at Tintern as early as the mid-sixteenth century, while in the late eighteenth century, the abbey's surrounds were home to an iron foundry that belched clouds of noxious smoke and fumes into the air. The charcoal that drove these activities was produced in the

'Iron Mills: A View near Tintern Abbey, Monmouthshire'. Drawn and engraved by J. Hassell, 28 February 1798

surrounding woods, while the hillside above the abbey was quarried for the making of lime. As Charles Heath's popular guidebook, *Descriptive Account of Tintern Abbey, Monmouthshire*, had put it in 1793, 'Before the introduction of this Manufactory, the woods around must have been grand indeed; but the works requiring such quantities of charcoal, they are now fallen in the course of every 12 or 14 years' (Heath 1793: vii). Reduced to poverty by the expansion of early capitalism, the workers and their families who served these industries at Tintern Abbey, together with a number of other impoverished vagrants from the Wye valley, were forced to make of the ruins a sordid, makeshift lodging. Inhabited by the destitute poor, and with its natural surrounds pillaged and polluted by the voracious demands of modern industry, Tintern Abbey was anything but the quiet pastoral scene that Wordsworth figures in his poem in 1798. When Gilpin described an earlier visit to Tintern Abbey in his *Observations on the River Wye* (1782), what he found there was considerably far removed from the tranquil, sylvan scene encountered in Wordsworth: the abbey was 'incompassed' [sic] by what Gilpin describes as 'shabby houses', and the ruin itself inhabited by poor and wretched squatters and vagrants: 'They occupy little huts, raised among the ruins of the monastery; and seem to have no employment, but begging: as if a place, once devoted to indolence, could never again become the seat of industry' (Gilpin 1789: 47, 50). Stebbing Shaw's popular guidebook, *A Tour to the West of England in 1788* (1789), paid as much attention to describing the iron industry at Tintern as the picturesque beauties of the ruin itself. Poverty, squalor and industrialisation were the realities at Tintern Abbey when Wordsworth made his second visit, Levinson maintains, the products of harsh political and economic pressures that the poet strategically overlooks, represses and occludes in order to write that great 'Romantic' poem that is, in more senses than one, 'above' the Abbey and everything that may be seen there.

Certainly, we get only the vaguest of references to these economic and political realities in the poem, such as Wordsworth's account of the 'vagrant dwellers in the houseless woods', or the 'wreathes of smoke / Sent up, in silence' that emanate not from the industrial works but from the domestic hearths of the 'pastoral farms' below. The Wordsworthian 'spot of time' that has, in the years between his two visits, consoled the persona 'in lonely rooms, and mid the din / Of towns and cities' is more the work of retrospective idealisation than accurate memory and recollection. As Levinson continues, Wordsworth also fails to make

Tintern Abbey. From The Romantic and Picturesque Scenery of England and Wales, from Drawings Made *[...]* by P. J. de Loutherbourg *[...]*, *1805*

mention of the fact that his visit to the site in July 1798 coincided with an historically significant moment, the nine-year anniversary of the Fall of the Bastille in Paris in July 1789, and the beginning of the French Revolution. Uncontested though it has not been, Levinson's reading of 'Tintern Abbey' is useful in reiterating the point made in Chapter 2 that the aesthetic of the picturesque – that decidedly eighteenth-century way of conceptualising architectural ruin – is often deeply ahistorical in nature: the ruined abbey attests not to the chaos of history, nor to the devastation of the present, so much as to the quiet, ruminative processes of the poet's own mind. At the very least, it is important to remember that, in the light of the tradition of ruined abbey poems addressed elsewhere in this volume, Wordsworth does not traffic in the anti-Catholicism of his age, but theologically participates, instead, in a pantheistic sense of 'God in nature'.

In several senses, other poems written in, about and to the ruined Cistercian abbey at Tintern in the eighteenth and nineteenth centuries actively confront many of the political, historical and economic realities on which Wordsworth's 'Tintern Abbey' remains resolutely silent. The first example is the anonymous 'Poetical Description of Tintern Abbey', a poem extracted from an earlier guidebook to the region and cited in full in Heath's *Descriptive Account*. Using Classical imagery that recalls Warner's description of the forge at Tintern, the persona in this poem is struck by the differences between the devout Catholic past and the enterprise of the modern present:

> Here now no bell calls Monks to morning prayer,
> Daws only chaunt their early matins here;
> Black forges smoke, and noisy hammers beat,
> Where sooty Cyclops puffing, drink and sweat;
> Confront the curling flames, nor back retire,
> But live, like Salamanders, in the fire;
> For at each stroke that's by the hammer giv'n,
> From the red iron fiery sparks are driven,
> In all directions round the forge they fly,
> Like lightning flash, and quick as lightning die.
> Here smelting furnaces like Aetna roar,
> And force the latent iron from the ore;
> The liquid metal from the furnace runs,

> And, caught in moulds of sand, forms pots or guns:
> Oft shifts its shape, like Proteus, in the fire,
> Huge iron bars here dwindle into wire:
> Assume such forms as suit the calls of trade,
> Ploughshare or broad-sword, pruning-book or spade.
> (quoted in Heath 1793: 48)

The quiet medieval piety at Tintern has been replaced and overtaken by industrial activity that, though in some senses alarming, possesses magical, creative and even sublime qualities of its own. Richard Warner echoed the sublime imagery of fire, volcanoes and Classical monstrosity in his description of his reactions to Tintern in *A Walk through Wales, in August 1797* (1799):

> This scene of bustle amidst smoke and fire, during the darkness and silence of midnight, which was only interrupted by the intonation of the bar-hammer, produced a most impressive effect on the mind. We saw Virgil's description realized, and the interior of Etna, the forges of the Cyclops, and their fearful employment, immediately occurred to us. (Warner 1799: 232)

Other poets, however, were more alarmed by the ruinous state in which Tintern Abbey existed in the modern present than ambivalently fascinated by the work that took place there. The anonymous poet of *A Series of Sonnets Written Expressly to Accompany Some Recently-Published Views of Tintern Abbey* (1816), for instance, reversed the tendency to see in the ruined abbey the felicitous signs of the Protestant Reformation so as to focus, instead, on the lamentable acts of architectural devastation that were licensed by Henry VIII's Dissolution of the Monasteries:

> No, ruthless HENRY! thine was not the flame
>   Of pious zeal – else, when thou gavest command
>   To drive forth from their homes that helpless band,
> And their free-manors bad'st thy nobles claim,
> If true religion then had been thy aim,
>   Thou would'st have guarded with thy kingly hand
> Those temples sacred to thy Maker's name,

> Nor left them thus despoil'd throughout the land. –
> But peace! – a warning voice hath reach'd my soul;
> It seems to say, 'Such vain regrets control:
>   'Can mortal with their works confer a grace
>   'On glory most ineffable – or trace
> 'His bounds who reigns o'er worlds that countless roll –
>   'that omnipresent GOD, whose temple fills all space?'
> (Anon. 1816: n.p.)

Appropriating the ruin as the portal to the faded realm of history, the persona across this sonnet sequence engages in an extended fantasy that details the rigorous discipline and admirable spiritual piety of Tintern Abbey's ancient monkish inhabitants. Edward Collins's *Tintern Abbey; or, the Beauties of Piercefield, a Poem* (1825) did much the same, constructing the abbey, in Book IV, as the ideal place for lifelong Catholic devotion, retirement and seclusion:

> At length the fertile vale with joy we hail,
> Of Tintern, where buried in monastic gloom,
> Dwelt those from the cares of life retir'd,
> In deep seclusion spent their fleeting days.
> Can we conceive, midst nature's various scenes,
> A place, where in abstracted thought, calm
> Contemplation, and religious awe, cou'd
> Be indulg'd to more advantage, than on
> The spot we see, pent in by hills on
> Every side, not merely soften'd to the
> Acclivitous form, but rising bold at once,
> In sylvan majesty they lift their heads,
> Throwing their lengthened shadows o'er the
> Clear and rapid stream.
> (Collins 1825: 130)

In 1854, by contrast, Frederick Bolingbroke Ribbans seized the opportunity occasioned by the rumour that the remains of Tintern were to be given back to the Catholic Church and turned into a working seminary to express vociferously anti-Catholic sentiments, views that bring to mind those that were characteristically articulated in much ruined-abbey poetry of the mid-eighteenth century. Presenting Tintern in its present, ruined picturesque condition as inestimably superior to its past of monkish superstition, lust and deceit, the poem equates Catholicism with debauchery and the powers of Protestantism with truth:

> May Popish craft and carnal crime no more
> > Pollute the grandeur of thy gorgeous halls!
> May Truth be in thee an abiding store,
> > And Holiness be written on thy walls!
> (Ribbans 1854: 11)

'I love thee better now in thy decay', the persona elsewhere notes, 'Than I had loved thee, if I could have seen / Thee, in thy early time of pride and youth', for then 'thy wast with falsehood fill'd, and sin' (Ribbans 1854: 6).

Of course, Ribbans's sense of the abbey as the site of Catholic lust and sexual perversion strays close to the notoriously anti-Catholic territory of the Gothic romance. However, when Francis Grose described the ruins in *The Antiquities of England and Wales*, he tempered his enthusiasm with the observation that, delightful though it undoubtedly was, Tintern Abbey was somewhat lacking in the rich powers of association demonstrated by other ecclesiastical ruins:

> On the whole, though this monastery is undoubtedly light and elegant, it wants that gloomy solemnity so essential to religious ruins; those yawning vaults and dreary recesses which strike the beholder with a religious awe, and make him almost shudder at entering them, calling into his mind all the tales of the nursery.
> (Grose c. 1784: 168)

Grose's reference, here, to 'gloomy solemnity', 'yawning vaults', 'dreary recesses' and 'all the tales of the nursery' serve as indexes of that literary mode that we now identify as Gothic, the literature and horror and terror that arose with, and in the wake of, Horace Walpole's *The Castle of Otranto* (1764). Charles Heath echoed Grose's impressions in his guidebook to Tintern of 1793, claiming that, of all the nation's monastical ruins, those at Tintern were the least amenable to Gothic-fictional appropriation. These reservations, however, did not prevent Sophia Ziegenhirt from penning *The Orphan of Tintern Abbey*, a three-volume Gothic romance that was published by the Minerva Press in 1816. The narrative opens with a description that would not be out of place in an early-nineteenth-century picturesque travel guide:

> The principal aisle, though unroofed, still retained striking proofs of former grandeur; the noble Gothic window, where the luxuriant ivy proudly usurped the place of many a painted pane, appeared now to have regained some of its former brilliant colouring, by the rays of a glorious setting sun darting its beams betwixt the ivy leaves. (Ziegenhirt 1816: vol. 1, 2)

And yet, the fiction develops in a direction that is quite different from the calm reveries of picturesque description. Set in and around the ruins of the abbey, Ziegenhirt's narrative concerns the fate of a foundling, the heroine Paulina, who, though initially of unknown parentage, is eventually restored to her legitimate familial dynasty. Jettisoning the historical distancing of earlier Gothic fictions, the story is set in the early-nineteenth-century present, and makes frequent reference to such topical concerns as the French Revolution and the eventual defeat of Napoleon Bonaparte. Indeed, refusing, unlike Wordsworth's poem, to forget the political and economic realities of its day, *The Orphan of Tintern Abbey* becomes a fiction of frank and urgent political exposure: its effects in no way dependent upon the supernatural, the 'supernumerary horror' of Ziegenhirt's ruined abbey is ultimately starkly material in nature.

When Alfred Tennyson responded to the ruins of Tintern Abbey in his 'Tears, Idle Tears', one of the songs included in the longer *The Princess; a Medley* of 1847, he returned to the lyrical mode of poetic expression that Wordsworth had employed to such effect in his poem of 1798. Like Wordsworth and others, the persona in 'Tears, Idle Tears' sees in the scene of architectural ruin evidence of the implacable passage of time:

> Tears, idle tears, I know not what they mean,
> Tears from the depth of some divine despair,
> Rise in the heart, and gather to the eyes,

> In looking on the happy Autumn-fields,
> And thinking of the days that are no more.
> (Tennyson 1847: 66)

As in much eighteenth-century poetry of the ruined abbey, the elegiac mode in 'Tears, Idle Tears' is the most appropriate for the confrontation of architectural ruin. However, bereft of the comfort that Wordsworth's poem recovers in the natural world, in memory and in the close and self-affirming relationship with his sister Dorothy, Tennyson's persona is forced to confront the devastations of time, death, loss and absence without any means of consolation. Indeed, if the faculty of memory for Tennyson is imbued with any salutary powers at all, it is only to bring back the thoughts of lost friends and loved ones as if 'from the underworld', as if they were mere spectres or ghosts, and without the immediacy, vitality and simulated presence of Wordsworth's spots of time. To a greater extent than in Wordsworth, then, the ruin of Tintern Abbey in 'Tears, Idle Tears' becomes gradually eclipsed in Tennyson's poem, quite receding beneath a watery veil of melancholia that knows no end.

Melrose Abbey

> Here is this Melrose, now, which has been be-rhymed, be-draggled through infinite guidebooks [...]; and yet [...] even for the sake of being original you could not, in conscience, declare you did not admire it. (Stowe 1854: 59)

Few ruins have owed the extent and the nature of their fame so overwhelmingly to one writer as the pinkly delicate ruins of the Cistercian chief house of St Mary's Abbey, Melrose. Founded in 1136 and formally disestablished in 1609, the abbey's ruins were for a century and more understood through Walter Scott's best-selling poem, *The Lay of the Last Minstrel* (1805), bringing them national and international fame as a tourist must-see.

In 1805, the abbey's ruins were already well known, if hardly as 'far-fam'd' as the enthusiastic Robert Burns had it (Leask 2015: 120). They had been painted by George Barret and by Thomas Girtin, and illustrated in Thomas Pennant's *A Tour in Scotland* (1776) and James

Fittler's *Scotia Depicta* (1804). They had showed up occasionally in travel writing such as William Hutchinson's *A View of Northumberland, With an Excursion to the Abbey of Mailross in Scotland* (1776–8). They had featured in the writings of the Scottish antiquarians, most notably Francis Grose's *The Antiquities of Scotland* (1797), which extracts a number of previous descriptions, including one dating from as early as 1649 on the tomb inscriptions, and Roger Gale's letter of 1742 recommending Melrose to the attention of antiquaries. Grose provided a handsome engraving to accompany an extensive and detailed description of the ruins, dwelling, as was by then conventional, on 'the elegance and finishing of the windows, and beauty of the ornaments, with which this building is profusely adorned' (Grose 1797: vol. 2, 122). Equally conventional was the short verse featured within the engraved frontispiece encouraging the pleasures of ruin visiting, part of which specifies how to visit abbey ruins, with an emphasis on the spectacle of nature breaching a previously sacred interior, thinning out the differences between roof and vault, arch and grave, and erasing evidence of past wealth, skill and identity:

> Let us explore the ruin'd Abbey's choir;
> The Sculptur'd Tombs o'ergrown with shrubs and brambles
> It's [sic] fretted roof and window of rich tracery,
> 'Midst broken arches, graves and gloomy vaults.
> (Grose 1797: vol. 1, frontispiece)

The effect of the publication of *The Lay of the Last Minstrel* on the number of visitors to the abbey was immediate: as John Bower's dedication to Scott in his 1813 guidebook remarked, 'you […] have certainly principally contributed to its being more generally known, and rendered it an object of much greater interest, not only in its more immediate vicinity, but also to strangers' (Bower 1813: iii). The *Lay* was also extraordinarily successful in changing the way in which contemporaries viewed Melrose; subsequent travel writing, formal and informal, and associated visual representations show that it set precise expectations of the 'proper' view of the place and the 'proper' emotional experience to take home as a souvenir. Scott's romance was so effective in re-scripting the tourist experience because it had much in common with the genre of the tourist guidebook. Canto II opens with the famous exhortation to visit Melrose, and instructions to the visitor as to how to view the ruins 'aright':

> If thou would'st view fair Melrose aright,
> Go visit it by the pale moonlight;
> For the gay beams of lightsome day,
> Gild, but to flout, the ruins grey.
> When the broken arches are black in night,
> And each shafted oriel glimmers white;
> When the cold light's uncertain shower
> Streams on the ruin'd central tower;
> When buttress and buttress, alternately,
> Seem fram'd of ebon and ivory;
> When silver edges the imagery,
> And the scrolls that teach thee to live and die;
> When distant Tweed is heard to rave,
> And the owlet to hoot o'er the dead man's grave,
> Then go – but go alone the while –
> Then view St David's ruin'd pile;
> And, home returning, soothly swear,
> Was never scene so sad and fair!
> (Scott 1951: Canto II, i)

Illustration to Scott's The Lay of the Last Minstrel, *by John C. Schetky, 1808*

Although the speaker here is supposed to be the aged and infirm 'last minstrel' of the title, entertaining his patroness (the seventeenth-century Duchess of Buccleuch) and her household with a lengthy narrative, this address comes close to falling out of the frame narrative and appearing as a direct and authoritative exhortation by the poet to his readers. The poet's apparent interest in how to view Melrose 'aright' aligns with the perennial and essentially modern tourist's problem of achieving a highly personal (and therefore solitary) experience which is nonetheless the 'right' one (which everyone else of sensitivity has managed to have, and which is certified in this instance by the poet), which can then be brought home in a souvenir-sized poetic sentiment: 'Was never scene so sad and fair!'. Thus this stanza provides a description of the authentic experience, instructions for gaining access to it, and what to think and say of it then and afterwards, while lending itself to helpful extraction in guidebooks and pensive recitation on the spot. John Carr remarked in 1807 on the consequent fashion for viewing the ruins by moonlight; thirty years later, Chauncy Hare Townshend would exclaim: 'To see Melrose by daylight, what a profanation!' (Carr 1809; Townshend 1840: 390).

The promised authentic tourist experience drew further power and excitement from its congruence with the experience of the protagonist of the minstrel's story, Sir William of Deloraine. The 'lay' which the minstrel offers the party deals with events of the sixteenth-century era of 'Border chivalry', when Mary Queen of Scots was still on the throne, and before the Reformation brought ruin to the abbey. Sir William of Deloraine journeys to 'Melrose's holy pile' on a nocturnal errand at the bidding of the Ladye of Branksome Tower:

Seek thou the Monk of St Mary's aisle.
Greet the Father well from me;
Say that the fated hour is come,
And tonight he shall watch with thee,
To win the treasure of the tomb:
For this will be St Michael's night,
And, though stars be dim, the moon is bright;
And the Cross, of bloody red,
Will point to the grave of the mighty dead.
(Scott 1951: Canto I, xxii)

Deloraine duly arrives at the abbey by moonlight and is ushered through the cloisters by the aged Father. The verse provides detailed, localised description of the cloisters:

> The pillar'd arches were over their head,
> And beneath their feet were the bones of the dead.
> Spreading herbs, and flowerets bright,
> Glisten'd with the dew of night;
> Nor herb, nor floweret, glisten'd there,
> But was carved in the cloister-arches as fair.
> (Scott 1951: Canto II, vii–viii)

Equally, it describes the interior, as Deloraine and his guide enter the chancel through the 'steel-clenched postern door':

> The darken'd roof rose high aloof
> On pillars lofty and light and small:
> The keystone, that locked each ribbed aisle,
> Was a fleur-de-lys, or a quatre-feuille;
> The corbells were carv'd grotesque and grim;
> And the pillars, with cluster'd shafts so trim,
> With base and with capital flourish'd around,
> Seem'd bundles of lances which garlands had bound.
> (Scott 1951: Canto II, ix)

Approaching the high altar, Deloraine looks up to the east window:

> The moon on the east oriel shone
> Through slender shafts of shapely stone,
> By foliaged tracery combin'd;
> Thou would'st have thought some fairy's hand
> 'Twixt poplars straight the ozier wand,
> In many a freakish knot, had twin'd;
> Then fram'd a spell, when the work was done,
> And chang'd the willow-wreaths to stone.
> (Scott 1951: Canto II, xi)

Deloraine's itinerary models that of the modern ruin tourist, although he is on a more obviously exciting and urgent quest. The 'treasure of the tomb' that Deloraine is hunting is the spell-book of the wizard Michael Scott, he who 'cleft the Eildon hills'. Deloraine assists at the exhumation of the wizard's body, miraculously preserved and emitting an unearthly light, and takes the 'Mighty Book' despite the unnerving discouragement of 'strange noises on the blast' (Scott 1951: Canto II, xxi–xxii).

The ways in which the *Lay* gripped the tourist imagination can be gauged from how it is used in successive editions of the guidebook to the abbey. Originally authored by John Bower in 1813, the guidebook was slowly adapted subsequently, making it possible to see changes in how the *Lay* is exploited. Although the edition of 1813 includes Scott's lines on viewing the abbey by moonlight, those describing the corbels and those on the 'east oriel' (Bower 1827: 28, 58–9, 66–7), the bulk of the verse included is by a much more obscure poet, J. Copland, and it is this that authorises Bower's recommendation to the reader to view Melrose in solitude, at midnight, and by moonlight (Bower 1827: 43). Later editions, however, excise Copland and give Scott increasing primacy, especially on the matter of moonlight. By 1878, the version by then-custodian Margaret Fairbairn provides the expected quotations from Scott but increasingly only in unattributed snippets embedded within the prose, suggesting that the poem was so well known by then that it did not need referencing in detail. Equally, extensive and all but obligatory quotation from the *Lay* characterised travel writing. One reason for quotation was the perceived accuracy of Scott's descriptive passages: in 1825 Amédée Pichot, quoting extensively, remarked that 'the poet is alone requisite to describe these characteristics' (Pichot 1825: vol. 2, 383); in the early 1830s the young American Henry Blake McLellan wrote in his journal on 'the remarkable accuracy of Scott's description of this imposing and splendid edifice' (McLellan 1834: 223). In 1845, an unusually thorough American visitor described how he set about viewing Melrose, firstly by sunset, then by moonlight, and lastly by sunrise. By moonlight 'the scene was one altogether of enchantment – a perfect realization of the poet's description' (Anon. 1845: 109).

Memorisable, quotable and above all accurate descriptions of the detailed 'beauties' of architecture and sculpture, Scott's lines begged verification on the spot. But tourists were lured too by the desire to shadow Deloraine's quest by undertaking a pseudo-supernatural errand to uncover the mysterious source of Scott's ability to enchant readers.

Under the guidance of the abbey custodian John Bower (who seems to have dramatised himself as a version of the 'aged monk'; see Bower 1827: 76), they accordingly visited by moonlight, passed through 'the steel-clenched postern door', sat on the very stone on which the monk and Deloraine sat, and carried copies of the poem to the high altar to read it there at midnight (see Botfield 1830: 8).

Although Victorian tourist experience of Melrose was primarily scripted by *The Lay of the Last Minstrel*, it would gradually expand to include imagining the figure of Scott within the ruins. The guidebook of 1878, for example, places the figure of Scott himself within the grounds of the abbey and near the wizard's grave:

> In this corner, is, according to the Lay of the Last Minstrel, the grave of the famous wizard, Michael Scott. [...] Beyond a footpath near these graves, on the north-east side of a heap of fragments, is a flat stone, which was a favourite seat with Sir Walter Scott, when he came to feast on the grand and varied beauty of the scene. (Fairbairn 1878: 6).

This formalised a widely felt desire to have Scott as a personal guide to the ruins. Although there is evidence that the abbey formed part of Scott's personal tour of the vicinity – when the Wordsworths visited in 1803, they were promptly shown the ruins (Wordsworth 1997: 206) – Scott eventually wearied of taking visitors round himself, so great was the desire on the part of friends and strangers alike for seeing them through his eyes. In October 1825, for instance, when the poet Thomas Moore showed up to be taken round the abbey by Scott, he confessed that he had been strongly tempted to come over earlier 'in order to see the Abbey by the beautiful moonlight we had then; but I thought it still better to reserve myself for the chance of seeing it with him, though I had heard he was not fond now of showing it' (Moore 1853–6: vol. 4, 339). In effect Moore had tossed up whether the experience would be more authentic if taken by moonlight or accompanied by the author and decided for the latter.

The desire to have Scott along as personal guide derived in large part from the practice of extracting or referencing passages from the poem, including in Scott's own spin-off illustrative, topographical and historical publications; in *The Border Antiquities of England and Scotland* (1814), for example, Scott quoted his own verse and explanatory notes in the entry on Melrose (Scott 1814: vol. 2, 97). The effect was to short-circuit the poem's frame narrative, putting the descriptive passages directly into Scott's mouth and so placing Scott as a figure in his own Romantic landscape. This effect was amplified by Scott's own sense of the locality as personal and imaginative territory, realised first in *The Minstrelsy of the Scottish Border* (1802–3), and then in the building of his baronial pile, Abbotsford, in Roxburghshire. It would become popularised after his death in the idea of 'Scott country', a terrain at once geographical and fictive branded by the idea of the author.

In the ruins of Melrose, tourists began to desire glimpses of Scott caught in the very act of imagination. Although this was, necessarily, a vain hope after Scott's death, it was given warrant by the way that the *Lay* holds out a fantasy of exhuming the still powerful and conjecturally immortal wizard. Just after Scott's death in 1832 and at the height of his own reputation, the American writer Washington Irving published an account of his visit to Abbotsford in 1817, which modelled the itinerary and sensibility of all subsequent literary tourists to Abbotsford and the country round about for close on a century, and was particularly important in enabling the foregrounding of the dead author as tourist guide to Melrose.

In 1817 Irving had travelled down from Edinburgh hoping 'to get a sight of the "mighty minstrel of the North"' (Irving 1835: 1). A letter of introduction secured a visit to Abbotsford that included a tour of Melrose. Irving identifies one of the more sophisticated and counter-intuitive pleasures of literary tourism – of *not* suspending disbelief, but discriminating between the actual setting and the romance naturalised there. Irving does this by gently poking fun at the zealous credulity of the custodian, 'Johnnie Bowers', who pointed out 'every thing in the Abbey that had been described by Scott in his "Lay of the Last Minstrel,"' and documented the accuracy of his account by repeating, 'with broad Scotch accent, the passage which corroborated it' (Irving 1835: 5). According to Irving, the demands of constructing a tour of the ruins that did sufficient justice to the poem had led Bower to elaborate further on Scott's realism of setting, or, in Irving's words, to go 'beyond Scott in the minuteness of his antiquarian research':

> for he had discovered the very tomb of the wizard, the position of which had been left in doubt by the poet. This he boasted to have

ascertained by the position of the oriel window, and the direction in which the moonbeams fell at night, through the stained glass casting the shadow of the red cross on the spot, as had all been specified in the poem. (Irving 1835: 6)

Bower had also developed an ingenious solution to the regular disappointment awaiting the many visitors who turned up hoping to see the ruins by moonlight:

This was a great double tallow candle stuck upon the end of a pole, with which he would conduct his visitors about the ruins on a dark night; so much to their satisfaction, that at length he began to think it even preferable to the moon itself. 'It does na' light up a' at once, to be sure,' he would say, 'but then you can shift it about, and show the auld Abbey, bit by bit, whilst the moon only shines on one side.' (Irving 1835: 9)

Irving distinguishes his own desire to see the abbey as the setting for the *Lay* from John Bower's desire to see and to show him the abbey as the place where the events of the *Lay* took place – a fine but critical distinction. He verges upon presenting Bower as a parody of Scott himself, doubling him in his willingness and ability to reinvent Melrose to suit the needs of romance, although ultimately he draws back from this position through asserting that Scott recognised Bower as his accidental creation: 'Scott used to amuse himself with the simplicity of the old man, and his zeal in verifying every passage of the poem, as though it had been authentic history' to the extent 'that he always acquiesced in his deductions'. In Irving's account, Bower eventually became so identified with the *Lay* that his identity became mixed up with its personages, becoming thus, even before Scott wrote his obituary, one of Scott's characters (Irving 1835: 6). The more pertinent parallel that threatens is that between Bower and Irving himself, a parallel that depends upon the likeness between the belief of guide and tourist. The difference resides in the distinction, especially fragile where Scott is concerned, between history and romance, a distinction expressed as a sharp class and commercial distinction between local guide and cosmopolitan tourist. What is sold is 'authentic history', but what is bought is a sophisticated game of the suspension of disbelief, given piquancy by social condescension modelled on that of Scott himself. In short, Irving – and by extension the tourist who follows in his footsteps – avoids becoming Bower through over-literalism by identifying with Scott's power to cast the spell of romance over locality. The result is the foregrounding of the figure of the (dead) author.

This negotiation is also evident in one of the earliest descriptions of 'doing' Melrose after Scott's death, provided by Thomas Dibdin, in his monumental *A Bibliographical, Antiquarian, and Picturesque Tour in the Northern Counties of England and in Scotland* (1838). Dibdin remarks severely that the Border landscape has been air-brushed by Scott ('the wand of the poet *only* has here created a fairy land') and, visiting Melrose, he notes that this too had been touched up: 'it would indeed require the keeping-down tint of "pale moonlight" to absorb all these vulgarities in a sort of poetical mist' (Dibdin 1838: vol. 2, 1007, 1003–4, 1015). (He was especially annoyed by a woman hanging out her linen.) This hard-headed waspishness, faced with the literal and modern realities, nonetheless gives way to the visionary: on entering the abbey, Dibdin writes,

> [I] fancied I saw the embodied spirit of the GREAT POET sitting upon the *identical spot* which it used to occupy in its more substantial form of flesh and blood [...] 'There, sir,' said the living genius of the place – (a Mr Bower – who has made every nook and recess of the ruin his own) 'there, Sir Walter Scott used to sit and look about him.' Of course, I was bound to sit and do the same. (Dibdin 1838: vol. 2, 1004)

Irving's suggestion that Bower was Scott's double here is realised by Dibdin – Bower acts as the 'living genius' of the place, Scott the dead one. But so too is Irving's suggestion that the tourist is Scott's double; the modern tourist, if sufficiently visionary, inherits the right to sit in the 'spot' of genius. Accordingly, Dibdin bought (and reproduces) the postcard of Scott sitting in the ruins that Bower sold to him.

Dibdin's double vision of Melrose, disappointment in the actuality coupled with admiration for Scott's imaginative powers, would echo in personal accounts and tourist's handbooks down the century. The question was how far you could as a mere tourist recreate Scott's vision by visiting Melrose. In 1854, Harriet Beecher Stowe's second moonlit visit ('Scott says we must see it by moonlight; it is one of the proprieties of the place as I understand' [Stowe 1854: 64]) was undertaken despite the deflating suggestion that Scott himself had never actually visited the abbey by 'the pale moonlight' that he recommended. Stowe's account oscillates self-parodically between hard-headed practicalities and experimentally romantic and Gothic ambitions:

> We walked up and down the long aisles, and groped out into the cloisters; and then I thought, to get the full ghostliness of the thing, we would go up the old, ruined staircase into the long galleries, that
>   'Midway thread the abbey wall'
> We got about half way up, when there came into our faces one of those sudden passionate puffs of mist and rain. [...] Whish! came the wind in our faces, like the rustling of a whole army of spirits down the staircase; whereat we all tumbled back promiscuously on to each other, and concluded we would not go up. In fact we had done the thing, and so we went home [...]. (Stowe 1854: 66)

Stowe is preoccupied with the extent to which her experience of the ruin lived up to the experience of reading the poem. On the one hand, Stowe commented, the description was 'as perfect in most details as if it had been written by an Architect as well as a poet – it is a kind of glorified daguerrotype' (Stowe 1854: 59); on the other, she amusingly recounts her disappointment at the discrepancy between the ruin that she saw and the ruin that Scott had imagined, before recasting the experience as a measure of Scott's magical ability to reconstitute the abbey:

> I fancied I could see him [...] gazing round the ruin, and mentally restoring it to its former splendour; he brings back the coloured light into the windows, and throws its many-hued reflexions over the graves; he ranges the banners along around the walls, and rebuilds every shattered arch and aisle, till we have the picture as it rises on us in his book. (Stowe 1854: 60)

With *The Lay of the Last Minstrel* Scott comprehensively overwrote well-established ruin thought-habits – enlightenment musing on factionalism, sentimental musing upon mortality, or Gothic fantasising of Catholic vices – in favour of a new way of seeing. J. M. W. Turner's watercolour *Melrose Abbey: Moonlight* of 1822 effectively depicts this.

Turner shows a solitary modern visitor struck by a flood of moonlight pouring through the east window, and in the foreground a stone inscribed with lines from the *Lay*. As Margaret Russett points out, 'those who view fair Melrose aright see, not the history of the abbey or even its architectural distinction, but the words of Scott himself, the Wizard of the North' (Russett 2016). Turner's visitor appears part-blinded, suggesting that seeing by moonlight is to see otherwise, like the poet. Indeed, when tourists came to Melrose Abbey they sought the possibility of enchantment, and often enough they found it. As one

'Melrose Abbey: Moonlight'. J. M. W. Turner, watercolour, 1822

enthusiast wrote, viewing the ruins at dawn after a late-night session: 'My moonlight visit to it seemed like a dream, and when I saw its grey walls in the morning light, it was as if a vision of the night had been embodied in stone' (Anon. 1845: 113). This sense of the ruins as liable to strange transformation is rooted in the famous lines about the 'east oriel':

> Thou woulds't have thought some fairy's hand
> 'Twixt poplars straight the ozier wand,
> In many a freakish knot, had twin'd;
> Then fram'd a spell, when the work was done,
> And chang'd the willow-wreaths to stone.
> (Scott 1951: Canto II, xi)

It is hard to overstate the oddity and originality of this way of viewing ruins, one that replaces human history with the idea of personal fancy and local enchantment; its profound influence is felt in Stowe's exclamation that 'it seems [...] for a thing so airy and spiritual to have sprung up by enchantment, and to have been the product of spells and fairy fingers, is no improbable account of the matter' (Stowe 1854: 62). This fairy petrification of the once living is a precisely reversed version of Scott's sorcerous ability to bring the stones of Melrose to life.

By the late nineteenth century, Scott's spell had resulted in such tourist numbers that achieving solitude by moonlight must have become less and less feasible: 'Cuthbert Bede' lamented that Melrose, as Scott's 'loved haunt, lying midway between his two earthly homes of Abbotsford and Dryburgh, is the convenient centre of a triple attraction for the quick-recurring throngs of visitors whom the railway carries to within a few yards of the Abbey' (Bradley 1863: 351–2). Such enthusiasm is unimaginable today; the Victorian thrill has vanished as Scott's poetry has faded from mainstream culture. Gone forever is the sense that Melrose might be simultaneously haunted by two spell-binding wizards named Scott, both capable of defying mortality through the power of their mighty books, both capable of changing the very landscape of the Borders through their spells.

Further Reading

Finley, Gerald. 1980. *Landscapes of Memory: Turner as Illustrator to Scott* (Berkeley and Los Angeles: University of California Press).

Haydon, Colin. 1993. *Anti-Catholicism in Eighteenth-Century England, c. 1714–80: A Political and Social Study* (Manchester and New York: Manchester University Press).
Hoeveler, Diane Long. 2014. *The Gothic Ideology: Religious Hysteria and Anti-Catholicism in British Popular Fiction, 1780–1880* (Cardiff: University of Wales Press).

References

Aikin, Anna Laetitia. 1773. 'On Monastic Institutions', in *Miscellaneous Pieces, in Prose*, by J. and A. L. Aikin (London: Printed for J. Johnson), 88–118.
Anon. 1768. *The Southampton Guide: or, An Account of the Antient and Present State of that Town* (Southampton: J. Linden).
Anon. 1775. *The Antiquarian Repertory: A Miscellany, Intended to Preserve and Illustrate Several Valuable Remains of Old Times*, 4 vols (London: Francis Blyth and T. Evans).
Anon. 1790. *Tour of the Isle of Wight*, 2 vols (London: Thomas Hookham).
Anon. 1816. *A Series of Sonnets Written Expressly to Accompany Some Recently-Published Views of Tintern Abbey* (London: Printed by J. Tyler).
Anon. 1841. *Melrose and Its Vicinity: Being an Account of Such Objects of Historical and Classical Interest as are to be Found in its Neighbourhood* (Edinburgh: J. B. Mould).
Anon. 1845. *A Transatlantic Tour: Comprising Travels in Great Britain, France, Holland, Belgium, Germany, Switzerland, and Italy* (Philadelphia: Perkin and Purves).
Bloomfield, Robert. 1807. *Journal of a ten days' tour from Uley in Gloucestershire, by way of Ross; down the River Wye to Chepstow, Abergavenny, Brecon, Hereford, Malvern. &c. &c. – August 1807*, British Library BL Add. MS 28267.
Botfield, Beriah. 1830. *Journal of a Tour through the Highlands of Scotland During the Summer of 1829* (North Hall, Northants: Printed for the Author).
Bower, John. 1813. *Description of the Abbeys of Melrose and Old Melrose, with their Traditions* (Kelso: Printed for the Author).
Bower, John. 1822. *Description of the Abbeys of Melrose and Old Melrose, with their Traditions*, 2nd edn (Edinburgh: Printed for the Author).
Bower, John. 1827. *Description of the Abbeys of Melrose and Old Melrose*, 3rd edn (Edinburgh: Printed for the Author).
Bowles, William Lisle. 1789. *Sonnets, Written Chiefly on Picturesque Spots, During a Tour* (Bath: R. Cruttwell).
Bradley, Edward [Cuthbert Bede]. 1863. *A Tour in Tartanland* (London: R. Bentley).
Bullar, John. 1799. *A Companion in a Tour Round Southampton* (Southampton: T. Baker).
Carr, John. 1809. *Caledonian Sketches, Or, A Tour Through Scotland in 1807* (London: For Mathews and Leigh).
Carter, Elizabeth. 1809. *A Series of Letters Between Mrs Elizabeth Carter and Miss Catherine Talbot, From the Year 1741 to 1770: To which are Added Letters from Mrs. Elizabeth Carter to Mrs. Vesey, Between the Years 1763 and 1787*, 4 vols (London: F. C. and J. Rivington).

Coleridge, Samuel Taylor and William Wordsworth. 2008. *Lyrical Ballads, 1798 and 1800*, edited by Michael Gamer and Dahlia Porter (Peterborough, Ont.: Broadview).

Colley, Linda. 2005. *Britons: Forging the Nation 1707-1837*, 2nd edn (New Haven and London: Yale University Press).

Collins, Edward. 1825. *Tintern Abbey; or, The Beauties of Piercefield, A Poem. In Four Books. Interspersed with Illustrative Notes* (Chepstow: Printed for the Author).

Dibdin, Thomas Frognall. 1838. *A Bibliographical, Antiquarian, and Picturesque Tour in the Northern Counties of England and in Scotland*, 2 vols (London: Printed for the Author).

Fairbairn, Margaret W. 1878. *Melrose Abbey: Notes Descriptive and Historical*, 2nd edn (Abbey Lodge, Melrose; Selkirk: Printed for the Author).

Gilpin, William. 1789. *Observations on the River Wye, and Several parts of South Wales, &c., Relative Chiefly to Picturesque Beauty; Made in the Summer of the Year 1770*, 2nd edn (London: Printed for R. Blamire).

Gilpin, William. 1798. *Observations on the Western Parts of England, Relative Chiefly to Picturesque Beauty* (London: T. Cadell and W. Davies).

Gray, Thomas. 1764. 'Thomas Gray to James Brown, 1 or 8 October 1764'. *Thomas Gray Archive*, http://www.thomasgray.org/cgi-bin/display.cgi?text=tgal0445 [last accessed 29 May 2017].

Grose, Francis. c. 1784. *The Antiquities of England and Wales, Vol. III* (London: Printed for S. Hooper).

Grose, Francis. 1797. *The Antiquities of Scotland*, 2 vols (London: For Hooper and Wigstead).

Hamley, Edward. 1789. *Poems of Various Kinds* (London: T. Cadell and W. Davies; New Haven and London: Yale University Press).

Heath, Charles. 1793. *Descriptive Account of Tintern Abbey, Monmouthshire. A Cistercian Monastery Founded in the Year MCXXXI. Six Hundred and Sixty-Two Years Ago, Selected from Grose, Gilpin, Shaw, Wheatley, and Other Esteemed Writers* (Monmouth: Sold by Charles Heath in the Market Place, and at all the Inns in the County).

Irving, Washington. 1835. *Abbotsford and Newstead Abbey* (Paris: A. W. Galignani & Co.).

Jerningham, Edward. 1765. *An Elegy Written Among the Ruins of an Abbey*, 2nd edn (London: Printed for J. Dodsley).

Keate, George. 1769. *Netley Abbey: An Elegy*, 2nd edn (London: J. Dodsley).

Leask, Nigel (ed.). 2015. *Robert Burns: Commonplace Books, Tour Journals and Miscellaneous Prose* (Oxford: Oxford University Press).

Levinson, Marjorie. 1986. *Wordsworth's Great Period Poems* (Cambridge: Cambridge University Press).

McLellan, Henry Blake. 1834. *Journal of a Residence in Scotland, and Tour through England* (Boston: Allen and Ticknor).

Mitford, Mary Russell. 1827. *Dramatic Scenes, Sonnets, and Other Poems* (London: George B. Whitaker).

Moore, Thomas. 1853-6. *Memoirs, Journal and Correspondence of Thomas Moore*, 5 vols (London: Longman, Brown, Green and Longman).

Norton, Christopher. 1986. 'Table of Cistercian Legislation', in *Cistercian Art and Architecture in the British Isles*, edited by Christopher Norton and David Park (Cambridge: Cambridge University Press), 315-93.

Pearce, William. 1794. *Netley Abbey: An Operatic Farce, in Two Acts* (London: W. Woodfall).

Pichot, Joseph Jean M. C. Amédée. 1825. *Historical and Literary Tour of a Foreigner in England and Scotland*, 2 vols (London: For Saunders and Otley).

Powicke, F. M. (ed.). 1994. *The Life of Aelred of Rievaulx*, by Walter Daniel (Kalamazoo: Cistercian Publications).

Ribbans, Frederick Bolingbroke. 1854. *Tintern Abbey: A Poem* (London).

Russett, Margaret. 2016. 'To view fair Melrose aright', *The Bottle Imp*, asls.arts.gla.ac.uk/SWE/TBI/TBIsup/TBIsupp3/Russett.html [last accessed 15 January 2017].

Scott, Walter. 1814. *The Border Antiquities of England and Scotland, Containing Specimens of the Architecture, Sculpture, and other Vestiges of Former Ages. Accompanied by Descriptions. Together with Illustrations of Remarkable Incidents in Border History and Tradition, and Original Poetry by Sir Walter Scott Esq.*, 2 vols (London: Printed for Longman, Hurst, Rees, Orme and Brown; J. Murray; Edinburgh: Constable & Co.).

Scott, Walter. 1951. *The Poetical Works of Sir Walter Scott with the Author's Introductions and Notes*, edited by J. Logie Robertson (London, New York and Tokyo: Oxford University Press).

Shell, Alison. 2007. *Oral Culture and Catholicism in Early Modern England* (Cambridge: Cambridge University Press).

Shenstone, William. 1764. 'The Ruin'd Abbey: or, The Effects of Superstition', in *The Works in Verse and Prose, of William Shenstone, Esq.*, 2 vols (London: Printed for R. and J. Dodsley), vol. 1, 308-21.

Simond, Francis. 1815. *Journal of a Tour and Residence in Great Britain, during the Years 1810 and 1811, by a French Traveller*, 2 vols (Edinburgh: Archibald Constable and Co.).

Stowe, Harriet Beecher. 1854. *Sunny Memories of Foreign Lands* (London: Piper, Stephenson and Spence).

Tennyson, Alfred. 1847. *The Princess; a Medley* (London: Edward Moxon).

Townshend, Chauncy Hare. 1840. *A Descriptive Tour in Scotland* (Brussels: Hauman and Co.; London: George Whitaker and Co.).

Walpole, Horace. 1937-83. *The Yale Edition of Horace Walpole's Correspondence*, edited by W. S. Lewis, 48 vols (New Haven: Yale University Press).

Warner, Richard. 1795. *Netley Abbey: A Gothic Story*, 2 vols (London: William Lane).

Warner, Richard. 1799. *A Walk through Wales, in August 1797* (Bath: Printed by R. Cruttwell).

Whaley, John (ed.). 1745. *A Collection of Original Poems and Translations* (London: Printed for the Author).

Wordsworth, Dorothy. 1997. *Recollections of a Tour Made in Scotland, A.D. 1803* (New Haven and London: Yale University Press).

Ziegenhirt, Sophia. 1816. *The Orphan of Tintern Abbey. A Novel. In Three Volumes* (London: Printed at the Minerva Press).

RUINS IN FOCUS

Tintagel Castle

Nick Groom

> Tintagel! day's pure ocean light
> Ne'er rolled o'er such poetic height;
> The seasons, led by nimble hours
> Ne'er circled stronger spell-bound towers [...]
> (Hogg 1827: 203)

The cultural revival of King Arthur that began at the end of the eighteenth century and culminated spectacularly in Alfred, Lord Tennyson's *Idylls of the King* (1859–85) was due in part to a renewed interest in the ruins of Tintagel Castle, Cornwall. A century after Edmund Spenser's comprehensive reinvention of Arthur in *The Faerie Queene* (1590–96), there had been attempts to revive Arthurianism in John Dryden and Henry

Tintagel. From W. H. Bartlett, The Ports, Harbours, Watering-places, and Coast Scenery of Great Britain. Illustrated by Views Taken on the Spot, *1842.*

Purcell's dramatic opera *King Arthur* (written 1684–5, performed 1691) and in Sir Richard Blackmore's epics *Prince Arthur* (1695) and *King Arthur* (1697). The response to Blackmore in particular was damning, best summed up by Thomas Brown who wrote a poem pointedly titled 'Upon seeing a Man light a Pipe of Tobacco in a Coffee-house, with a Leaf of *King Arthur*' (Brown 1702: 16). It was not only Blackmore who was ridiculed, for Arthur himself became a ludicrous figure in the first half of the eighteenth century: Henry Fielding's burlesque play, *Tom Thumb* (1730) is, for example, set at 'The Court of King Arthur'. Thomas Gray did make passing reference to the legendary king in *The Bard* (1757) – 'No more our long-lost Arthur we bewail. / "All-hail, ye genuine kings, Britannia's issue, hail!"' (Gray 1764: 19) – yet he also undercut this elsewhere with an arch note on the mythical monarch: 'It was the common belief of the Welch nation, that King Arthur was still alive in Fairy-Land, and should return again to reign over Britain' (Gosse 1884: vol. 1, 389).

And yet Arthur's supposed birthplace – the now-ruined Tintagel Castle on the north coast of Cornwall – was celebrated as 'one of the Wonders of the World' (Simpson 1746: vol. 1, 141). The castle had a breathtaking position: it stood on a high and rocky island linked to the mainland by an elm-tree drawbridge over a vertiginous isthmus. The sixteenth-century poet and antiquary John Leland described it as 'marvelus strong [...and] on a great an high terrible cragge environid with the Se' (Hearne 1710–12: vol. 2, 60). Tintagel Castle became a byword for an impregnable fortress: in *University Education* (1726), Richard Newton of Hart Hall, Oxford, noted that 'The Doors of Your *Prison* are *open* indeed, but It is not less a *Prison*, if, like King *Arthur*'s Castle at *Tintagel*, it be surrounded by a *Precipice*' (Newton 1726: 112).

So despite the burlesque mockery, it became generally accepted that Arthur was an historical figure who had had his seat of power (and even his Round Table, too) at the castle. Tintagel Castle thus became woven into national myth: sublime, picturesque and politically Whiggish – a stupendous instance of the forces of history. By the end of the century, William George Maton had canonised the castle as a place, like Gray's country churchyard, to reflect on the past and on British history and the relentless pursuit of liberty and freedom:

> Associating the idea of its former splendor and importance, – of its having been the palace of the princes of *Danmonium*, – with the

wild sublimity and commanding aspect of the situation, we felt at the scene before us an involuntary awe. Its desolation and decay gave rise to reflections on the early periods of our history; on the bold stand made by our warlike ancestors in defence of their race and native soil; on the heroic chiefs whom these struggles for independence and freedom from foreign rule called forth; and on the vicissitudes which towns, tribes, whole nations, languages, and all human institutions and ideas undergo. These walls, now mouldering into rubbish, once 'frowned a proud pile,' and contained apartments in which appeared the pomp and pageantry of a court. Fancy figured 'thronging knights' resorting hither to the throne of their warlike sovereign, and partaking of the military honors of his *round-table*, whilst the royal standard of Britain waving above proclaimed this the seat of supreme authority! – Now desolation holds her reign. (Maton 1797: vol. 1, 260–1)

It was here, then, that Tennyson came in May 1848 to resume his Arthurian interests that had diverted him since his youth ('The Lady of Shalott' was published in 1832, when Tennyson was aged twenty-three), and to speak with Robert Stephen Hawker, vicar of nearby Morwenstow, who was working on his own Arthurian epic. In 1859 the first four poems of *Idylls of the King* were published: *Enid, Vivien, Elaine* and *Guinevere*. The *Idylls* would become Tennyson's – and Victorian poetry's – crowning achievement.

References
Brown, Thomas. 1702. *Commendatory Verses*, 2nd edn (London).
Gosse, Edmund (ed.). 1884. *The Works of Thomas Gray*, 4 vols (London: Macmillan & Co.).
Gray, Thomas. 1757. *Odes by Mr Gray* (London: Printed at Strawberry Hill, for R. and J. Dodsley).
Hearne, Thomas (ed.). 1710–12. *The Itinerary of John Leland the Antiquary*, 9 vols (Oxford: Printed for James Fletcher and Joseph Pote).
Hogg, Thomas. 1827. *The Fabulous History of the Ancient Kingdom of Cornwall* (London: Printed for Longman, Rees, Orme and Co.).
Maton, William George. 1797. *Observations Relative Chiefly to the Natural History, Picturesque Scenery, and Antiquities, of the Western Counties of England, made in the Years 1794 and 1796*, 2 vols (Salisbury: Printed and Sold by J. Easton).
Newton, Richard. 1726. *University Education* (London: Printed for G. Strahan).
Simpson, Samuel. 1746. *The Agreeable Historian*, 2 vols (London: R. Walker).

Harlech Castle

David Punter

> High on a rock, where ocean's waves are spread,
> Fair Bronwen's Tower erects its stately head;
> Since known by *Collwyn*, then by *Lear's* name:
> A fairer structure ne'er was known to fame.
> (quoted in Cathrall 1828: 249)

Harlech Castle, Gwynedd, is one of the most prominent of all Welsh castles in the arts and letters, which is hardly surprising, considering its spectacular setting above the sea and – from the angle from which it was most famously represented – the presence of Snowdon in the background. The pictures of it are countless: there is at least one engraving by the Buck brothers (1742); there is a well-known drawing by John Sell Cotman (c. 1800–2); and there are paintings by Henry Gastineau, Paul Sandby, John Varley and J. M. W. Turner, among many others. In prose it was eloquently described by Thomas Pennant in *A Tour in Wales* (1778–83).

Harlech Castle. Engraving from Picturesque Views in England and Wales, from Drawings by J. M. W. Turner *[...], 1838*

The castle was originally built between 1283 and 1289, after the death of Gruffudd ap Llywelyn, and the work was directed by the fabled James of St George, a Savoyard who later became constable of the castle. Because of its location, it was impossible to supply from the Welsh hinterland, and its supplies came by sea from Ireland, to enter through the water gate and the famous 'way to the sea' up the precipitous cliff flank.

Harlech Castle has, unlike many other castles, had a significant military and, as some would say, colonial history. It played a key role in the uprising of Owain Glyn Dŵr, and an inventory of supplies of the time shows the extreme difficulty that the English had in maintaining it as a military base. Unsubstantiated accounts claim that it was at Harlech that Owain was formally crowned Prince of Wales. It was recaptured by Harry of Monmouth, the future King Henry V, in 1409. During the Wars of the Roses it gave shelter to Queen Margaret of Anjou, and it was held for almost a decade by a Welsh constable for the Lancastrians; the Yorkist siege which ended this period is supposed to have given rise to the popular song 'Men of Harlech', and was described by the fifteenth-century Welsh poet Hywel Dafi thus: 'seven thousand men shooting in every port, their bows made from every yew tree' (quoted in Williams 2002: 202).

By 1564, however, the castle was in 'utter ruin', with most buildings being 'utterlie in ruyn and prostrate'. Part of it was saved and again rendered habitable during the reign of Elizabeth by her decision to hold the Merioneth Assizes there – 'the said Castle has been quite ruinated and decayed, if the Justices of assise had not restored to it, as aforesaid, & will daylie decay hereafter, if they bee not compelled to keepe their Sessions in that towne' (Westwood and Williams 1850: 32) – but after the Civil Wars it was rendered unusable, although spared an advised complete demolition. From the eighteenth century, however, it became a favourite site for artists and antiquaries, and it is now on the World Heritage list of sites of 'outstanding universal value'. What can be seen today looks, from a certain distance, remarkably complete: the entire outer shell has survived the centuries. In fact, although such a fact might have been of little interest to those who came to prize the ruin for its own sake, Harlech had, in a magnified form, the advantages and problems of so many medieval castles: almost impossible to attack, it was simultaneously almost impossible to supply and thus fell a victim, in true 'ruins of empire' fashion, to its own spectacular grandiosity.

References

Cathrall, William. 1828. *The History of North Wales, Vol. II* (Manchester: Printed by J. Cleave and Sons).

Westwood, John Obadiah and John Williams. 1850. *Observations on the Stone of St. Cadfan, at Towyn* (London: W. Pickering).

Williams, Glanmor. 2002. *Renewal and Reformation: Wales c. 1415–1642* (Oxford: Oxford University Press).

Chapter 5:
The Haunting of Britain's Ruins

Hamish Mathison and Angela Wright

> With all the chances against her of house, hall, place, park, court, and cottage, Northanger turned up an abbey, and she was to be its inhabitant. Its long, damp passages, its narrow cells and ruined chapel, were to be within her daily reach, and she could not entirely subdue the hope of some traditional legends, some awful memorials of an injured and ill-fated nun. (Austen 1998: 147)

As she looks forward to her visit to Northanger Abbey, the family home of her suitor Henry Tilney, Jane Austen's heroine Catherine Morland embodies the excitement of visiting anything that had the appendage of 'Abbey' attached to it during the Romantic period. '[T]raditional legends' had a tendency to gather round the ruined relics of religious sites, and where the Protestant Reformation loomed large in England, 'some awful memorials of an injured and ill-fated nun', made so fashionable in the Gothic literature of the 1790s, such as in Matthew Lewis's tale of the Bleeding Nun in *The Monk* (1796), were desirable commodities. In what follows, the risks and rewards of investing British literary practice with the heft of a haunted past will be explored.

There is a particular thrill of anticipation attendant upon the experience of visiting and writing about ruins. Part of the poetic frisson of visiting a feudal, ruined space lies in the prospect of encountering the restless ghosts of its former inhabitants. Revenants who were perhaps unjustly treated during their lives, or who conversely were embodiments of awful tyranny, can tell us about a past that is infinitely more terrifying than the present. Whether victims of violence and tyranny, or perpetrators of the same, apparitions can reassure us about the rational present in their terrifying embodiments of the past.

Britain's ruins are renowned for being haunted by spectral visitants. John Mason's *Haunted Heritage* (1999), which covers reputedly haunted ruins in the care of English Heritage, lists blue ladies, grey ladies, white ladies, cowled monks and even a phantom leper who haunt the grounds of priories, monasteries and castles which they reputedly inhabited during their lifetimes. They are identified primarily by their former roles or class, and the legends surrounding them are just sufficiently tangible to arouse the curiosity of the traveller, who may pause a while and attempt to see them. Authors of the Romantic period capitalised upon the appetite for ghouls and spectres that accreted around particular ruins, with titles that often incorporated or invented local legend. *The Grey Friar, and the Black Spirit of the Wye: A Romance* (1810) by John English, for example, epitomised this vogue for literature to combine local legend, ruined monasteries and ghostly presences known only by the colour of their cowls and habits. Situated in the Wye valley, close to the ruined Cistercian Tintern Abbey that Wordsworth had enshrined so memorably in his 'Lines Written a Few Miles from Tintern Abbey, on Revisiting the Banks of the Wye During a Tour, July 13, 1798' in *Lyrical Ballads* (1798), English's two-volume romance lured in its readership by its promise of a ghostly friar around the environs of Tintern Abbey. For Jane Austen's fictional reader Catherine Morland, as for many others, ruined abbeys and castles promised the potential, at least, to encounter the ghosts of the past.

In the Prologue to her *Tales of Superstition and Chivalry* (1802), the Romantic poet Anne Bannerman foregrounded the imaginative potential of the 'dim regions of monastic night' that could be found in Britain's ruined churches and abbeys:

> Yet in their cavern'd, dark recesses, dwells
> The long-lost Spirit of forgotten times,
> Whose voice prophetic reach'd to distant climes,
> And rul'd the nations from his witched cells;
>
> That voice is hush'd! [...] But still in Fancy's ear
> Its first unmeasur'd melodies resound!
> Blending with terrors wild, and legends drear,

> The charmed minstrelsy of mystic sound,
> The rous'd, embodied, to the eye of Fear,
> The unearthly habitants of faery ground.
> (Bannerman 1802: n.p.)

For Bannerman, the anticipation of encountering a ghost among the 'dark recesses' of 'monastic night' opened up 'Fancy's ear'. The imagination could provide the acoustics of the 'unmeasur'd melodies' even if the ghosts themselves did not materialise among the ruins. Blending 'legends drear' and 'terrors wild', 'mystic sound' could then rouse 'unearthly habitants'. Ghostly visitations, then, were a consequence of careful orchestration in the vision of Anne Bannerman, an orchestration that combined location, legend and imagination in equal measure. *Tales of Superstition and Chivalry* included dramatic monologues by a range of ghostly visitants: among others, there was 'The Perjured Nun', 'The Dark Ladie' and 'The Penitent's Confession'. Bannerman's list of characters drew upon the conventions of local legend in their functional anonymity. The naming of Bannerman's spectral characters in *Tales of Superstition and Chivalry* was deliberately vague; identified either by their Catholicism or by their station in life, the ghostly narrators were able to gesture towards a more feudal version of Britain embodied in the buildings that they haunted. They ventriloquised the past, bringing to life just a handful of the ruins of Britain. As Bannerman astutely pointed out to other authors aspiring to write in the same supernatural vein, however, local legend (from whence the tales of hauntings arise) must be combined carefully with a ruined building, a keen imagination and a sense of sound and atmosphere in the creation of a ghost.

The Ghosts of Furness Abbey

Before and after Bannerman, the combination of architectural ruin, imagination and attentiveness to atmosphere characterised the work of many authors who sought to evoke the supernatural in the ruins that they visited. When visiting the ruined Cistercian Furness Abbey, in what was then the county of Lancashire, in 1794 as part of a larger tour to the Lakes, for example, the Gothic romancer Ann Radcliffe underlined how the ruined structure of the monastery was intrinsic to her imaginative recreation of the monks who once inhabited it:

Furness Abbey. From Thomas Hearne, Antiquities of Great Britain *[...] Engraved (by W. Byrne) from Drawings Made by T. Hearne, London, 1786*

As, soothed by the venerable shades and the view of a more venerable ruin, we rested opposite to the eastern window of the choir, where once the high altar stood, and, with five other altars, assisted the religious pomp of the scene; the images and the manners of times, that were past, rose to reflection. The midnight procession of monks, clothed in white and bearing lighted tapers, appeared to the 'mind's eye' issuing to the choir through the very door-case, by which such processions were wont to pass from the cloisters to perform the matin service, when, at the moment of their entering the church, the deep chanting of voices was heard, and the organ swelled a solemn peal. To fancy, the strain still echoed feebly along the arcades and died in the breeze among the woods, the rustling leaves mingling with the close. It was easy to image the abbot and the officiating priests seated beneath the richly-fretted canopy of the four stalls, that still remain entire in the southern wall, and high over which is now perched a solitary yew-tree, a black funereal memento to the living of those who once sat below. (Radcliffe 1795: 490–1)

Radcliffe here artfully combines nature and culture through the repetition of the word 'venerable', suggesting how, united, they can lead the 'mind's eye' to see the monks that formerly inhabited Furness passing into the church in procession. The 'solitary yew-tree', which casts its shadow across the stalls where the monks once sat, provides a 'funereal memento' of the monks in procession. Radcliffe brings the spectral monks back to life in her 'mind's eye' by paying close attention to the visual and aural cues of nature. Sound plays just as important a role in the imaginative remembering of Radcliffe, with the 'rustling leaves' of the present combining with the 'solemn peal' of the organ of the abbey's past.

Dating back to 1123, Furness Abbey had long been a major landmark of tours to the Lake District. Although Thomas Gray's journal of his tour of the Lake District in 1769 (published in 1775 under the title of a 'Memoir' of Gray by W. A. Mason) did not engage extensively with Furness Abbey itself, Gray's picturesque engagement with the Lake District clearly inspired Radcliffe, as he detailed 'the points of Furness shooting far into the sea' (Gray 1775: 370). Radcliffe drew quite significantly from Gray's journey in terms of her own itinerary and her own literary engagement with the area. Thomas West was another influence upon Ann Radcliffe. Author of the widely cited and popular *Guide to the Lakes* of 1778, West first wrote the more localised but nonetheless extensive study *The Antiquities of Furness* in 1774. Radcliffe was inspired by West's historical attention to detail in her own lengthy account of Furness, particularly as she later drilled into the detail of the change in colour of the monks' cassocks from grey to the stricter white as the abbey became a member of the Cistercian order. West's more factual account, however, becomes endowed with the imaginative potential of the supernatural in Radcliffe's more literary treatment. In referring to the 'mind's eye' in the passage above, Radcliffe invokes Act I, scene ii of Shakespeare's *Hamlet*, where Hamlet confesses to Horatio that 'Methinks I see my father' before he encounters the ghost of Old Hamlet later, in scene v of the same act. It is an early moment in the play that points up the rich and fertile imagination of Hamlet as he anticipates his unearthly visitant. Radcliffe's citation of Hamlet, as she herself imagines the procession of monks, prognosticates, and even sanctions, the possibility that ghostly monks lurk in the ruins of Furness Abbey.

Furness Abbey has long enjoyed the reputation of being haunted by one of its former monks, being nominated by the *Daily Mail* in 2015 as one of Britain's 'spookiest' locations, owing to the monk's being frequently spotted 'climbing a staircase and also walking towards the gatehouse before vanishing into a wall' (Greenaway 2015). Whereas Radcliffe sought to invoke the ghostly monks, however, others who engaged with Furness Abbey during the Romantic period in travel journals and poetry did not draw upon or refer to its haunted reputation. In 1844 and 1845, William Wordsworth wrote two sonnets entitled 'At Furness Abbey'. The earlier poem focuses upon the erosion of man-made pride as nature's 'Ivy clasps the Sacred Ruin' and the abbey's 'mouldered walls' are rejuvenated by blossoming flowers (Wordsworth 1909: 785); the second concentrates upon a group of devout and humble railway labourers who visit the abbey, and who sit and walk 'Among the Ruins, but no idle talk / Is heard'. Instead, 'from one Voice a Hymn with tuneful sound / Hallows once more the long-deserted Quire / And thrills the old sepulchral earth, around' (Wordsworth 1909: 787). The abbey remains resolutely 'sepulchral' in the visions of Wordsworth, only reanimated by nature and fellow men. In and of themselves, the 'ruins' of Furness Abbey speak of death and desertion to Wordsworth rather than of any reanimated ghostly visitants. It is the role of the living (nature and men) to animate the abbey. This inevitability for Wordsworth, however, is no ghostly *reanimation*, but an organic and gradual process. The reasons for Wordsworth's conscious distancing of himself in these poems from the hauntings of Furness Abbey are numerous. Wordsworth's own self-conscious rejection of the Gothic began in 1798 with the publication of *Lyrical Ballads*, and remained a preoccupation throughout his career. In a later (1800) preface to that collection, he sought to promote a form of poetry that was invested more in the common language of men than in the thrills and sensations of supernatural fiction. Particularly in these sonnets addressed to Furness, Wordsworth wished to promote the preoccupations of, and reverence for, the rail workers visiting the abbey over the belief in the ghosts of any bygone feudal age.

Alloway Auld Kirk

Wordsworth's recombination of the quick and the dead was shaped, in part, by the work of Robert Burns. The siblings Dorothy and William

Kirk Alloway. Engraving from Edinburgh Magazine, *1803*

Wordsworth had made a study of Burns's work, conducting a tour in 1802 that included a summer visit to the Scottish poet's graveside. William Wordsworth was to write in an open letter of 1816 how 'The poet, penetrating the unsightly and disgusting surface of things, has unveiled with exquisite skill the finer ties of imagination and feeling' that promoted 'intelligent sympathy' for lesser mortals (Low 1974: 286). The poem that he had in mind at that point was 'Tam o'Shanter', which Robert Burns had completed in the winter of 1790/91, and which first saw publication in the *Edinburgh Herald* on 18 March 1791. It was hailed from its first appearance as one of Burns's finest performances, displaying, in the words of Burns's contemporary Alexander Fraser Tytler in 1791, 'a power of imagination that Shakespeare himself could not have exceeded' (Low 1974: 95); it was his '*opus magnum*', as Byron had it in a letter to John Murray of 1821 (Low 1974, 326). The reception of Burns's poem sheds important light on how his contemporary readers and near-contemporary reviewers took a tale of haunted space and ghaistly goings-on, for while willing to praise the piece, the British literati struggled to place a tale of humour, pathos, credulity and the supernatural realm. Unlike so many treatments of the supernatural in the period, Burns's poem is unashamedly comic in tone, but not at all unsophisticated in purpose. The origins of its awkward reception lie in the origins of the poem's composition. The poem was commissioned by the antiquary Francis Grose, and having appeared in the Edinburgh periodical press in March 1791, it appeared in the second volume of Grose's two-volume *The Antiquities of Scotland* that same spring. One of the ironies raised by the poem is the rather unremarkable quality of the building itself: when *The Edinburgh Magazine* later published an engraving of the Kirk in May 1803, the accompanying text rather downplayed the building's significance: '[it] is this ruin which Burns mentions in his poem of *Tam o'Shanter* [...] and from this circumstance alone, are we induced to present it to our readers, more than from its external appearance, which is neither very picturesque or romantic' (J. D. 1803: 326).

After a lengthy drinking session in the town of Ayr, Tam (the poem's titular 'hero') is very drunk indeed as he rides home on his 'gray mare' Meg. His way will take him past old, ruined Alloway Kirk. That building, 'Whare ghaists and houlets nightly cry', became synonymous with the poem, and is itself framed by a darkling vision of the Scottish countryside. Tam traverses no pastoral retreat, no productive georgic field or enlightened agrarian space. Instead he negotiates a thickly painted scene of horrific folk memory:

> By this time he was cross the ford,
> Whare, in the snaw, the chapman smoor'd;
> And past the birks and meikle stane,
> Whare drunken *Charlie* brak's neck-bane;
> And thro' the whins, and by the cairn,
> Whare hunters fand the murder'd bairn;
> And near the thorn, aboon the well,
> Whare *Mungo's* mither hang'd hersel'.—
> (Burns 1968: vol. 2, 560, lines 89–96)

The poem will shortly reveal to the drunken Tam Satan himself, the central figure of high Presbyterian moral will – but the width and eschatological reach of the Presbyterian Church of Scotland is quite beyond him. His focus is on the immediate and the local: Mungo's mother, the chapman, Charlie with his broken neck. This cast of characters is aggressively local in its being, these peers, fellows and contemporaries of Tam so local as to require merely their first name or occupation at their time of demise (later, we will find Satan offered in the similarly familiar 'auld Nick'). The landscape prefigures Burns's key spatial and temporal gestures in the poem, where the supernatural and the eternal are rendered local and absolute and bounded – bounded by a moment, an instant, by the four ruined walls of a very specific location: Alloway Kirk, South Ayrshire.

One of Burns's most recognised techniques in the poem is the speed and precision with which he transitions between an elevated register that recalls the higher strains of eighteenth-century verse, and a more demotic Scots lexis. As Tam nears the church it would appear that 'glimmering thro' the groaning trees, / *Kirk-Alloway* seem'd in a bleeze'. What is important here is the strong juxtaposition of simplicity and complexity, of the local and the general. The complexity and dexterity of the alliteration ('glimmering / groaning') and the rhyme across English and Scots lexis ('trees / bleeze') is set against the reductive conclusion: it just 'seem'd in a bleeze'. Notice the continuing equivocation towards the building: it 'seem'd', rather than 'was'. In the minutiae of verse, Burns takes the fabric of the building and punts the certainty of the actual fabric of Kirk Alloway towards an altogether more generalised conclusion (or holding position): that it 'seemed' to be other than its rightful self. Further equivocation exists at the level of perception: precisely to whom does the building seem to be 'in a bleeze'? The obvious answer, given that Tam is our focaliser here (through his eyes we perceive the scene), would be Tam himself. Consider the tense, however; just when did Kirk Alloway seem so? When precisely was it 'in a bleeze'? The answer really cannot have been on the night itself (imagine 'Kirk Alloway *was* in a bleeze'); there is a disjunction because of the word – even then a contraction – 'seem'd': a disjunction between the experience and the telling. If we want to imagine that it 'seems' to be in Tam's retelling of the tale to the narrator, then we enter into all sorts of possible fictional realms and times of telling – Tam's experience, Tam's recollection of the experience, the narrator's imagination of how Tam perceived it, the narrator's deliberately reductive account for our benefit at the point of (re)telling, and so forth.

All of which would be nit-picking were it not for the fact that Burns is quite deliberate in his strategy as he approaches the treatment of the ruined building's haunted space. To enfold an apparent simplicity of proposition within an accomplished and ambivalent poetic technique helps to create a sense of tension between the local supernatural event that is unfolding and a much broader sense of how literature must rest upon a broader base of poetic accomplishment if it wishes to tell this tale. Just as the fabric of the locally haunted space has to accommodate wider tensions between the realm of faith and the sphere of the supernatural, so the fabric of the poem has to accommodate a tension between a simplicity of proposition and a sustainable sophistication of verse: reading a poem about a drunk man's perceptions can be fun; not so much simply listening to a man, drunk. The agony of the poem over the use of the word 'seem'd' thus encapsulates precisely how and why Burns was praised for this performance, and why its low subject yet profound sophistication of telling the tale of Kirk Alloway wowed yet puzzled his peers and near contemporaries.

Thus Burns introduces one of British poetry's most abiding haunted spaces, Kirk Alloway. Before we are allowed, as it were, into the building we have to negotiate not only the contextual frame put in place by the countryside surrounding it, but also the interpretative frame put in place by Burns's sophisticated treatment of demotic perception. Tam's senses, which may or may not have gathered that something supernatural was in play, are about to be further enriched, for from the Kirk 'loud resounded mirth and dancing'. Mirth, dancing: neither sanctioned by the Presbytery of Ayr. Tam, peering into the church, 'saw an unco sight':

Warlocks and witches in a dance;
Nae cotillion brent new frae *France*,
But hornpipes, jigs, strathspeys, and reels,
Put life and mettle in their heels.
A winnock-bunker in the east,
There sat auld Nick, in shape o' beast;
A towzie tyke, black, grim, and large,
To gie them music was his charge:
He screw'd the pipes and gart them skirl,
Till roof and rafters a' did dirl.—
Coffins stood round, like open presses,
That shaw'd the dead in their last dresses;
And by some devilish cantraip slight
Each in its cauld hand held a light.—
(Burns 1968: vol. 2, 560–1, lines 115–28)

The haunting of the church is deeply bathetic: what, asks the poem, do coffins freshly raised by Satan from the earth look like? The answer is 'like open presses' – like open cupboards. Ramming the astonishment of the supernatural into the profound mundanity of domestic storage by means of a deliberately blunt simile is another example of Burns's fashioning of the improbably haunted space as one only conceivable in the most quotidian terms. This effect is not just visual but aural: Satan offers no exotic 'cotillion brent new frae *France*' to fill the space, but rather 'hornpipes, jigs, strathspeys, and reels'. Kirk Alloway, represented here in the 1790s as Britain contested state legitimacy as well as a European and colonial future with France, becomes a metonym for a much wider conflict between states of being and embodied values; again, the local and the general are invoked by, and contained within, the profoundly haunted space of an unremarkably ruined church.

The ruination of the space is both contrasted to and compared with the physical state of the dead who are dancing to Nick's bagpipes. On the one hand, as we might imagine the undead to be, there are 'wither'd beldams, auld and droll, / Rigwoodie hags wad spean a foal' (Burns 1968: vol. 2, 562, lines 159–60): witches of the popular imagination, precisely the kind of elderly women burned, hanged and drowned by Britons well into the 'enlightened' eighteenth century. Tam's eyes, or the telling of Tam's eyes should one have begun to distrust the narrator's motives, are taken rather with a much younger member of the 'hellish legion': Nanny. Nanny has merely a 'cutty sark', a short undergarment, between her modesty and Tam's licentious gaze; amidst the hellish company, it is Nanny who haunts the local memory and Kirk Alloway in particular:

There was ae winsome wench and wawlie,
That night enlisted in the core,
(Lang after kend on *Carrick* shore;
For mony a beast to dead she shot,
And perish'd mony a bony boat,
And shook baith meikle corn and bear,
And kept the country-side in fear:)
Her cutty sark, o' Paisley harn,
That while a lassie she had worn,
In longitude tho' sorely scanty,
It was her best, and she was vauntie,—

> Ah! little kend thy reverend grannie,
> That sark she coft for her wee Nannie,
> Wi' twa pund Scots, ('twas a' her riches),
> Wad ever grac'd a dance of witches!
> (Burns 1968: vol. 2, 562–3, lines 164–78)

The specificity is remarkable, and local: the cutty sark (price 'twa pund Scots') made by her grandmother (from 'Paisley harn') is short in longitude (not latitude) as it graces the 'dance of witches'. Price, origin, co-ordinates: the material of this haunting is foregrounded. There is an absolute and concrete bearing to this apparition, conjured as it is not within some indeterminate space but within a poem that bears (in Francis Grose's 1791 *Antiquities of Scotland*) a precise visual representation. Alongside the image, we are asked to populate the church represented in antiquarian daylight with its midnight inhabitants. Kirk Alloway and its environs, by night, holds not the generalised thought of the undead, but teems rather with named witches whose (scanty) nightwear has a local, verifiable, provenance. Enamoured of Nannie, Tam shouts his appreciation; all falls dark, and Tam flees: 'the witches follow, / Wi' many an eldritch skreech and hollow' (Burns 1968: vol. 2, 563, lines 199–200). By jumping over a stream of running water, Maggie the horse saves her rider the drunk – at the cost of her tail. The poem concludes with a phatic and homosocial moral: beware drink and, when in drink, beware women. The poem cannot conclude firmly, built as it is around such a stunning representation of the haunted space that is the particularity of Kirk Alloway: there is nowhere for it (or for Tam) to go in general, other than 'away'. Quite deliberately, Maggie the horse is left without a tail: having passed Kirk Alloway she, like the poem, lacks an end.

Byron's Ghostly Friar

That sense of ambiguity and of uncertainty, the thrill of the unexpected, was furthered in verse by Lord Byron – perhaps recalling his 1821 assessment of Burns's *'opus magnum'* – as he tackled the late Cantos of *Don Juan*. Byron's depiction of a ghost in the so-called Norman Cantos of the poem entertained both the scepticisms and thrills of the age in its insertion of the ghost of a friar. In Canto XV, Byron teased and tantalised his readers about the forthcoming ghost in Canto XVI of the poem, asking:

> Grim reader! did you ever see a ghost?
> No; but you have heard – I understand – be dumb!
> And don't regret the time you may have lost,
> For you have got that pleasure still to come:
> And do not think I mean to sneer at most
> Of these things, or by ridicule benumb
> That source of the sublime and the mysterious:–
> For certain reasons, my belief is serious.
> (Byron 2008: 842, Canto XV, stanza 95, lines 753–60)

In an age of increasing scepticism and anxiety about the way in which the Gothic romance had saturated the credibility of its readership by over-exposure to ghosts, the poetic voice in *Don Juan* discourages its readership from believing that the intention is to 'ridicule' or 'sneer' at ghosts, and draws attention to the poem's own ghost in Canto XVI as a 'pleasure still to come'. But while acknowledging the lure of the ghost as pleasure, Byron claims for himself that 'my belief is serious'. Pursuing his reasons in the following stanza, the poetic voice claims 'I say I do believe a haunted spot / Exists – and where?' but refuses to disclose the precise spot, relying instead upon the supernatural as a source of the 'sublime and mysterious' (Byron 2008: 842, Canto XV, stanza 96, lines 763–4).

Canto XVI of *Don Juan* takes place in Amundeville Abbey, a fictional pile which was modelled closely upon Byron's ancestral home, Newstead Abbey. Amundeville Abbey has a ghostly friar whom Don Juan encounters one evening as he prepares for bed. The stanzas describing Juan's encounter with the ghostly friar in Canto XVI capture brilliantly the heady combination of curiosity and physical petrification that accompanies the encountering of a ghost:

> It was no mouse, but lo! a monk, arrayed
> In cowl and beads, and dusky garb, appeared,
> Now in the moonlight, and now lapsed in shade,
> With steps that trod as heavy, yet unheard;
> His garments only a slight murmur made;

> He moved as shadowy as the sisters weird,
> But slowly; and as he passed Juan by,
> Glanced, without pausing, on him a bright eye.
>
> Juan was petrified; he had heard a hint
> Of such a spirit in these halls of old,
> But thought, like most men, there was nothing in't
> Beyond the rumour which such spots unfold,
> Coined from surviving supersitition's mint,
> Which passes ghosts in currency like gold,
> But rarely seen, like gold compared with paper.
> And *did* he see this? or was it a vapour?
>
> Once, twice, thrice passed, repassed – the thing of air,
> Or earth beneath, or heaven, or t'other place;
> And Juan gazed upon it with a stare,
> Yet could not speak or move; but on its base
> As stands a statue, stood: he felt his hair
> Twine like a knot of snakes around his face;
> He taxed his tongue for words, which were not granted,
> To ask the reverend person what he wanted.
> (Byron 2008: 848–9, Canto XVI, stanzas 21–3, lines 161–84)

These stanzas are notable for their initial refusal to make light of Juan's encounter with the 'reverend person' of the monk, no more than Burns's earlier poem had challenged the invocation of the 'reverend grannie' in 'Tam o' Shanter'. While they attest to what E. J. Clery has identified as the commercial potential of ghosts in the lines 'Coined from surviving superstition's mint, / Which passes ghosts in currency like gold' from stanza 22, Byron's philosophical stance instead draws upon what we *cannot* know, with the questioning of whether Juan does in fact see a ghost or a vapour (Clery 1995). Rather than drawing from the well of scepticism and literary exhaustion of his age, as was his wont in many other cantos of *Don Juan*, Byron, like Radcliffe before him, chose to draw here from Act I, scene v of *Hamlet*. There Horatio, interrupting Hamlet's encounter with the ghost of his father, is admonished thus: 'There are more things in heaven and earth, Horatio, / Than are dreamt of in your philosophy' (*Hamlet*, Act I, scene v, lines 166–7). Byron plays with Hamlet's corrective stance on ghosts in stanza 23, as the ghostly monk is described as 'the thing of air, / Or earth beneath, or heaven, or t'other place'. Although the phrase 't'other place' sounds at first dismissive in tone, the stanzas as a whole are characterised by uncertainty, hesitation and a refusal to ridicule or rationalise what Juan sees before him. The overarching impression of gravity lends this particular part of *Don Juan* a different edge, one which refuses to poke fun at belief in hauntings and revenants.

The character who tells the legend of the 'Black Friar' in Canto XVI of *Don Juan* is the Lady Adeline of Amundeville. Her husband Lord Henry, the sire of Amundeville, jokes with their guests that 'Adeline is half a poetess' and, 'smiling', begs of the audience to indulge Adeline's recitation of the legend. Byron makes fun of Adeline's 'charming hesitation' as 'with eyes fixed to the ground / At first, kindling into animation', she begins to recite her lyric on the legend of the Black Friar. The target of the satire, however, is less the subject of the legend, the Black Friar, and more the gendering, artfully improvised recitation of such legends. Adeline recites:

1.

Beware! Beware! of the Black Friar,
 Who sitteth by Norman stone,
For he mutters his prayer to the midnight air,
 And his mass of the days that are gone.
When the Lord of the Hill, Amundeville,
 Made Norman Church his prey,
And expelled the friars, one friar still
 Would not be driven away.

2.

Though he came in his might, with King Henry's right,
 To turn church lands to lay,
With sword in hand, and torch to light
 Their walls, if they said nay,
A monk remained, unchased, unchained,
 And he did not seem formed of clay,
For he's seen in the porch, and he's seen in the church,
 Though he is not seen by day.

3.
And whether for good, or whether for ill,
    It is not mine to say;
But still to the house of Amundeville
    He abideth night and day.
By the marriage bed of their lords, 'tis said,
    He flits on the bridal eve;
And 'tis held as faith, to their bed of death,
    He comes – but not to grieve.

4.
When an heir is born, he is heard to mourn,
    And when aught is to befall
That ancient line, in the pale moonshine
    He walks from hall to hall.
His form you may trace, but not his face,
    'Tis shadowed by his cowl;
But his eyes may be seen from the folds between,
    And they seem of a parted soul.

5.
But beware! beware! of the Black Friar,
    He still retains his sway,
For he is yet the church's heir
    Who ever may be the lay.
Amundeville is lord by day,
    But the monk is lord by night.
Nor wine nor wassail could raise a vassal
    To question that friar's right.

6.
Say nought to him as he walks the hall,
    And he'll say nought to you;
He sweeps along in his dusky pall,
    As o'er the grass the dew.
Then Gramercy! for the Black Friar;
    Heaven sain him! fair or foul,
And whatsoe'er may be his prayer,

Let ours be for his soul.
(Byron 2008: 853-5, Canto XVI, lines 321-68)

These stanzas, composed and then recited by the Lady Adeline, are segregated from the rest of the Canto, nestling in between stanzas 40 and 41. Their separation indicates the distance that the poetic voice wishes to establish between himself and their alleged author. Characterised by poor scansion and clichéd warnings about the ghost, their only interest lies in their telling of the violent tale of the Protestant Reformation that displaces the Black Friar from his monastery. Replaced by a newly titled family, the Black Friar exists as a ghostly reminder of the abbey's monastic past. Despite the questionable merit of the Lady Adeline's narration of this tale, this ghostly friar in the Norman Cantos of *Don Juan* is not discredited – that is, not until the voluptuous Duchess of Fitz-Fulke, having learned of the legend from Adeline's tale, is discovered at the end of Canto XVI to be masquerading as the Black Friar in her attempts at seducing the younger Juan. Despite the bathetic sense of the 'explained supernatural' at work here, *Don Juan* ends on a note of teasing supernatural indecision: 'I leave the thing a problem, like all things', the persona notes; 'Ghost, or none, / 'Twere difficult to say – but Juan looked / As if he had combatted with more than one' (Byron 2008: 879, Canto XVII, lines 97-107). Though seemingly eradicated by the disclosure of the Duchess's amorous intentions, ghostliness the following morning persists, spilling out into the rituals of everyday, waking reality: Don Juan looks 'wan and worn', the Duchess 'pale and shivered' (Byron 2008: 879, Canto XVII, lines 108-11). Juan's encounter with the ghost is thus curiously free from the contempt of the many other Gothic parodies of Byron's time, indicating that Byron's own professed encounter with a ghost was something, at least, in which he believed.

Thus it is that the haunted ruins of Britain are our reward for becoming a literate and critical nation in the centuries following the invention of the British state at the start of the eighteenth century. The works treated here in prose and verse, from Burns to Byron, or from Radcliffe to Austen, helped to shape a second order of popular literary criticism brought into being during the literary period known as 'Romanticism': consistently they invite us to tease apart the voice that tells a story from the truthfulness of the tale. We are rewarded for recognising that only the most credulous reader of 'Tam o'Shanter' or Adeline's stanzas in *Don Juan* would take them at face value. It is in this sense that to call back into being the bygone inhabitants of Britain's ruins was and continues to be appealing, reassuring even. As all the texts above indicate, however, there are also risks in such a venture: the risk of inauthentic cliché; of searching for what was never there, or, for Wordsworth, of misconstruing the world of sense as one casts about in memory for an irrecoverable past. As Britain emerged from the eighteenth century, the nation's haunted ruins came to offer authors and readers fantastic spaces for the expression of increasingly suppressed anxieties of class, religion, opportunity and nationhood. Never before had such spectral ground and haunted space been woven into the fabric of British literary identity: the haunting continues to this day.

Further Reading
Brooks, J. A. 1990. *Britain's Haunted Heritage* (Norwich: Jarrold).
Hanks, Michele. 2015. *Haunted Heritage: The Cultural Politics of Ghost Tourism, Populism, and the Past* (London and New York: Routledge).

References
Austen, Jane. 1998. *Northanger Abbey* (1818), edited by Claire Grogan (Peterborough, Ont.: Broadview).
Bannerman, Anne. 1802. *Tales of Superstition and Chivalry* (London: James Swan).
Burns, Robert. 1968. 'Tam o'Shanter', in *The Poems and Songs of Robert Burns*, edited by James Kinsley, 3 vols (Oxford: Oxford University Press), vol. 2, 557–64.
Byron, Lord George Gordon. 2008. *Don Juan*, in *Lord Byron: The Major Works*, edited by Jerome J. McGann (Oxford: Oxford University Press), 373–879.
Clery, E. J. 1995. *The Rise of Supernatural Fiction, 1762–1800* (Cambridge: Cambridge University Press).
English, John. 1810. *The Grey Friar, And the Black Spirit of the Wye: A Romance*, 2 vols (London: Minerva Press).
Gray, Thomas. 1775. *The Poems of Thomas Gray. To Which are Prefixed Memoirs of His Life and Writings by W. Mason* (London: Dodsley).
Greenaway, Naomi. 2015. 'Inside the Real Haunted Houses: From Aggrieved Murder Victims to Phantom Monks, Britain's Spookiest Homes Revealed (and unsurprisingly most are up for sale)', *Mail Online*, http://www.dailymail.co.uk/femail/article-3294731/Inside-real-haunted-houses-Britain.html [last accessed 14 March 2017].
J. D. 1803. 'Description of Alloway Kirk – With a View', in *The Edinburgh*

Magazine or Literary Miscellany (May 1803): 321–6.

Low, Donald (ed.). 1974. *Robert Burns: The Critical Heritage* (London: Routledge & Kegan Paul).

Mason, John. 1999. *Haunted Heritage* (London: Collins and Brown).

Radcliffe, Ann. 1795. *A Journey Made in the Summer of 1794, through Holland and the Western Frontier of Germany, With a Return down the Rhine: To Which are Added Observations during a Tour to the Lakes of Lancashire, Westmoreland, and Cumberland* (London: G. Robinson).

Roberts, William (ed.). 2001. *Thomas Gray's Journal of his Visit to the Lake District in 1769* (Liverpool: Liverpool University Press).

West, Thomas. 1774. *The Antiquities of Furness; or, an Account of the Royal Abbey of St. Mary, in the vale of Nightshade, near Dalton in Furness, belonging to the Right Honorable Lord George Cavendish* (London: Joseph Johnson).

West, Thomas. 1778. *A Guide to the Lakes: Dedicated to the Lovers of Landscape Studies, and to all who have Visited, or Intend to Visit the Lakes in Cumberland, Westmorland, and Lancashire. By the author of The Antiquities of Furness* (London: Richardson and Urquhart).

Wordsworth, William. 1909. *The Complete Poetical Works of William Wordsworth*, edited by John Morley (London: Macmillan and Co.).

The Haunting of Minster Lovell Hall

Alicia Edwards

> At length an oak chest, that had long lain hid
> Was found in the castle—they raised the lid—
> And a skeleton form lay mouldering there,
> In the bridal wreath of that lady fair!
> Oh! Sad was her fate!—in sportive jest
> She hid from her lord in the old oak chest.
> It closed with a spring!—and, dreadful doom,
> The bride lay clasp'd in her living tomb! (Bayly 1844: 233)

Where the high ground of the Wynchwood Forest slopes down to the river Windrush stand the ruins of a manor house. Situated halfway between Witney and Burford in Oxfordshire, the ruin of Minster Lovell Hall is a picture of tranquillity, but a tranquillity haunted by a past of bloodshed, betrayal and tragedy. The recorded history of the site dates to the building of a ninth-century priory dedicated to the boy martyr

Minster Lovell Hall. From Monastic Remains and Ancient Castles [...] drawn on the spot by James Moore Esq. F.A.S., and executed in aquatint by G. J. Parkins Esq. *vol. 1, 1792*

St Kenelm, Prince of Mercia, murdered by a greedy relative despite the warning given by a prophetic dream (Taylor 2003: 16). From the site's inception, with its dedication to a victim of familial ambition, to the mysterious corpse discovered there in 1708, and the tale of a festive game of hide-and-seek gone awry that was immortalised in the nineteenth-century ballad 'The Mistletoe Bough', Minster Lovell Hall has been steeped in tales of murder, greed and mystery.

The land came into Lovell hands in c. 1124, the gift of Henry I to William Lupellus (the first Lovell). In the fifteenth century, the priory itself, historically attached to the Benedictine abbey of Ivory in Normandy, was seized by the Crown, as part of a wider programme of seizures of alien priories, and gifted to the Lovells. The manor house, whose ruins survive today, was built in the early fifteenth century by William, 7th Baron Lovell of Tichmarsh, as an assertion of his wealth and prosperity. The Lovell name was used to distinguish this hall from the adjacent manor, Little Minster, owned by the Earls of Pembroke (Taylor 2003: 16–18). What tantalises the literary imagination in relation to the site, however, is not the building itself but rather the owner who was trapped in its halls. It is the mysterious disappearance of Richard III's notorious 'Dog', Viscount Francis Lovell, that has so marked the literary rewritings of the site in both Clara Reeve's *The Old English Baron* (1778) and Thomas Haynes Bayly's 'The Mistletoe Bough' (Manning 1851: 128).

Clara Reeve's novel was first published anonymously in 1777 under the title *The Champion of Virtue*, but revised and republished as *The Old English Baron: A Gothic Story* under Reeve's own name a year later. The phrase *'Ficta voluptatis causa sint proxima'* (fictions meant to please should approximate the truth) that adorns the cover of the first edition of Reeve's text hints at the potential for truth harboured in the fantastical tale through its connection to the Lovell estates, the extra-fictional inspiration for its fictional location. Reeve's emphasis on the appearance of ghosts that are within 'the utmost *verge* of probability' in the narrative is, perhaps, a nod to the location's 'real' history of haunting (Reeve 1778: vi). The ghost that haunts Minster Lovell Hall is that of Viscount Francis Lovell, a figure whose end is shrouded in mystery. The historical Lovell was a Yorkist supporter of Richard III who fled to the continent after the King was slain at the Battle of Bosworth Field. Speculation concerning his demise was rife after his apparent disappearance following the failed support of Simnel the Pretender at the battle of Stoke. The earliest speculations on his fate after the battle can be found in the writings of Sir Francis Bacon in his *Historie of the Reigne of King Henry the Seventh*: 'But another report leaves him not there, but that he lived long after in a Cave or Vault' (Bacon 1629: 35). Unverified reports of his flight from the battle received further grisly support when, in 1708, a skeleton was found in a vault at Minster Lovell Hall. As William Cowper, Esq., related in 1737, the posited identity of this skeleton was that of the missing Lord Lovell:

> On the 6th May, 1728, the present Duke of Rutland related in my hearing, that about twenty years before, viz., in 1708, upon occasion of new laying a chimney at Minster Luvel [Oxfordshire], there was discovered a large vault or room under ground, in which was the entire skeleton of a man, as having been sitting at a table, which was before him, with a book, paper, pen, &c. &c. In another part of the room lay a cap, all much mouldered and decayed, which the family and others judged to be this Lord Luvel, whose exit has hitherto been so uncertain. (quoted in Burke 1852: 239)

In the eighteenth century, the story was already taking on a life of its own, spawning numerous variants and alternative narratives. By the time of the publication of James Anderson's *History of the House of Yvery* (1742), for example, a dramatic twist had been added: 'the body whom was yet entire when the workmen entered, but upon admission of the air soon fell to dust' (Anderson 1742: 290). Clara Reeve's *The Old English Baron* was the first, and most famous, avowedly fictional reworking of the tale.

The Old English Baron does not retell but rather echoes the tale with a number of obvious allusions. The narrative recounts the story of Edmund, whose soldier father, Lord Arthur Lovel, was murdered by a treacherous kinsman on his return from a battle. 'Soon after [his death] it was reported that the Castle was haunted, and that the ghosts of Lord and Lady Lovel had been seen by several of the servants. Whoever went into this apartment were terrified by uncommon noises, and strange appearances' (Reeve 1778: 44). Edmund, raised as a peasant, is returned to his rightful inheritance thanks to the intervention of his father's ghost, a *Hamlet*-style spectre who leads him to the discovery of his own corpse, hog-tied in a trunk in a hidden chamber. The discovery of a body in a hidden subterranean chamber, the figure of the loyal servant, the issue of disputed inheritance (not only within the context of the building itself but equally within the national context) and the mystery surrounding the disappearance of a military figure collapse the boundaries between the purely historical and the literary.

In the nineteenth century, there was a resurgence of interest in the ruined pile and the legends around it in the pages of *Notes and Queries*, as well as in historical and antiquarian enquiries on the subject of Sir Francis Lovell. The 1830s witnessed the rise in popularity of 'The Mistletoe Bough', a festive ballad that, in its subject, echoes the trend to associate Christmas with the telling of ghost stories. Several compositions around this time, such as Samuel Roger's 'Ginevra' (1822) and John Heneage Jesse's 'The Bride of Modena' (1830), related similar stories. 'The Mistletoe Bough', however, was unique for its direct mentioning of the house of Lovell; the victim, the young woman who died locked in a chest after an unfortunate game of hide-and-seek on her wedding night, is identified as 'young Lovell's bride' (Bayly 1844: 232). The story has been transformed again: here, it is a bride, not a soldier, who is confined unto death; it is merely a melancholy accident, and there is neither malice nor persecution behind her death. However, beyond these differences, the core of the tale remains: mysterious death haunts the Lovell family, and the motif of confinement and betrayal, however accidental, remains.

References

Anderson, James. 1742. *A Geneological History of the House of Yvery; In its Different Branches of Yvery, Luvel, Perceval, and Gournay*, vol. I (London: Printed by H. Woodfall).

Bacon, Francis. 1629. *The Historie of the Reigne of King Henry the Seventh* (London: Printed by I. Haviland and R. Young).

Bayly, Thomas Haynes. 1844. *Songs, Ballads, and Other Poems, Vol. I, edited by his Widow* (London: Richard Bentley).

Burke, John Bernard. 1852. *A Visitation of the Seats and Arms of the Noblemen and Gentlemen of Great Britain*, vol. I (London: Colburn and Co.).

Manning, James Alexander. 1851. *The Lives of the Speakers of the House of Commons, from the Time of King Edward III to Queen Victoria, Comprising the Biographies of Upwards of One Hundred Distinguished Persons, and the Copious Details of the Parliamentary History of England, from the Most Authentic Documents* (London: George Willis).

Reeve, Clara. 1778. *The Old English Baron: A Gothic Story* (London: Printed for Edward and Charles Dilly).

Taylor, A. J. 2003. *Minster Lovell Hall: Oxfordshire* (London: English Heritage).

Conwy Castle

David Punter

> CONWAY, deserted pile, in whose exhausted halls
>   The discontented winds fresh wrath engender,
> Whose figure knightly times to Fancy oft recalls,
>   Take the sole boon a passenger can render,
>
> Who to thy tow'rs august in giddy wonder clings,
>   Thy mien unhumbled by mishap rehearses,
> Thine aged arches grey and sea-worn rampart sings,
>   And moss-clad battlements, in plaintive verses.
> (White 1789: 3)

Conwy Castle, on the north coast of Wales, is well known to scholars of late-eighteenth-century Gothic literature as the setting of Matthew Lewis's 1797 play, *The Castle Spectre*; but Conwy is not merely a castle, it is an entire walled town. Planned, like so many other defensive structures, by Edward I, the entire town was raised during four building seasons from 1283 to 1287. It now contains the most intact set of monarchical residential buildings anywhere in Wales or England; Edward sheltered there during the Welsh rebellion of 1294-5. Figuring again on the Royalist side during the Civil Wars, it was deliberately ruined shortly afterwards, and later became noted for its picturesque qualities.

    There is a remarkable painting, even by the artist's own standards, by J. M. W. Turner dating from *c.* 1803, which features not only the castle itself but the boats and shores which form its hinterland. The slighting of Conwy Castle probably took place between 1655 and 1665. In addition to Turner's depiction, the castle became the subject of paintings and engravings by Paul Sandby, Moses Griffith, Julius Caesar Ibbetson and Thomas Girtin, among others. The watercolour by Girtin is particularly remarkable, showing two of the great arches in the Hall range along with the masses of fallen masonry to which much of the castle had been reduced.

Great Hall, Conwy Castle. Thomas Girtin, watercolour, c. 1798

The history of Conwy also reflects on developments in industrialisation and transport during the nineteenth century, when some of the previously prized vistas were all but destroyed by, first, Thomas Telford's suspension bridge of 1826, then a road bridge, and finally Robert Stephenson's tubular bridge which brought the Chester and Holyhead Railway below the south wall of the castle. There is now also a modern road bridge. However, although views and a certain kind of antiquarian interest may have suffered damage, the upshot was also that tourism boomed, leading to a certain amount of much-needed restoration.

And the views from Conwy towards Snowdonia remained, of course, untrammelled and magnificent, accentuating the design and sheer immensity of the castle itself. But for Matthew Lewis, it was the aptness of the medieval castle itself, as he conceived it, for the appearance of the supernatural that was its most important feature. 'You are to know', says one of his characters in a typical passage, 'that since the late Earl's death the Castle is thought to be haunted: the servants are fully persuaded that his ghost wanders every night through the long galleries, and parades the old towers and dreary halls which abound in this melancholy mansion' (Lewis 1798: 22).

> Had I minded [he continues a little later] all the strange things related of this Castle, I should have died of fright [...] Why, they say that Earl Hubert rides every night round the Castle on a white horse; that the ghost of Lady Bertha haunts the west pinnacle of the Chapel-Tower; and that Lord Hildebrand, who was condemned for treason some sixty years ago, may be seen in the Great Hall, regularly at midnight playing at foot-ball with his own head! (Lewis 1798: 23).

And there is more – much more – in this foundational work of Gothic drama that seeks, through a tale of haunting, to restore Conwy to its eclipsed sanguinary glory.

References
Lewis, Matthew Gregory. 1789. *The Castle Spectre: A Drama, in Five Acts* (London: Printed for J. Bell).
White, James. 1789. *Conway Castle: A Poem* (London: Printed for J. Dodsley).

Rosslyn Chapel

James A. McKean

> Through the cold twilight of the haunted aisle
>   The lunar beam of shadowy Autumn falls,
> And the low winds, like whispering voices, steal,
>   Thro' the arch'd casements of the gothic walls.
>
> And ghastly, mid the visionary gloom,
>   The awful phantoms of forgotten years
> Bend o'er the slumbering warrior's ruin'd tomb,
>   And bathe the marble with unearthly tears.
>
> ('Adeline' 1811: 121)

The view of Rosslyn Chapel, Midlothian, that was vividly projected onto cinema screens across the globe in Ron Howard's 2006 film *The Da Vinci Code* was by no means the first time that it had been shown to the public on such a grand scale. In 1824, nearly two hundred years before, Louis-Jacques-Mande Daguerre displayed *L'Abbaye de Roslyn, effet de soleil* as one of his first Dioramas to the Parisian public. This large-scale popular visual entertainment was made up of painted screens measuring approximately 24 yards in width and 15 yards in height (22 × 14 metres) (Maggi 2008: 24). The Diorama utilised sunlight to illuminate Daguerre's paintings, creating a dramatic and awe-inspiring effect, and much was written at the time about how impressive Daguerre's exhibitions were (Maggi 2008: 24–5). Angelo Maggi puts the popularity of the Rosslyn Chapel Diorama down to the success of Sir Walter Scott's *The Lay of the Last Minstrel* (1805), since light was used in an unpredictable and almost supernatural way in both mediums (Maggi 2008: 25).

The construction of Rosslyn Chapel was begun in 1446 by Sir William St Clair. It is a cacophony of different architectural styles and was purportedly built to house a provost, six prebendaries and two singing boys (Grose 1797: vol. 1, 43). The nineteenth-century antiquary John Britton completed one of the first and most comprehensive studies of the chapel, but he remained perplexed by the seemingly multi-faceted approach to the architectural design. His study cited the opinion of the architectural draughtsman and artist Joseph Michael Gandy, who described the building as a 'combination of Egyptian, Grecian, Roman and Sarasenic styles' (quoted in Britton 1812: 59). Over the centuries, however, more has been made of the many legends associated with Rosslyn Chapel than of the architectural structure of the building itself. In particular, several myths today surround its connection to the Knights Templar, and the location of the Holy Grail of Arthurian legend and apocryphal history, aspects of Rosslyn's lore that were exploited in Dan Brown's best-selling thriller *The Da Vinci Code* (2003) and the later film version (Wallace-Murphy and Hopkins 1999). Undoubtedly, it is the appeal of Brown's story-telling that has revived popular interest in, and tourism to, Rosslyn Chapel today.

Indeed, the place seems to be steeped in lore and legend. Other tales associated with Rosslyn concern physical features to be seen within the chapel itself. The most popular concerns the story of the 'Prince's Pillar' or 'Apprentice's Pillar'. According to this tale, a master builder went to Rome further to study the plans of the chapel. Upon his return, the story goes, he found that a pier inside the chapel had been ornately carved in his absence by his apprentice, whose only reward for his deed was a fatal blow to the head with a hammer. Although little credence has been given to this tale, it is mentioned time and again in literature concerning Rosslyn. John Britton tells a lesser-known story concerning how the land on which the chapel is built came into the possession of Sir William St Clair by way of a bet that he made with Robert the Bruce. St Clair wagered that his two dogs could catch a deer that had outwitted Bruce's dogs many times before. Britton recounts a nail-biting finale that sees the deer getting halfway across the March-burn brook before St Clair's dogs manage to take it down. This accounts for why Sir William St Clair's tomb in the chapel renders his likeness in armour with a greyhound at his feet, along with a column with the sculptured features of a dog and a deer surrounding it.

For the poet identifying herself only as 'Adeline', Rosslyn Chapel was haunted by the mournful, lovesick ghost of the wife of St Clair of 'Roslin', a knight who undertook a pilgrimage to the Holy Land with the heart of Robert the Bruce. His vessel blown by rough winds onto the

The 'Apprentice Pillar', Rosslyn Chapel. From William Howitt, Ruined Abbeys and Castles of Great Britain, *1862*

coast of Spain, St Clair was slain in battle with the Moors, leaving the ghost of his distraught widow to mourn perpetually at his tomb:

> And still when falls the pale autumnal even
> The lone Enthusiast lingers in the dell,
>   To hear soft mingling with the breath of Heaven
> The widow'd mourner the aerial vespers swell.
> ('Adeline' 1811: 122)

Other stories attached to the chapel were immortalised by the work of Sir Walter Scott. In *The Lay of the Last Minstrel*, for instance, Scott provides the following evocative description of the interior of the chapel being consumed by fire:

Seem'd all on fire that chapel proud
    Where Roslin's chiefs uncoffin'd lie;
Each baron, for a sable shroud,
    Sheathed in his iron panoply.
(Scott 1805; 191, Canto XXIII)

Scott was clearly drawing upon local lore and legend in describing Rosslyn in these terms. In his *Theatrum Scotiae* (1693), the first-ever pictorial survey of Scotland, John Slezer noted in his account of Rosslyn the tradition that 'before the Death of any of the Family of Roslin, this Chapel appears all in Fire' (Slezer 1693: 63). The antiquarian Francis Grose, too, made mention of this legend in his *Antiquities of Scotland* (Grose 1797: vol. 1, 47). Despite these earlier antiquarian accounts, this legend was said by many to have originated with Scott's poem: in 1839, Henry Ince claimed that it was he who was responsible for reviving 'the legends, traditions and superstitions of ancient time' that circulated around Rosslyn (Ince 1839: 569). As with the Apprentice Pillar and the tomb of Sir William St Clair, though, this fire is probably attributable to something more physical than supernatural: a trick of the eye caused by the fall of the light on the stained-glass windows on the western-facing wall.

References

'Adeline'. 1811. 'Stanzas Written in the Chapel of Roslin', in *The Poetical Register, and Repository of Fugitive Poetry, for 1806–1807* (London: Printed for F. C. and J. Rivington), 121–2.

Britton, John. 1812. *The Architectural Antiquities of Great Britain*, vol. III (London: Printed by Longman, Hurst, Rees, Orme and Brown).

Grose, Francis. 1797. *The Antiquities of Scotland*, 2 vols (London: Printed for Hooper and Wigstead).

Ince, Henry (ed.). 1839. *The Wonders of the World in Nature and Art* (London: Grattan and Gilbert).

Maggi, Angelo. 2008. *Rosslyn Chapel: An Icon through the Ages* (Edinburgh: Burlinn).

Scott, Walter. 1805. *The Lay of the Last Minstrel, A Poem*, 2nd edn (London: Printed for Longman, Hurst, Rees and Orme; Edinburgh: A. Constable and Co.).

Slezer, John. 1693. *Theatrum Scotiae* (London: Printed by John Leake for Abell Swalle).

Wallace-Murphy, Tim and Marilyn Hopkins. 1999. *Rosslyn: Guardian of the Secrets of the Holy Grail* (Shaftesbury: Element Books).

RUINS IN FOCUS

Berry Pomeroy Castle

Nick Groom

> In the west of England are yet to be seen the ruins of Berry Pomeroy Castle, formerly a place of great strength, but now, like the proud ancient possessors, almost forgotten, and daily mingling with the dust. (Montague 1806: vol. 1, 1)

The opening sentence of Edward Montague's novel *The Castle of Berry Pomeroy* (1806) alludes to *The Worthies of Devon* (1701) by the Reverend John Prince, who wrote of this wreck that 'all this Glory lieth in the Dust, buried in its own Ruins, there being nothing standing but a few broken Walls, which seem to mourn their own approaching Funerals' (Prince 1701: 492). Berry Pomeroy was a vast memento mori, dust returning to dust. But it was also troubled by a ferocious history. Montague's opening continues:

> Many are the dark deeds said to have been perpetrated within its walls, as the yet blood-stained stones and flitting shades that nightly

Berry Pomeroy Castle, Devon. Painted by Thomas Walmsley, engraved by J. Hassell, 24 June 1801

hover over their sad remains, entombed amongst the ruins, or buried without sepulchral rites, are sad mementos of. Often do their wailing shrieks vex the nocturnal breeze, that else would sleep in the quiet amidst the shady branches of the surrounding woods. (Montague 1806: vol. 1, 12)

The ensuing tale is a wild Gothic extravaganza of dynastic power politics, corrupt monks, multiple murders, kidnap, piracy, shipwrecks, incarceration, torture, beheadings and live burial, enlivened with gratuitous nudity, nightmares, restless ghosts, and atrocious weather – A *Game of Thrones* for a Regency readership. It was not long before morbid visitors were attracted to the site. In 1811 a lengthy description of the castle appeared in *The Weekly Entertainer*: 'The magnificence of these venerable and great remains cannot fail to impress the reflecting mind with a degree of surprise and awe'; it is, wrote the author 'J. C.', 'one of the largest and most interesting ruins I ever beheld' ('J. C.' 1811: 663–6).

Berry Pomeroy Castle itself occupies a dramatic position: built on high crags, overlooking verdant woodland and gazing imperiously north towards Dartmoor. The contrast between the picturesque arboreal setting and the brutal history of the ruined citadel was terrifying. A decade before Montague's sensational novel appeared, William George Maton had noted that the unnerving disparity between natural beauty and medieval ruins was 'almost unparalleled' (Maton 1797: vol. 1, 113). Reached through 'a thick wood', the setting was 'beautiful [...] romantic [...] peaceful' – until, that is, one perceived 'the frowning turrets however, massy walls, and gloomy dungeons [...] wholly at variance with the beauty and serenity of the spot', whereupon the imagination was filled with 'sieges, chains, torture, and death' (Maton 1797: vol. 1, 111–12). The castle had its own grisly folklore, most notoriously the story of one of the Pomeroy dynasty who, faced with being taken by the enemy, rode his blindfolded horse from the battlements in a suicidal leap into oblivion.

Despite the ghosts that haunted Montague's novel, then, Berry Pomeroy was not, in the early nineteenth century, noted for the supernatural but for the violent contrast between the picturesque and the blood-spattered history it represented. In such cruel company nature became threatening, eerie, and so the woodland that hems in the castle is dangerous – indeed, in Montague's story, in which the castle is already entangled in briars, the forest is home to ferocious wild boar.

It is in this same menacing picturesque wilderness that Eliza Bray begins her 1841 novel *Henry de Pomeroy: or, The Eve of St John*. Bray visited the ruins herself, and began her novel with an account of this visit, accompanied by a 'nice little girl' who kept the keys (Bray 1884: 3). Again the foliage is so dense that it obscures the castle, as if nature were supplanting history: 'We could not help saying that Berry Pomeroy would be a most interesting ruin, if it were not so encumbered with brambles and trees, as in many places you can see nothing else'. Exploring the site was a dangerous undertaking, the trees being so thick in places that 'you are scarcely conscious you are near a precipice till on its very verge' (Bray 1884: 5). Nevertheless, Bray's 'little fairy-footed guide' takes her up to the crags to tell the story of Sir Henry de Pomeroy riding his horse over the edge.

Although *Henry de Pomeroy* is an antiquarian novel filled with period detail and Saxon–Norman politics rather than Gothic atmospherics, when the castle itself finally does feature in all its original and solemn splendour, it is actually as the backdrop against which the ghost of the Norman knight Sir Ralph de Pomeroy appears (Bray 1884: 284–91, 291–3). The apparition is a premonition of calamity that presages Sir Henry's dramatic mounted plunge. This reckless episode binds Bray's medievalist narrative to the contemporary retellings of folklore that she had heard recounted at the castle – what she called 'traditional fragments' (Bray 1884: 5). But the fleeting appearance of the fatal ghost worked a stranger alchemy, and the weird brew of wildwood and ruin was to prove a heady combination for visitors. Within a few years, Berry Pomeroy Castle had become a notorious tourist attraction: the most haunted place in Britain.

References

Bray, Eliza. 1884. *Henry de Pomeroy: or The Eve of St John*, new edn (London: Chapman and Hall).

'J. C.'. 1811. 'Description and History of Berry Church, Berry House, and Berry Pomeroy Castle', *The Weekly Entertainer* 51 (26 August): 663–6.

Maton, William George. 1797. *Observations Relative Chiefly to the Natural History, Picturesque Scenery, and Antiquities, of the Western Counties of England, made in the Years 1794 and 1796*, 2 vols (Salisbury: Printed and Sold by J. Easton).

Montague, Edward. 1806. *The Castle of Berry Pomeroy: A Novel*, 2 vols (London: Printed at the Minerva Press).

Prince, John. 1701. *Danmonii orientales illustres: or, The Worthies of Devon* (Exeter: Printed by Samuel Farley for Awnsham and John Churchill).

Chapter 6:
The Politics of Ruin

James Kelly

Ruins speak of human finitude. Moss on a fallen lintel stone or grass in an empty nave can eloquently tell of the folly of human ambition, the grandeur of the past, or the settled peace of the present. During the long eighteenth century in Britain and Ireland ruins were recuperated not only aesthetically but politically, with the very idea of ruination allowing for meditation on historical conflicts both resolved and still open, and anticipation of the moment when current grandiloquent structures would fall to fragments. Ruins were often read differently by visitors in Britain and Ireland, the latter seeing present degradation in contrast to a rich past where the former saw assurance about the progress from superstition to a bright modernity. Many eighteenth-century poets prefaced their philosophical meditations on specific ruins with a reference to lines from John Webster's Jacobean tragedy, *The Duchess of Malfi* (1614):

> I do love these ancient ruins.
> We never tread upon them but we set
> Our foot upon some reverend history.
> (Act V, scene iii, lines 11–13)

'Reverend history', though, could be a matter of perspective. Often relics of the Reformation and subsequent historical conflict, ruins could not fail to be tinged with sectarian assumptions in a century that saw fractious confessionalism and political revolutions. The growing aesthetic of ruins had important historical overtones. Philosophical meditation on the depredations of time could easily slide into political advocacy of history's victims. Awed introspection on the fall of once-great structures could prompt cautionary advice to present-day society. And political beliefs handed down from prior generations could as easily be venerated or castigated as Gothic ruins in the national landscape. In *A Vindication of the Rights of Men* (1790), her passionate defence of democratic ideals against Edmund Burke's conservative *Reflections on the Revolution in France* published earlier in the same year, Mary Wollstonecraft imagined that:

> [The] time may come, when the traveller may ask where proud London stood? when its temples, its laws, and its trade, may be buried in one common ruin, and only serve as a by-word to point a moral, or furnish senators, who wage a wordy war, on the other side of the Atlantic, with tropes to swell their thundering bursts of eloquence. (Wollstonecraft 1790: 83)

Ruins in the eighteenth and early nineteenth centuries were able to point a moral, and furnished many writers with tropes that served to heighten political and rhetorical points. Ruins were powerfully evocative, combining in their sepulchral beauty multiple potentialities of interpretation.

A Tale of Two Parliaments

Edmund Burke asked in his *Philosophical Enquiry into the Origin of our Ideas of the Sublime and Beautiful* (1757) a rhetorical question designed to complicate a complacent rush to appreciate ruins without thinking fully of the suffering that may have gone into their creation:

> This noble capital, the pride of England and of Europe, I believe no man is so strangely wicked as to desire to see destroyed by a conflagration or an earthquake, though he should be removed himself to the greatest distance from the danger. But suppose such a fatal accident to have happened, what numbers from all parts would croud [sic] to behold the ruins, and amongst them many who would have been content never to have seen London in its glory? (Burke 1990: 44)

Londoners were to see a spectacle of ruination in action for themselves on the night of 16 October 1834, when a massive conflagration burned through the ancient Palace of Westminster, a building more commonly known as the Houses of Parliament. Many drank in the solemnity of such a sublime moment, although some sections of the crowd made their own less-exalted observations: 'Instead of regretting the dreadful event as a national calamity, many appeared to consider it as a well-merited visitation, and actually openly expressed their regret that the Lords and Commons were not sitting at the time' (Anon. 1834a: 665). Indeed, the potential for satirical comment proved irresistible for many. One writer for the *New Monthly Magazine* noted that the fire had only briefly passed through the Court of Chancery: 'Nothing can get through the Court of Chancery; lucky is the fire, or anything else, that, once in, can escape out of it' (Anon. 1834c: 352).

Flame and ruination could provide material for satire, but what is more remarkable is the alacrity with which plans were drawn for rebuilding and redesign. The burnt remains of Parliament attracted visitors (and, at least in some early days, looters). In the following week King William IV visited the remains of the palace and St Stephen's Chapel, where 'inquisitiveness, as regards minor objects, seemed to merge in the one painful feeling of afflicting thought on the ruin of so politically sacred

'View of the Conflagration of the Houses of the Lords & Commons, as it appeared on the Night of Thursday October 16th 1834. Sketch on the Spot & On Stone'. J. Hitchins

a spot' (Anon. 1834b: 682). While there would follow some discussion about relocating Parliament elsewhere, majority opinion favoured a rebuilding in Westminster. The style in which this act of rebuilding was to be undertaken was the cause of much controversy. While many favoured the Classicism of ancient Greece and Rome, others looked to the Gothic as the appropriate architectural style for one of the nation's most symbolic edifices. In a debate on 'The New Houses of Parliament', Lord Henry Petty-Fitzmaurice, Marquess of Lansdowne, returned to the organic relationship between architectural style, historical location and the political idea of the nation:

> [If] a Grecian style were to be adopted, the uniformity with Westminster Hall would be lost, and an alteration would be attended with great inconvenience and expense. It was, he conceived, proper that the new buildings should assimilate with those great monuments so intimately connected with the history of this country, in the neighbourhood of which they were to be placed. (Hansard 1837: vol. 37, col. 1390)

The idea of Westminster being a particularly sacred spot illustrates the manner in which locations and buildings were intimately tied to memory and politics. The same writer who satirised the Court of Chancery went on to elaborate on a wider feeling of the intimate emotional ties that resonate from locations identified with the nation:

> The past has been called the heir-loom to the world. The places, then, that have witnessed its deeds are to some extent, as it were, the freehold wherein that heir-loom should descend for the inheritance of posterity. It is very well to say that the words or deeds of distinguished Englishmen will be had in grateful remembrance, notwithstanding the ruin of the places where they were spoken or performed, – to a great extent we trust this is so; but it were very vain indeed to deny, that the existence of those places do not more immediately connect us with the actors of those words and deeds – do not impress us with a nearer and more personal feeling – do not enthral us with a dearer sympathy, and encourage within us something that is greater and more reasonable than reason – a fond and loving imagination. (Anon. 1834c: 355)

'College Green, Dublin [...] to the right is seen the Bank, formerly the Parliament House'.
T. S. Roberts del., engraved by R. Havell & Son, 1816

Politics in the age of reason was as much a matter of sympathetic imagination as reasonable deduction. Particular locations could be imbued with a political charge far more potent for its appeal to history, identity and tradition. The three decades that preceded the great fire at Westminster, though, had seen frequent meditations on the ruin of another Parliament building, this time in Dublin. The Acts of Union between Great Britain and Ireland that came into law in January 1801 abolished the Irish Parliament, and the Parliament building was taken over by the Bank of Ireland. While the structure was not physically ruined, the Union prompted a rhetoric of ruination in its opponents, with frequent prognostications in the run-up to it that College Green, the grand civic space in front of Parliament House, would fall to nature. As one pamphlet had it:

> [If] it should be the case that Dublin will loose [sic] so much, why then the shop-keepers may shut up their shops, for there will be a plentiful scarcity of every thing; and as a ballot [sic] singer in this country says,
> Turnips will grow in the Royal Exchange
> And Cabbages down along Dame Street.
> (Anon. 1800: 6)

The trope of streets running to nature recurs in the poet Adelaide O'Keefe's *National Characters Exhibited in Forty Geographical Poems* (1818), a book for children in which she imagines the monologue of an Irish officer returning wounded from the Napoleonic wars:

> Oh when a youth I took such pride
> Into the House of Parliament to glide,
>   Debates to hear:
>   A member bid me by his side,
>   And archly smiling cried,
>   'A future patriot I fear,
>   A GRATTAN he will grow.'
> Tis now a Bank they say – well be it so.
>   And in the Courts and Streets springs grass
>   I'm told;
>   Spirit is dead – its grave-stones we behold.
> (O'Keefe 1818: 25)

In the same year the Gothic novelist Charles Robert Maturin published his novel *Women; or, Pour et Contre*, which featured a hyperbolic and macabre panorama of College Green in Dublin. A central character speaks in similar terms to O'Keefe's officer, seeing the buildings shorn of their animating spirit, their hulking frames looming now over a cowering modern populace:

> '[Dublin's] beauty continues,' said Zaira, 'but it is the frightful lifeless beauty of a corse; and the magnificent architecture of its public buildings seems like the skeleton of some gigantic frame, which the inhabiting spirit has deserted; like the vast structure of the bones of the Behemoth, which has ceased to live for ages, and around whose remains modern gazers fearfully creep and stare.'
> (Maturin 1818: vol. 2, 184)

Maturin finds the change in use from Parliament to bank particularly galling:

> I behold a building which would have embellished Athens in the purest days of its architectural pride – It was the Senate-house of

Ireland – It is now the Bank; and along those steps, worthy of
a temple of Minerva or of Jupiter, the inhabitants of this
impoverished city, without trade and without wealth, are crawling
to pay bills; and among those splendid passages which once echoed
to the eloquence of a Flood, a Grattan, a Foster, and a Plunkett,
is heard the jargon of runners and tellers; and in that splendid
apartment of the House of Peers still hung with the triumphs of
William, the directors meet to ascertain dividends, and strike a
bonus. (Maturin 1818: vol. 2, 185)

A third Irish literary text from 1818 placed the panorama of College Green and the Houses of Parliament within a rhetoric of ruins that would have been far more recognisable to the late eighteenth- and early nineteenth-century traveller, not simply seeing the buildings as indicators of post-Union degradation, but going even further in projecting towards a future in which foreign travellers might use their actual ruins as spurs to philosophical meditation:

'It is a beautiful thing of its kind,' said De Vere, rather apostrophizing
the building than addressing his companion, who stood silent and
self-wrapped. 'Beautiful even now, entire and perfect in all its parts
– what will it be centuries hence, when its columns, touched by the
consecrating hand of time, shall lie prostrate, and its pediments and
architraves be broken and moss-grown – when all around it shall be
silence and desolation? Then, haply, some strife of elements may
conduct the enterprising spirit of remote philosophy to these coasts;
may cast some future Volney of the Ohio or Susquehanah upon the
shores of this little Palmyra, when he may surmise and wonder, may
dream his theories, and calculate his probabilities; and, bending
over these ruins, may see the future in the past, and apostrophize the
inevitable fate of existing empires.'
   'Or an American freeman,' observed the Commodore, 'the
descendants of some Irish exile, may voluntarily seek the bright
green shores of his fathers, and, in this mouldering structure, behold
the monument of their former degradation.' (Morgan 1818: vol. 1, 49–50)

The Irish novelist Sydney Owenson (later Lady Morgan) was able to draw on a well-developed rhetoric of ruins from the eighteenth century, and her anticipatory attitude to ruination was by no means original, with sentiments akin to hers having been voiced by a range of writers and thinkers across the mid-eighteenth to early nineteenth centuries. The reference that Morgan makes to the Marquis de Volney's *The Ruins: or, A Survey of the Revolutions of Empires* (1791; translated into English in 1792) places the Irish Houses of Parliament in a tradition of eighteenth-century ruin meditation that had explicitly political aims. Ruins both extant and anticipated were sites for poetical and, increasingly, political meditations on current social formations.

Ruins and Memory

The poet Anna Laetitia Aikin (later Barbauld) described a walk in 1773 through the ruins of an unnamed abbey, when, 'like a good Protestant', she 'began to indulge a secret triumph in the ruin of so many structures which [she] had always considered as the haunts of ignorance and superstition' (Barbauld 1825: vol. 2, 195). While Barbauld is able to acknowledge that monasteries acted to preserve some vestiges of learning in the Dark Ages, and that they provided many, including women, with refuge during troubled times, the emotions provoked by the ruins remain a mixture of 'exultation and dread': 'Farewell, ye once venerated seats! enough of you remains, and may it always remain, to remind us from what we have escaped, and make posterity for ever thankful for this fairer age of liberty and light' (Barbauld 1825: vol. 2, 196).

Ruins allowed Barbauld a rhetorical space in which to consider the progress of Britain from superstitious Catholicism into the rational freedom of the present day. The artist and landscape theorist William Gilpin had a similar, arguably stronger, reaction when viewing the ruins of Glastonbury, Somerset. While acknowledging that the history of alms-giving in monasteries might appear 'great and noble', he claims that true meditation on the significance of ruins leads to more than just an aesthetic satisfaction:

> On the other hand, when we consider five hundred persons, bred up in indolence, and lost to the commonwealth; when we consider that these houses were the great nurseries of superstition, bigotry, and ignorance; the stews of sloth, stupidity, and perhaps intemperance;

when we consider, that the education received in them had not the least tincture of useful learning, good manners, or true religion, but tended rather to vilify and disgrace the human mind; when we consider that the pilgrims and strangers who resorted thither, were idle vagabonds, who got nothing abroad that was equivalent to the occupations they left at home; and when we consider, lastly, that indiscriminate alms-giving is not real charity, but an avocation from labour and industry, checking every idea of exertion, and filling the mind with abject notions, we are led to acquiesce in the fate of these great foundations, and view their ruins, not only with a picturesque eye, but with moral and religious satisfaction. (Gilpin 1798: 138–9)

Gilpin, who was the leading theorist of the picturesque and immensely influential in shaping British attitudes to landscape, wrote that ruins of abbeys 'being naturalized to the soil, might indeed, without much impropriety, be classed among its natural beauties' (Gilpin 1786: vol. 1, 13). This process of naturalisation could lead to a form of philosophical meditation that saw history as either a teleological move from Catholic idleness and superstition to Protestant liberty and labour, or moved the ruin out of human history entirely to stand instead as a marker of the inexorable march of time. As Anne Janowitz argues, examples of the latter rhetoric 'naturalizes [...] the violence of nation-making, which evacuates from cultural artifacts the labor that made them, the human events that took place in them, and the cost to both ancient and local defeated communities' (Janowitz 1990: 4). Certainly, reactions to ruins varied across the British Isles, and the 'feeling of satisfaction' that Gilpin felt looking at the ruins of Glastonbury was not shared universally. Ruins in Ireland could speak not so much to a celebratory advance or abstract sense of mutability as to an ongoing bitterness at sectarian conflict and its visible legacy on the landscape. To some writers, ruins were far more likely to provoke anger and even threats of retribution than a satisfied melancholy.

The mid-century ruin poem became a form for pious reflection on the folly of human ambition. The antiquarian John Brand described elegy as 'the eldest *Daughter of Meditation*' and suggested that when encountering ruined buildings it finds its clearest thematic focus on the mutability of the human condition:

When her Theme contemplates the short Duration of all earthly Grandeur in the awful Ruins of Temples, Towers, and other superb Edifices, become a Prey to Time, we are naturally led by her to a Reflection on the empty Efforts of ambitious Art, the Imbecility of mortal Power, and the changing Inconstancy and Vicissitude of all sublunary Things. (Brand 1765: n.p.)

As in many mid-century poems, Brand's ruin contemplations take place at evening, and involve a retreat from the crowded social life of Georgian Britain. 'An elegy upon a pile of sacred ruins' opens with this quintessential turn away from shallow society to pensive solitude:

Soon as cool *Ev-ning* clos'd the Sun-scorch'd *Day*,
    I left the *laughing Throng* in *thoughtful Mood*;
And, where the *sacred Scene* before me lay,
    Thus sigh'd, in aw'd Attention as I stood. (Brand 1765: 2)

The evidence of 'hoary *Time's* all-changing Pow'r' removes the unnamed abbey from secular history into moral exemplum. 'Silence reigns where once the social *Crowd* / Responsive chaunted to the lauding Lay' (Brand 1765: 3). Ruins are powerful signifiers of temporal mortality to the 'laughing throng' and social crowd. As Jean Starobinski points out, 'for a ruin to appear beautiful, the act of destruction must be remote enough for its precise circumstances to have been forgotten' (Starobinski 1987: 180). The underlying eschatological message of ruin poetry deflected the process of ruination into an abstracted, personified Time. Examples abound in mid-century poetry. In the same year as Brand's collection of poems, the poet Edward Jerningham elegised another unnamed abbey in similar terms:

Of human Grandeur mark the fleeting Day,
How frail each Purpose, and each Wish how vain!
The strong-built Domes, the cloister'd Fanes decay,
And Ruin hovers round the desert Scene.
(Jerningham 1765: 7)

Likewise, John Cunningham four years earlier presented yet another anonymous pile of ruins as markers of the unstoppable march of time:

Inexorably calm, with silent pace
    Here TIME has pass'd – What ruin marks his way!
This pile, now crumbling o'er its hallow'd base,
Turn'd not his step, nor could his course delay.
(Cunningham 1761: 3)

When confronted with a more specific ruin, however, it is harder to ignore the conflict that led to present ruination. George Keate's *The Ruins of Netley Abbey* (1764) contains the standard reference to 'all-conquering TIME', yet in a second edition in 1765 Keate added a preface giving a history of the monastery in order to '[clean up] a mistake, under which many people lay, who fancied it was time only that had decayed this noble edifice' (Keate 1765: 8).

The sectarian violence and conflict of the Reformation that lay behind the melancholy solitude of ruined abbeys was arguably more visible in those nations of the United Kingdom that had seen religious conflict continue beyond the sixteenth century. John Copland's ruin poem on St Andrews in Scotland opens with a typical evening setting and desire for solitude:

Now is the time for contemplation sweet,
And cool reflection, in a calm retreat
From care, and business; and the jarring noise
Of crouds impertinent.
(Copland 1776: 6)

However, rather than evacuating the ruins of historical conflict, it heightens in rhetorical intensity as it considers the execution of the Protestant preacher George Wishart in 1545 by the then archbishop David Beaton (named Bethune in the poem):

Bethune! whose savage heart what can express?
A bloody tiger in a prelate's dress!
A furious bigot upward from his youth,
From earliest dawn to persecute the truth.
Behold that window, with his guilty blood
Embru'd! where, erst, in princely state, he stood,
With hellish joy to sate his brutal ire;

> When Wishart, all-resigned, to the fire
> Condemn'd by him, a faultless victim dy'd.
> (Copland 1776: 15)

Copland's abbey is harder to shift out of the political arena and into the contemplative melancholy of earlier examples. Even the most famous ruined Scottish abbey, Melrose, while celebrated by Sir Walter Scott and a host of subsequent poets, retained, if looked at closely enough, troubling signs of past conflict: 'Many parts of the abbey are still in a state of tolerable preservation; the marks of cannon-shot and fire are visible on the walls in some places, the abbey having been bombarded by Oliver Cromwell, with his usual zeal against every thing that adorned the country' (Anon. 1827: 445).

Castles and abbeys formed the two kinds of ruin that added to the picturesque beauty of the British landscape. Gilpin voiced a common eighteenth-century opinion that ruined abbeys resulted from the Dissolution of the Monasteries during the Reformation of Henry VIII, while ruined castles were the result of the Civil Wars of the seventeenth century and could be attributed largely to Oliver Cromwell:

> What share of picturesque genius Cromwell might have, I know not. Certain however it is, that no man, since Henry the eight, has contributed more to adorn this country with picturesque ruins. The difference between these two masters lay chiefly in the style of ruins, in which they composed. Henry adorned his landscapes with the ruins of abbeys; Cromwell, with those of castles. (Gilpin 1786: vol. 2, 122)

Certainly, the martial associations of castles could lead to a literature more aware of historical violence than the sacral ruins of abbeys. John Brand's 'Fragment, supposed to have been written among the RUINS of Tinmouth Castle and Monastery, Northumberland', in the same 1765 collection as his elegy on an unnamed abbey, provides a more immediate sense of the violence that is implicitly inscribed within the named ruin:

> In Lethean Years, long, long elaps'd,
> The swift-wing'd Bullet of Destruction,
> Loud-lab'ring from the brazen Cannon's Womb,

Pierc'd hence with Light'ning Speed, the perv'ous Air,
And roar'd, re-echoed from yon murmuring Main,
Death's thund'ring Summons, and sulphurous Call.
(Brand 1765: 10)

The Cromwellian invasion of Ireland left a far more bitter legacy, and Jonathan Swift in 1726 provided a panoramic view of ruins in the region of Drogheda in Co. Dundalk:

When I arriv'd at [Drogheda] the first mortifying sight was the ruins of several churches batter'd down by that usurper Cromwell [...] Examine all the eastern towns of Ireland and you will trace this horrid instrument of destruction, in the defacing of churches, and particularly in destroying whatever was ornamental, either within or without them [...] When I passed from Dundalk, where this cursed usurper's handy-work is yet visible, I cast mine eyes around from the top of a mountain, from whence I had a wide and a waste prospect of several venerable ruins. (Swift 1729: 49, 51-2)

Far from leading to any type of 'secret triumph', Swift notes that the 'sights and occurrences' of his trip instead lead to a 'Mixture of Rage and Compassion' (Swift 1729: 53). A slightly different inflection of rage and compassion is caught by Thomas Crofton Croker in his *Researches in the South of Ireland* (1824), when he outlines the history of the Catholic Irish family of the MacCartys of Muskery in Co. Cork, who had lost their land during the Williamite wars of 1688-91:

A considerable part of the forfeited estates of that family, in the county Cork, was held by Mr. S— about the middle of the last century. Walking one evening in his demesne, he observed a figure, apparently asleep, at the foot of an aged tree, and, on approaching the spot, found an old man extended on the ground, whose audible sobs proclaimed the severest affliction. Mr S— inquired the cause, and was answered – 'Forgive me, sir; my grief is idle, but to mourn is a relief to the desolate heart and humbled spirit. I am a Mac Carty, once possessor of that castle, now in ruins, and of this ground; – this tree was planted by my own hands, and I have returned to water its roots with my tears. Tomorrow I sail for Spain, where I have long

A view in black chalk of the interior of Tynemouth Priory and barracks. J. W. Cooke, c. 1800

been an exile and an outlaw since the Revolution. I am an old man, and tonight, probably for the last time, bid farewell to the place of my birth and the home of my forefathers.' (T. C. Croker 1824: 305)

Eighteenth-century ruin sentiment came into contact with powerful local attachments in Ireland, attachments that coloured the sentimental abstractions of time and mutability with concrete examples of historical violence. Irish ruins, as Kevin Whelan has argued, were 'mausolea of memory, the site of rupture not of aesthetic rapture' (Whelan 2004: 301). The eponymous Celtic rebel of Charles Maturin's *The Milesian Chief* (1812) corrects a visitor to a ruin who would presume to make a typically eighteenth-century meditative point about the passage of time:

> 'The nameless ruins,' said he, 'which are supposed to commemorate greatness now unknown, and virtues that have no other memorial; ruins amid which fancy sits down at leisure to dream of what its tenants might have been; such may suggest an abstract and indefinite melancholy – a melancholy without passion, and without remembrance.' His voice trembled as he added, 'But here is a local genius: a spirit of eloquence and mortality seems to have taken up his residence between the living and the dead, and to interpret to one the language of the other. I feel who lies below: every step I take awakes the memory of him on whose tomb I tread, and every hour seems weary till I lie down with them, and are forgotten.' (Maturin 1812: vol. 1, 186–7)

In Maturin's novel the Milesian Chief himself, Connal O'Morven, goes on to lead a short but bloody rebellion. Rebels in Maria Edgeworth's *Ennui* (1809) meet 'at night in the great cave, where the smugglers used to hide formerly, under the big rock, opposite the old abbey' (Edgeworth 1999: 258). And in Charlotte Elizabeth Tonna's *The Rockite* (1829), a murderous band of rebels meet in the dungeon of a ruined castle. Too deep a preoccupation with past wrongs in the Irish setting leads to the danger of reliving and recreating historical violence rather than emerging into a peaceful and prosperous modernity.

Classical and Future Ruins

In Henry Home, Lord Kames's *Elements of Criticism* (1762), advice is offered on whether a garden should be 'decorated' by a constructed ruin, and if so whether it should be Gothic or Grecian: 'Whether should a ruin be in the Gothic or Grecian form? In the former, I say; because it exhibits the triumph of time over strength, a melancholy but not unpleasant thought. A Grecian ruin suggests rather the triumph of barbarity over taste, a gloomy and discouraging thought' (Home 1762: vol. 3, 313).

Ruins from Classical Greece and Rome were far more likely to lead not to Barbauld's 'secret triumph' but to thoughts on the passing of empires. In the eighteenth century this could lead to a licence to consider Britain's inheritance of the mantle of empire, liberty and civilisation, or to a melancholic anticipation of the fall of our own structures into ruination.

The former attitude is clearly expressed in John Dyer's *The Ruins of Rome* (1740), which provides a wide panorama of the ancient city:

> Fall'n, fall'n, a silent Heap; her Heroes all
> Sunk in their Urns; behold the Pride of Pomp,
> The Throne of Nations fall'n; obscur'd in dust;
> Ev'n yet Majestical: The solemn Scene
> Elates the soul, while now the rising Sun
> Flames on the Ruins, in the purer air
> Tow'ring aloft, upon the glitt'ring plain,
> Like broken Rocks, a vast circumference;
> Rent Palaces, crush'd Columns, rifted Moles,
> Fanes roll'd on Fanes, and Tombs on buried Tombs.
> (Dyer 1740: 2)

Dyer's poem is partly a tourist guide to various sites which, in reality, lay scattered across the Eternal City, brought by the poem into striking proximity and leading to a strengthened feeling of patriotism. The ruins 'high ambitious Thoughts inflame / Greatly to serve my Country, distant Land' (Dyer 1740: 7–8). And while these thoughts may be initially based in a desire for personal fame as a virtuous patriot, they move into a more general account of how Britain is now the home and sanctuary of political liberty:

>   O Liberty,
> Parent of Happiness, celestial born;
> His sacred genius Thou; Be Britain's Care;
> With her secure, prolong thy lov'd retreat;
> Thence bless Mankind; while Yet among her Sons,
> Ev'n Yet there are, to shield thine equal laws,
> Whose bosoms kindle at the sacred Names
> Of Cecil, Raleigh, Walsingham and Drake.
> (Dyer 1740: 12)

Dyer's poem ends by warning Britons to take a warning from the example of Rome. While once the Romans 'were Free / Were Brave, were Virtuous', liberty was extinguished when 'Tyranny [...] Deign'd to walk forth a while in pageant state' (Dyer 1740: 27). In what is a standard account of reasons for the fall of Rome, Dyer blames 'Luxury', a self-centred indulgence in excessive pleasures, and a word that would recur in eighteenth-century ruin poetry that was concerned with the falling of empires. For Dyer, Luxury is at the cause of all ancient ruin, and the poem ends by moving from the panoramic view of Roman ruins to an abstract panorama of various ruined cities across Rome and the Middle East:

> O Luxury,
> Bane of elated Life, of affluent States,
> What dreary Change, what Ruin is not thine?
> How doth thy Bowl intoxicate the Mind?
> To the soft Entrance of thy Rosy Cave
> How do'st thou lure the Fortunate and Great.
> Dreadful Attraction! while behind thee gapes
> Th' unfathomable Gulph where Ashur lies
> O'erwhelm'd, forgotten; and high-boasting Cham
> And Elam's haughty Pomp, and beauteous Greece;
> And the great Queen of Earth, Imperial Rome.
> (Dyer 1740: 28)

In the mid-eighteenth century a new interest in the ancient ruins at Palmyra and Baalbek provided a powerful rhetoric of ruination to writers. The Irish-born antiquarian Robert Wood travelled through Syria from Turkey in 1750–1 with two other Oxford scholars, John Bouverie and James Woods, as well as the Italian draughtsman Giovanni Battista Borra. Wood's aim, as he later stated it, was to visit 'the most celebrated scenes of ancient story, in order to compare their present appearance with the early classical ideas we had conceived of them' (Wood 1767: i). In his Preface to his book on Palmyra, Wood argued for the mutual interaction between literature and place:

> Circumstances of climate and situation, otherwise trivial, become interesting from that connection with great men, and great actions, which history and poetry have given them: The life of Militiades

or Leonidas could never be read with so much pleasure, as on the plains of Marathon or at the straits of Thermopylae [...]. The particular pleasure, it is true, which an imagination warmed upon the spot receives from those scenes of heroic actions, the traveller only can feel, nor is it to be communicated by description. (Wood 1753: n.p.)

Wood was not the first British traveller to Palmyra; reference was made to the ruins by William Halifax in 1691. Another English writer, Abednego Seller, published *The Antiquities of Palmyra, alias Tedmor* in 1705, with a focus on recovered coins and inscriptions, although he also noted that 'were there nothing else at Palmyra to be seen, but the noble Ruins of the Temples and Places, according to the best and boldest Rules of the ancient Architecture, I should think a Journey thither on that Errand alone worth the Undertaking' (Seller 1705: n.p.).

Wood's *The Ruins of Palmyra, Otherwise Tedmor, in the Desart* (1753), however, brought the ruins to the consciousness of a much wider public primed by a growing wider culture of melancholy reflection and ruin literature. Borra's illustrations, in particular, aided the appeal of Wood's book (Borra would go on to a moderately successful career incorporating Palmyrene motifs into interior decoration). The popularity of Wood's books was reflected in Gavin Hamilton's stylised painting of

Plate from Robert Wood, The Ruins of Palmyra, Otherwise Tedmor, in the Desart, *1753*

James Dawkins and Robert Wood Discovering the Ruins of Palmyra (1758), with the two explorers dressed in togas being led by their Turkish guides towards a ruined arch in the distance. Wood opened his book by outlining a history of the Syrian city that would have resonated strongly with British readers. Palmyra's growth, due to its favourable position on trading routes and the gradual accumulation of wealth, led Wood to make the connection between ancient Palmyra and modern Britain explicit: 'The desert was in a great measure to Palmyra what the sea is to Great Britain, both their riches and defence' (Wood 1753: 20). The fall of Palmyra and its almost total erasure from history left the ruins a melancholic metonym for the weakness of historical memory: 'How much is to be regretted that we do not know more of a country, which has left such monuments of its magnificence?' (Wood 1753: 23). These were ruins all the more potent in their symbolism as the Palmyrene language was lost, and there was no literature to illuminate the purpose of the structures that the traveller could view. Almost completely divorced from an easily accessible historical memory, Palmyra would become a recurring allusion in ruin literature. Wood followed his immensely popular book on Palmyra with *The Ruins of Balbeck* (1757), giving an account of the city in modern-day Lebanon (often referred to by the variant spelling of Baalbek) which further cemented the oriental desert as the appropriate setting for the literary topos of mutability.

Palmyra and Baalbek were a faded backdrop to the later eighteenth century, but their beauty was not simply a matter of introspective reflection on the great leveller, time. The ruins of Palmyra also fed into eighteenth-century debates about the dangerous effects of luxury on the national polity. By an extension of Wood's comparison between the city and Britain made in his preface, some eighteenth-century writers were willing to allude to Palmyra as a warning to a Britain in the midst of a consumer revolution. A correspondent to *The General Magazine of Arts and Sciences* in May 1764, having spent 'several days feeding my eyes with those delicious remains of ancient architecture, the ruins of Palmyra', suggested that Borra's images depicted 'ruins [...] built at a time when an unbounded luxury had over-run the state, and almost extinguished the natural taste for truth and propriety' (Anon. 1764: 205, 205–06). Horace Walpole was an early enthusiast of Wood's writings. In a private letter he voiced an early example of a late-eighteenth-century sub-genre – the anticipatory ruin meditation:

The next Augustan age will dawn on the other side of the Atlantic. There will perhaps be a new Thucydides at Boston, a Xenophon at New York, and in time a Virgil at Mexico, and a Newton at Peru. At last some curious traveller from Lima will visit England and give a description of the ruins of St Paul's, like the editions of Balbec and Palmyra – but am I not prophesying contrary to my consummate prudence, and casting horoscopes of empires like Rousseau? (quoted in Skilton 2007: 97)

The anticipatory ruin meditation was used by Thomas Lyttleton, who combined Walpole's 'horoscope' with censure of luxury in his posthumously published poem 'The State of England in the year 2199' (1780). The Lyttleton family home at Hagley Hall, Worcestershire, had given evidence of eighteenth-century ruin-philia, with an elaborate mock-medieval ruined castle built in the grounds by the Gothic Revivalist architect Sanderson Miller in the middle of the century. Lyttleton's poem, however, eschews the medieval ruin for the anticipated ruin of London. By 2199 Britain has 'fallen from that envy'd height' when:

She rul'd the subject nations, and beheld
The Spaniard crouch beneath her spear, and all
The Gallic lilies crimson'd o'er with blood.

Now, however, those glories are extinguished, and:

[Her] sun
That once enlighten'd Europe with his beams,
Sunk in the West, is set, and ne'er again
Shall o'er Britannia spread his orient rays!
(Lyttleton 1780: 2)

The narrator's thoughts on the faded glory of Britain lead to a passage that applies a familiar Palmyrene rhetoric of ruins to London, with only St Paul's Cathedral somehow being preserved amidst the waste:

These were my thoughts whilst thro' a falling heap
Of shapeless ruins far and wide diffus'd,
Paul's great Cathedral, from her solid base,

High tow'ring to the sky, by heav'n's command
Amidst the universal waste preserv'd
Struck my astonish'd view!
(Lyttleton 1780: 2)

Lyttleton's narrator is guided by 'a poor emaciate Briton' who explains that the cause of the destruction of London was corruption resulting from commerce. Much as the earlier writer for *The Gentleman's Magazine* warned against the corrupting influence of luxury, so Lyttleton's anticipatory ruin poem provides a vivid parable for the dangers of unfettered greed and national debt ('public credit'):

[What] time
The fall of public credit, that had long
Totter'd upon her airy base, involv'd
In sudden and promiscuous ruin all
The great commercial world. – Then fell,
Struck to the heart by dark corruption's arms,
The British Lion.
(Lyttleton 1780: 5)

While Lyttleton might legitimately be labelled an eccentric, he was not alone in tracing a link between unfettered greed and ruination. Oliver Goldsmith's *The Deserted Village* (1770) had lamented the decline of a rural community through depopulation due to avaricious landowners:

Sunk are thy bowers, in shapeless ruin all,
And the long grass o'ertops the mouldering wall;
And, trembling, shrinking from the spoiler's hand,
Far, far away, thy children leave the land.
Ill fares the land, to hastening ills a prey,
Where wealth accumulates, and men decay.
(Goldsmith 1770: 3–4)

An introductory note by Goldsmith complained that his poem's attack on luxury might provoke 'the shout of modern politicians', as 'it has been the fashion to consider luxury as one of the greatest national advantages; and all the wisdom of antiquity in that particular, as erroneous' (Goldsmith 1770: vii). Certainly, negative reactions to Goldsmith's poems could not compare with the hostility that greeted Anna Laetitia Barbauld's *Eighteen Hundred and Eleven* (1812). Barbauld gave perhaps the most significant anticipatory ruin poem of the period, all the more galling during Britain's long experience of the Napoleonic wars. In a deeply political poem, Barbauld imagines a future in which the light of liberty and empire has passed from Britain:

> Night, Gothic night, again may shade the plains
> Where Power is seated, and where Science reigns;
> England, the seat of arts, be only known
> By the gray ruin and the mouldering stone.
> (Barbauld 1825: vol. 1, 238–9)

Like Lyttleton, Barbauld goes on to imagine a traveller from the New World touring classic sites of Britain, including Skiddaw, Edinburgh and Melrose Abbey, incorporating in the last case a reference to Sir Walter Scott's famous ruin poem, *The Lay of the Last Minstrel* (1805):

> With curious search their pilgrim steps shall rove
> By many a ruined tower and proud alcove,
> Shall listen for those strains that soothed of yore
> Thy rock, stern Skiddaw, and thy fall, Lodore;
> Feast with Dun Edin's classic brow their sight,
> And visit 'Melross by the pale moonlight.'
> (Barbauld 1825: vol. 1, 240)

John Wilson Croker in the conservative *Quarterly Review* was led by these lines to point out that 'while all our modern edifices are to be in such a lamentable state of dilapidation, Time is to proceed with so cautious and discriminating a step, that Melrose Abbey, which is now pretty well in ruins, is not to grow a bit older, but to continue a beautiful ruin still' (J. W. Croker 1812: 311). Much as Dyer had provided a panoramic view of the ruins of Rome in 1740, Barbauld imagines that her traveller 'from the blue mountains, or Ontario's lake' (Barbauld, 1825: 1, 239):

[...] of some crumbling turret, mined by time,
The broken stairs with perilous step shall climb,
Thence stretch their view the wide horizon round,
By scattered hamlets trace [London's] ancient bound,
And, choked no more with fleets, fair Thames survey
Through reeds and sedge pursue his idle way.
(Barbauld 1825: vol. 1, 241–2)

While its imagery anticipates later post-apocalyptic fiction such as Richard Jeffries' *After London* (1885), Barbauld's poem also clearly links back to earlier eighteenth-century warnings against the danger to the polity of commerce and imperial expansion. After a survey of the faded glories of London, the moral lesson chimes with earlier meditations by Lyttleton and Goldsmith:

But fairest flowers expand but to decay;
The worm is in thy core, thy glories pass away;
Arts, arms and wealth destroy the fruits they bring;
Commerce, like beauty, knows no second Spring.
(Barbauld 1825: vol. 1, 249)

A reference to the 'desert solitudes' where 'Tadmor [Palmyra] sleeps' (Barbauld 1825: vol. 1, 246) places Barbauld's prophetic poem firmly within the eighteenth-century tradition, although it was a tradition that had been significantly changed between 1812 and Lyttleton's earlier anticipatory ruin poem by the work of Constantin-François Volney.

Volney's *Les Ruines; ou, Méditation sur les revolutions des empires* (1791) had brought the meditative contemplation of Palmyrene ruins into conversation with radical, and atheist, French political theory. Volney's work opens with a poetic 'invocation' to the ruins: '[Though] the profane and vulgar mind shrinks with dismay from your august and awe-inspiring aspect, to me ye unfold the sublimest charms of contemplation and sentiment, and offer to my senses the luxury of a thousand and enchanting thoughts!' (Volney 1799: ix–x). The contemplation of temporal mutability and the decline of structures into oblivion is transformed by Volney into a pointedly anti-tyrannical reading that situates ruin meditation as a fundamental part of wider revolutionary thinking:

> When oppressed humanity bent in timid silence throughout the globe beneath the galling yoke of slavery, it was you that proclaimed aloud the birthright of those truths, which tyrants tremble at while they detest; and which, by sinking the loftiest head of the proudest potentate, with all his boasted pageantry, to the level of mortality with his meanest slave, confirmed and ratified by your unerring testimony the sacred and immortal doctrine of *Equality*. (Volney 1799: x–xi)

Volney brought ruin meditation into clear dialogue with French Revolutionary ideals. The Revolution itself led to one of the most spectacular acts of ruination of the eighteenth century with the storming of the Bastille in July 1789. Ruin rhetoric also percolated into British debates about the revolution. Edmund Burke's *Reflections on the Revolution in France* (1790) is haunted by the ruination of social and political structures under the force of Revolutionary ideology. For Burke, the French state was left in ruins by the Revolution, and he imagines an alternative in which the older constitution had been restored: 'Your constitution, it is true, whilst you were out of possession, suffered some waste and dilapidation; but you possessed in some parts the walls, and in all the foundations of a noble and venerable castle. You might have repaired those walls; you might have built on those old foundations' (Burke 1790: 50). Sympathisers with the Revolution responded in kind, arguing for the removal of all traces of such antiquated political structures, often relying on precisely the progressive meditations that had characterised ruin literature in the earlier decades of the century.

Conclusion: Ruined Cottages

Contemplating the remains of Wricklemarsh House in Kent, the radical philosopher John Thelwall confessed that 'I pass by such monuments of the instability of Grandeur with much less emotion or concern than I behold, as I sometimes do, the ruins of a little farm house, or the much more common spectacle of a desolated cottage' (Thelwall 1793: vol. 1, 180). It is perhaps a fitting manner in which to conclude a survey of the political implications of ruin literature in the long eighteenth century. Certainly, the 1790s saw two poets respond to historical violence by composing poems entitled 'The Ruined Cottage'. The more famous of the two, by William Wordsworth, written in 1797, was eventually published in his long poem *The Excursion* (1814), where its meditation on a cottage ruined during the American War of Independence was enfolded within a longer meditation on the dejection that follows the betrayal of early liberal political enthusiasm. The Irish Quaker poet Mary Leadbeater's 'The Ruined Cottage' was published in her 1808 collection of poems, but it is set during the Irish Rebellion of 1798. Both poems let the ruin act as a synecdoche for the wider ruination brought about by conflict. Beautiful, picturesque, melancholy: ruins viewed, imagined, or anticipated were complex carriers of political sentiments as well as aesthetic appreciation and philosophical contemplation. During a period that recovered them from oblivion, they spoke to their audiences with a quiet but clear eloquence.

Further Reading

Sir John Soane's Museum. 1999. *Visions of Ruin: Architectural Fantasies and Designs for Garden Follies, with 'Crude Hints Towards a History of My House' by John Soane* (London: The Soane Gallery).

Woodward, Christopher. 2002. *In Ruins* (London: Vintage).

Wright, Julia M. 2014. *Representing the National Landscape in Irish Romanticism* (New York: Syracuse University Press).

References

Anon. 1764. 'Concerning the Ruins of Palmyra', *The General Magazine of Arts and Sciences, Philosophical, Philological, Mathematical, and Mechanical* 14 (May): 205-7.

Anon. 1800. *Letter [A] from Murtagh Feagan cousin German to Denis Feagan of Edenderry in answer to Darby Tracy of London, chairman, srewing [sic] (nothing but truth)*. Dublin, http://www.actofunion.ac.uk [last accessed 30 May 2017].

Anon. 1827. 'Recollections of Melrose Abbey', *The Mirror of Literature, or Amusement and Instruction* 10, no. 290 (29 December): 445-7.

Anon. 1834a. 'The Destruction of Both Houses of Parliament', *The Examiner* (19 October): 656-66.

Anon. 1834b. 'The Great Fire at Westminster', *The Examiner* (26 October): 682-3.

Anon. 1834c. 'Destruction of the Houses of Parliament', *New Monthly Magazine* 42, no. 167 (November): 352-7.

Barbauld, Anna Laetitia. 1825. *The Works of Anna Laetitia Barbauld*, edited by Lucy Aikin, 2 vols (London: Longman, Hurst, Rees, Orme, Brown and Green).

Brand, John. 1765. *A Collection of Poetical Essays* (Newcastle upon Tyne: Printed by I. Thompson).

Burke, Edmund. 1790. *Reflections on the Revolution in France* (London: J. Dodsley).

Burke, Edmund. 1990. *A Philosophical Enquiry into the Origin of our Ideas of the Sublime and Beautiful*, edited by Adam Phillips (Oxford: Oxford University Press).

Copland, John. 1776. *Saint Andrews; or, A Sentimental Evening Walk Near the Ruins of that Ancient City* (Edinburgh).

Croker, John Wilson. 1812. 'Eighteen Hundred and Eleven', *Quarterly Review* 7, no. 14 (June): 309-13.

Croker, Thomas Crofton. 1824. *Researches in the South of Ireland, Illustrative of the Scenery, Architectural Remains, and the Manners and Superstitions of the Peasantry* (London: John Murray).

Cunningham, John. 1761. *An Elegy upon a Pile of Ruins* (London: Printed for H. Payne and W. Cropley).

Dyer, John. 1740. *The Ruins of Rome: A Poem* (London: Printed for Lawton Gilliver).

Edgeworth, Maria. 1999. *Ennui. Castle Rackrent, Irish Bulls, Ennui*, edited by Jane Desmarais, Tim McLoughlin and Marilyn Butler. *The Novels and Selected Works of Maria Edgeworth*, General editors Marilyn Butler and Mitzi Myers (London: Pickering and Chatto).

Gilpin, William. 1786. *Observations, Relative Chiefly to Picturesque Beauty, Made in the Year 1772, On Several Parts of England; Particularly the Mountains and Lakes of Cumberland and Westmoreland*, 2 vols (London: Printed for R. Blamire).

Gilpin, William. 1798. *Observations on the Western Parts of England* (London: Printed for T. Cadell jun. and W. Davies).

Goldsmith, Oliver. 1770. *The Deserted Village, A Poem* (London: W. Griffin).

Hansard. 1837. *HL Deb. Vol. 37 cc 1389-90*, 18 April 1837.

Home, Henry, Lord Kames. 1762. *Elements of Criticism*, 3 vols (London: Printed for A. Millar; Edinburgh: Printed for J. Bell).

Janowitz, Anne. 1990. *England's Ruins: Poetic Purpose and the National Landscape* (Cambridge, Mass.: Basil Blackwell).

Jerningham, Edward. 1765. *An Elegy Written Among the Ruins of an Abbey*, 2nd edn (London: Printed for J. Dodsley).

Keate, George. 1765. *The Ruins of Netley Abbey*, 2nd edn (London).

Lyttleton, Lord Thomas. 1780. *Poems, by a Young Nobleman, of Distinguished Abilities, Lately Deceased* (London: Printed for G. Kearsley).

Maturin, Charles. 1812. *The Milesian Chief: A Romance*, 4 vols (London: Printed for H. Colburn).

Maturin, Charles. 1818. *Women; or, Pour et Contre, A Tale*, 3 vols (Edinburgh: Archibald Constable and Co.; London: Longman, Hurst, Rees, Orme and Brown).

Morgan, Lady. 1818. *Florence Maccarthy: An Irish Tale*, 3 vols (London: Printed for Henry Colburn).

O'Keefe, Adelaide. 1818. *National Characters Exhibited in Forty Geographical Poems* (London: Printed for Darton, Harvey and Darton).

Seller, Abednego. 1705. *The Antiquities of Palmyra, alias Tedmor, built by King*

Solomon. (London: Printed for S. Smith and B. Walford).

Skilton, David. 2007. 'Tourists at the Ruins of Empire: The Metropolis and the Struggle for Empire', *Cercles* 17: 93–119.

Starobinski, Jean. 1987. 'Melancholy among the ruins', in *The Invention of Liberty, 1700-1789* (New York: Rizzoli), 179–81.

Swift, Jonathan. 1729. 'No. 6: A Representation of the present Condition of Ireland' (1726). *The Intelligencer* (London): 46–57.

Thelwall, John. 1793. *The Peripatetic; or, Sketches of the Heart, of Nature and Society*, 3 vols (London).

Volney, Constantin-François. 1799. *The Ruins; or, A Survey of the Revolutions of Empires* (Philadelphia: Printed by J. Lyon).

Whelan, Kevin. 2004. 'Reading the Ruins: The Presence of Absence in the Irish Landscape', in *Surveying Ireland's Past: Multidisciplinary Essays in Honour of Anngret Simms*, edited by Howard B. Clarke, Jacinta Prunty and Mark Hennessy (Dublin: Geography Publications), 292–328.

Wollstonecraft, Mary. 1790. *A Vindication of the Rights of Men* (London: Printed for J. Johnson).

Wood, Robert. 1753. *The Ruins of Palmyra, Otherwise Tedmor, in the Desart* (London).

Wood, Robert. 1767. *A Comparative View of the Antient and Present State of the Troade. To Which is Prefixed an Essay on the Original Genius of Homer* (London).

Beaumaris Castle

David Punter

> [Beaumaris Castle] covers a great extent of ground, but wants height to give it dignity; and though massive and ponderous, it has not the imposing effect of other structures of the same age. (Black and Black 1864: 99)

Beaumaris Castle on the isle of Anglesey, North Wales, is a low-lying castle without much of the sublime about it; instead, it is an architectural gem, outstandingly picturesque, standing within its own moat and equipped with its own dock on the south coast of the island. Despite later depredations, much of what was originally built in the late thirteenth century by Edward I during his campaigns to conquer Wales is still standing; it was never completed, nor was it destroyed or slighted, although by 1609 we read that its interior was 'utterlie decayed' (quoted in Taylor 2004: 15). Like so many other castles in Wales and elsewhere, it was brought back into fighting, or at least defensive, condition for the Civil Wars, and there was apparently a great deal of reported 'robbing' around 1660.

J. M. W. Turner visited the castle in 1798, and he painted it much later, in c. 1835. The painting is far from topographically accurate, but it is immensely atmospheric, succeeding in converting a rather domestic

North view of Beaumaris Castle. Samuel and Nathaniel Buck, 1742

setting and scenario into a hazy and highly coloured apparition of high Romanticism. All through the eighteenth century, gentle decay had been continuing, both alleviated and emphasised by the enormous growths of ivy pictured, for example, in a Victorian engraving by Alfred Sumners (1852). By his time, the castle ruins had become mainly a backdrop for aristocratic pleasure outings; in 1832 it was the site of a so-called Royal Eisteddfod, attended by, among others, the young Princess Victoria.

Beaumaris figured large in the highly popular poem *Beaumaris Bay* (1800) by Richard Llwyd, the 'Bard of Snowdon':

Here earth is loaded with a mass of wall,
The proud insulting badge of Cambria's fall,
By haughty Edward rais'd; and every stone
Records a sigh, a murder, or a groan.
The Muse of Britain, suffering at its birth,
Exulting, sees it crumbling to the earth.
Ah! What avails it that the lordly tower
Attracts the thoughtless stare and vacant hour
If ev'ry Bard with indignation burns,
When to the tragic tale the eye returns;
If for his haunted race, to distant times,
There's still reserved a vengeance for his crimes.
(Llwyd 1800: 13–14)

As Jane Aaron eloquently puts it, 'Britain' and 'British' in the poem clearly signify for the Bard of Snowdon:

an ethnicity whose modern-day representatives are the Welsh and whose historical oppressor is that England which excluded their ancestors to the rural outskirts of post-conquest castle towns like Beaumaris. And the poem suggests that this past history is still haunting contemporary Britain: the castle's crumbling walls still echo to the groans of old atrocities and endure as a monument to horror and oppression. (Aaron 2013: 45)

Beaumaris is now a World Heritage site, an accolade that seems particularly justified by the remarkable chapel, originally designed for the private use of the king and his family, with trefoil-headed twin doorways and a magnificent, though small-scale, ribbed-stone vault. It also has watching chambers to each side, still complete, and it was possible to close off the entire chapel complex from the remainder of the castle.

References

Aaron, Jane. 2013. *Welsh Gothic* (Cardiff: University of Wales Press).
Black, Adam and Charles Black. 1864. *Black's Picturesque Guide through North and South Wales*, 13th edn (Edinburgh: Adam and Charles Black).
Llwyd, Richard. 1800. *Beaumaris Bay, A Poem* (Chester: Printed by J. Fletcher).
Taylor, Arnold. 2004. *Beaumaris Castle*, 5th edn (Cardiff: Cadw).

Shobdon's Folly

Peter N. Lindfield

The redevelopment of the Shobdon estate in Herefordshire is an important example of Georgian architectural reconstruction and 'improvement', a highly politicised term that, for some concerned antiquaries in the late eighteenth century, was indistinguishable from deliberate acts of architectural destruction. The main protagonist involved in this quasi-mysterious and undocumented series of works is Dickie Bateman, a friend and correspondent of Georgian Britain's arch-Gothicist, Horace Walpole of Strawberry Hill, Twickenham. We know that Walpole spent 'many pleasing days [at Bateman's house] with him and Lady Hervey', and Bateman would almost certainly have mentioned the work going on at Shobdon – especially the recasting of the ancient church in a thoroughly modern and simultaneously 'historicist' Gothic style – after Walpole had taken Chopp'd-Straw-Hall and begun transforming it into Strawberry Hill from 1747 (Walpole 1937–83: vol. 32, 241; Reeve 2013; Lindfield 2016: 158–9).

Bateman supervised the works on the Shobdon estate, architectural

Shobdon's Folly. From George Robert Lewis, The Ancient Church of Shobdon, Herefordshire, Illustrated and Described, *London, 1852*

'improvements' which saw, among other things, the refurbishment of the country seat, Shobdon Court, in the Classical mode by Henry Flitcroft, and the complete reimagining of the church. The genuine Romanesque structure built by Oliver de Merlimond in c. 1130 was, save the tower, pulled down in 1752 and the spoils, including sculptural panels, were used to create a Norman-Gothic triumphal arch, Shobdon Arches. In Bateman's correspondence, these are purported to be a fragmentary legacy of an ancient priory on the site; the body of the 'new' church was designed in the highly theatrical Georgian Gothic style of William Kent in the 1750s.

Despite the fact that the surviving carvings from Shobdon's Romanesque church are celebrated today as some of the finest examples of the dramatic school of twelfth-century Herefordshire carving, Bateman's plans were firmly set upon 'improvement'. In 1746, he wrote: 'We have a new Bishop [James Beauclerk] who I hope will make no difficulty as soon as he is consecrated of granting us all we have to ask, in relation to the Church and C yard. So that in all probability you will see Shobdon much improved this summer' (Hereford 1746: f. 1v). The twelfth-century fabric lacked the architectural drama and ornament so desirable in certain fashionable circles of the day. Recreating the church in the most up-to-date style not only created a fashionable Gothic fabric, but also a highly visible folly on the estate. The folly's arches are round-headed with appropriate dog-tooth moulding, yet the structure's form and other ornament, including battlements and a trefoil punctuating the gable, are disparate. Nevertheless, the intention to create a ruined folly out of the Romanesque fabric speaks of the importance of medieval ruins to the picturesque country house landscape (Baxter 2010).

References
Baxter, Ron. 2010. 'Whose Heritage? The Problem of Shobdon Arches', *Journal of the British Archaeological Association* 163, no. 1: 154–76.

Hereford. 1746. Herefordshire Record Office, G39/III/E/110 f. 1v.

Lindfield, Peter N. 2016. *Georgian Gothic: Medievalist Architecture, Furniture and Interiors, 1730–1840* (Woodbridge: Boydell & Brewer).

Reeve, Matthew. 2013. 'Dickie Bateman and the Gothicization of Old Windsor: Architecture and Sexuality in the Circle of Horace Walpole', *Architectural History* 56: 99–133.

Walpole, Horace. 1937–83. *The Yale Edition of Horace Walpole's Correspondence*, edited by W. S. Lewis, 48 vols (New Haven: Yale University Press).

Conclusion
Conserving Britain's Ruins, 1700 to the Present Day

Marion Harney

The Allure of Ruins

The subject of art, literature and philosophical reflection, Gothic remains were valued over the course of the long eighteenth century as tangible structures, but equally cherished for their ability to induce intangible melancholic romantic responses, moods of contemplation and reverie, thoughts about the passage of time, visions of an ideal medieval past and feelings of mortality and transience. As the chapters in this book have shown, the eighteenth century witnessed a proliferation of literary and artistic responses to the effect of ruins on the aesthetic sensibility; the 'pleasing decay' and 'romantic gloom' that they inspired amounted to a 'cult' of ruin sensibility that had a profound effect on the history of taste. Admiration and awe for romantic ruins reached a zenith when they were appreciated for their Gothic form and valued for their architecturally dramatic state of irresistible decay: crumbling edifices swamped by nature located in isolated settings inspired the curiosity and creative imagination with notions of an irrecoverable past. Frequently the subject of literary and artistic effusion, ruins evoked numerous creative responses, with artists such as J. M. W. Turner and several amateur picturesque travellers making ruined abbeys and castles a central feature of their landscape paintings, and poets and novelists such as Percy Bysshe Shelley, Walter Scott, Lord

Byron, William Wordsworth and many others giving them literary form and expression.

As the individual 'Ruins in Focus' studies included in this volume demonstrate, ruins cannot be separated from the sites in which they occur. Their meaning and value are inextricably linked to a physical space, their presence creating the *genius loci* or presiding spirit of the place. In the eighteenth- and nineteenth-century British psyche, this was inevitably linked to their associations with the social, historical and political events of the past. The antiquary John Williamson made this connection particularly clear in his account of Glastonbury Abbey, Somerset, in 1852: 'And though this Abbey now lies, like some ancient tomb, in sad and mournful ruin, yet still it demands and enjoys intense veneration, as much for the influences – social, political and religious – it once distributed, as for its ancient and artistic splendour' (Williamson 1852: 7). Similarly perceiving ruin as a visible reminder of a turbulent historical narrative, the antiquary John Aubrey in the late seventeenth century said of monastic ruins that 'the eie and mind is no less affected with these stately ruines than they would be if they were standing and entire. They breed in generous minds a kind of pittie; and set the thoughts aworke to make out their magnificence as they were in perfection' (quoted in Woodward 2001: 130). However, as Rose Macaulay pointed out in 1953 in her magisterial study *Pleasure of Ruins*, the appeal of ruins then, as now, is as much legendary as it is historical:

> The ascendancy over men's minds of the ruins of the stupendous past, the past of history, legend and myth, at once factual and fantastic, stretching back and back into ages that can be but surmised, is half-mystical in basis. The intoxication, at once so heady and so devout, is not the romantic melancholy engendered by broken towers and mouldered stones; it is the soaring of the imagination into the high empyrean where huge episodes are tangled with myths and dreams; it is the stunning impact of world history on its amazed heirs. (Macaulay 1953: 40)

Irrespective of whether the associations that they bring to mind are the stuff of myth or history, ruins since the eighteenth century have been powerfully charged with the ability to instil awe and wonder in the minds of those who perceive them.

The presence of Gothic ruins in Britain rose dramatically following the Dissolution of the Monasteries (1536–40), a strategy of deliberate architectural vandalism that resulted in the destruction of approximately 650 monastic communities by Henry VIII and Thomas Cromwell. This alone left a vast proliferation of abandoned religious sites across the British countryside. The English Civil Wars (1642–51) and the period of the Commonwealth (1649–60) created yet another layer of castles and fortified houses lying in ruin across the landscape, many of these structures having been 'slighted' or partially demolished by Republican forces in an attempt at rendering them unusable to the Royalist cause. Only fifty years after the Dissolution, the effects of ecclesiastical ruin on the poetic imagination were already being registered. In Shakespeare's Sonnet 73, the persona refers to the emotional and aesthetic impact of ruined churches in the line 'Bare ruined choirs, where late the sweet birds sang' (Shakespeare 2008: 1970). In John Webster's Jacobean tragedy *The Duchess of Malfi* (1613–14), Antonio appreciates walking among the ruins of an ancient abbey for their potential to evoke historical imaginings: 'I do love these ancient ruins: / We never tread upon them, but we set / Our foot upon some reverend history' (Act V, scene iii, lines 9–11; Webster 1986: 93). John Denham's *Cooper's Hill* (1642), often cited as the first British topographical poem, reflects on the destruction caused during the Dissolution of the Monasteries as a precursor to the political and cultural upheaval likely to be occasioned by the more recent outbreak of the English Civil Wars:

> My wandring eye, an emulous Hill doth bound,
> My more contracted sight, whose top of late
> A Chappell crown'd, till in the common fate
> The neighbouring Abbey fell, (may no such storme
> Fall on our times, where ruine must reform.
> (Denham 1642: 8)

The chapters and shorter articles included in the 'Ruins in Focus' sections of this book have explored the extraordinary imaginative powers of ruins beyond these localised examples.

Such evocations of the ruin's imaginative properties were soon coupled with an interest in their preservation. In an often-cited memorandum of 1709 to the Duke and Duchess of Marlborough, Sir

John Vanbrugh petitioned for the retention of the old ruined manor at Blenheim, 'so that all the Buildings left (which is only the Habitable Part and the Chapell) might Appear in two Risings amongst 'em', claiming that 'it wou'd make One of the Most Agreable Objects that the best of the Landskip Painters can invent' (quoted in Harney 2013: 42–3). As he continued, the 'Small Remains of ancient Woodstock Manour' had associative potential through their links to British history, their appeal to the senses and their ability to stimulate the historical imagination:

> There is perhaps no One thing, which the most Polite part of Mankind have more universally agreed in; than the Vallue they have ever set upon the Remains of distant Times. Nor amongst the Severall kinds of those Antiquitys, are there any so much regarded, as those of Buildings; Some for their Magnificence, or Curious Workmanship; And others; as they move more lively and pleasing Reflections (than History without their aid can do) on the Persons who have Inhabited them; On the Remarkable things which have been transacted in them, Or the extraordinary Occasions of Erecting them. (quoted in Harney 2013: 42–3)

Vanbrugh's response to the ruinous remains at Blenheim prefigured the antiquarian drive towards a better understanding and appreciation of the past. But he is also an early example of the cultural urge to conserve Gothic architectural remains, an impulse that was reflected, too, in the antiquarian desire to draw them so as to record what was increasingly being seen as the indigenous or native style of British or 'Gothic' architecture.

Recording Ruins

The year 1717 saw the formalisation of meetings and proceedings of the Society of Antiquaries of London, the informal establishment of which in 1707 heralded a new interest in medieval ancestry and British antiquities. The intellectual and social elite were key players in the antiquarian community, and their research and publications informed eighteenth-century ideas of cultural identity and patriotism. Edmund Gibson's revision of William Camden's pioneering chorographical survey of the British Isles, *Britannia* (1695), was a seminal text for any antiquary interested in early history, and the first in a series of county histories that combined topographical regional and medieval textual studies. The development of learned antiquarian studies in the late seventeenth and the eighteenth centuries significantly influenced intellectual culture, and its main legacies of archaeology and history remain apparent today.

Though not always in a spirit of conservation, several ruins were salvaged in the eighteenth century through acts of architectural appropriation and repurposing. Of the 650 or so monastic buildings seized during the Dissolution, one-third have been lost due to benign neglect, having been unroofed and stripped of valuable materials. Approximately one-third remain as abandoned sites, having been wilfully destroyed or disintegrated. Many others, however, were converted to domestic dwellings, while others still were converted for commercial use. Bath Abbey is one example of a site that was rescued by the populace and converted into a parish church. Other ecclesiastical buildings found a new secular function as substantial private residences, the most prominent examples including Lord Byron's ancestral home, the Augustinian priory Newstead Abbey, Nottinghamshire, founded c. 1170; the thirteenth-century convent at Lacock Abbey, Wiltshire; and Hailes Abbey, Gloucestershire, originally built c. 1245 and partially inhabited until the seventeenth century, when much of its remains were again demolished. The twelfth-century Benedictine monastery Malmesbury Abbey, Wiltshire, was converted for use as a woollen mill, the looms still operational when John Aubrey, discoverer of Avebury Henge, visited the site in 1660.

Those ruins that remained continued to be valued both as historic structures and for their aesthetic qualities, and some of these were bought and creatively incorporated as picturesque visual objects in a view or incorporated into designed landscapes. The latter accounts for the survival of some of the most spectacular ruins, such as: Fountains Abbey in Yorkshire; Tintern Abbey in the Wye valley; and Old Wardour Castle, Wiltshire, slighted and ruined in the Civil Wars and deliberately retained to be viewed as a picturesque object from the new Palladian Wardour Castle (1769–76) designed by James Paine. Other Gothic structures were used as quarries and pillaged for spolia, their building materials stripped and reappropriated for construction work elsewhere. Such was the fate of Halesowen Abbey, Worcestershire, a Premonstratensian abbey founded in 1214 and surrendered to the Crown in 1538. The monastic buildings were partly demolished in 1540, with the remaining parts later incorporated into the north barn of Manor Farm. The poet William Shenstone developed a *ferme ornée* or 'ornamented farm' at The Leasowes, Worcestershire, between 1743 and 1763, removing fragments from the abbey to incorporate into a Gothic folly that he was creating in his own garden adjacent to the abbey ruins. The north transept of Netley Abbey that Horace Walpole so admired when he visited it in 1755 is another example of spolia architecture that was removed and erected as an eye-catcher in the grounds of Cranbury Park, Worcestershire, in 1765 by the MP Thomas Dummer, where it remains to this day. The south transept is still in its original location and is now in the care of English Heritage.

If eighteenth-century landowners did not have an aesthetically pleasing Gothic survival ruin of their own, they merely created a sham or fake one. As several case studies in this volume have shown, these sham ruins were acts of creativity in their own right, and fostered several others, too. The first English Gothic garden pavilions were of a 'political' or 'patriotic' nature, often signifying political allegiances and ideologies. The Gothic Temple (after 1717) at Shotover, Oxfordshire, attributed to William Townshend, and Alfred's Hall (1721–32) at Cirencester Park, Gloucestershire, constructed by the Tory peer Lord Bathurst, were expressive of a time of political liberty that their patrons believed to have been destroyed and compromised by Whig politics. The Gothic Temple, or Temple of Liberty, at Stowe, Buckinghamshire, completed between 1741 and 1749 by James Gibbs, is another well-known example of a building constructed to convey a political ideology. Other instances of Gothic garden buildings include the Cuttle Mill (c. 1740) at Rousham, Oxfordshire, by William Kent, and Edgehill Castle Tower (1745–7) at Radway, Warwickshire, built by Sanderson Miller for himself (Harney 2013: 122). Sanderson Miller's Gothic mock-ruined castle at Hagley, Worcestershire, dates from 1746. The antiquary William Stukeley removed spolia as a means of conservation, incorporating the salvaged architectural fragments and stained glass from churches undergoing 'modernisation' to construct a Gothic hermitage in his garden at Stamford in 1738. Horace Walpole records in his private correspondence a visit to Miller's mock-ruined castle at Hagley and his emotional response to the ruin set in the landscape, asserting its associative qualities and political resonances with the Wars of the Roses (1455–85): 'There is extreme taste in the park: the seats are not the best, but there is not one absurdity. There is a ruined castle, built by Miller, that would get him his freedom even of Strawberry: it has the true rust of the Barons' War' (Walpole 1973: 148). Joseph Heely recorded a similar range of historical associations evoked by the mock-Gothic ruins at Hagley in *Letters on the Beauties of Hagley, Envil, and the Leasowes* (1777):

> one cannot resist an involuntary pause—struck with its character, the mind naturally falls into reflections, while curiosity is on the wing, to be acquainted with its history; and I make no doubt that an antiquarian like my friend, would sigh to know in what æra it was founded, and by whom:—what sieges it had sustained;—what blood had been spilt upon its walls:—and would lament that hostile discord; or the iron hand of an all-mouldering time, should so rapaciously destroy it. Believe me, the appearance of this antique pile has the power of stamping these impressions on the mind, so masterly is it executed to deceive. (Heely 1777: vol. 1, 173–4)

Textual and Visual Conservation

Gothic ruins were captured through the permanence of paintings and poetry but also through the tradition of recording ruins and antiquities in topographical prints and engravings. Eighteenth-century antiquaries had a learned interest in studying ruins as historical objects, and the increasing volume of antiquarian publications such as *Archaeologia* (1770–2007) stimulated the patriotic agenda through recording antiquities and making them available to a wider public readership. This, in turn, led to greater curiosity and interest in British history and architecture, and encouraged domestic travel and sightseeing within Britain. From its inception, the Society of Antiquaries of London had employed an engraver for the drawing and engraving of ruins, and George Vertue was one of the earliest to assume this role. Vertue influenced, and was largely responsible for, the Society's regular publication of engravings depicting medieval antiquities in this period. The antiquaries' methods demonstrated that knowledge and evidence could be derived from sources other than texts, and those such as Charles Lyttelton and

Richard Gough played a pivotal role in establishing the systematic study of architectural history, their re-evaluation of the Gothic style of architecture contributing to a historicist approach to the past (Sweet 2004: xvi). By the late eighteenth century, artists and engravers such as Thomas Hearne were prolific in producing depictions of Gothic antiquities in picturesque settings, their creations fulfilling an increasing public demand for picturesque tourism.

Horace Walpole had a passion for the architectural remains of Britain, and his influence on the aesthetic taste for picturesque Gothic architecture in the mid-eighteenth century cannot be underestimated. In his *Anecdotes of Painting in England* (1762) Walpole describes the aesthetic and emotional power of Gothic architecture, famously stating that 'One must have taste to be sensible of the beauties of Grecian architecture; one only wants passions to feel Gothic' (Walpole 1762: 107–8). This sense of 'passion' is perfectly illustrated in his own reaction to Netley Abbey, discussed in Chapter 4 of this book. Walpole and his coterie formed the architectural 'Strawberry Committee', whose intention it was to foster and promote Gothic or Old English taste in architecture, literature and art. He undertook a series of 'Gothic Pilgrimages' with his friend John Chute, decades before it was fashionable to do so, and his observations of Gothic ruins represent an early manifestation of a concern with the conservation of important Gothic monuments. His collection and interpretation of antiquarian prints are also indicative of his desire to record and preserve Gothic architectural precedents, undertaken so as better to understand the underlying principles and development of the style. Of course, his impulse to preserve the native British style was also evidenced by incorporating these Gothic elements, designs and fragments into the fabric of his 'little Gothic castle' at Strawberry Hill, Twickenham. Rather than prefiguring the nineteenth-century Gothic Revival, which was based upon a set of different and quite specific religious and patriotic beliefs, the precepts delineated in Walpole's theories on Gothic architecture anticipated the picturesque school of Uvedale Price, Richard Payne Knight, Humphry Repton and John Nash (Harney 2013: 279–80).

Later in the century, the highly accomplished architectural draughtsman and artist John Carter became the most passionate advocate of the conservation of Gothic ruins. As the one-time draughtsman for the Society of Antiquaries' *Vetusta Monumenta* series, he specialised in depicting Gothic buildings and architectural antiquities, making them available to a wider social spectrum. Carter was enthralled by the medieval chivalric fantasies expressed in the proliferation of contemporary romance literature and poetry, such as Richard Hurd's *Letters on Chivalry and Romance* (1762) and Thomas Percy's *Reliques of Ancient English Poetry* (1765), and emphasised the sublimity and mystery of the Gothic style in his writings in *The Gentleman's Magazine* and other widely distributed periodicals and publications. Carter's indefatigable endeavours in the late eighteenth and early nineteenth centuries brought Gothic architecture to the attention of a wider reading public, and had the effect of raising the national consciousness of Gothic style as an indigenous part of our history and heritage.

The urge to conserve national monuments was driven by events beyond Britain's shores, too: the destruction of the architectural relics of the *ancien régime* during the ten tumultuous years of the French Revolution (1789–99) had the effect of heightening awareness of the need to preserve local British antiquities. To Carter and others, architectural demolition such as that wreaked on the Bastille in Paris in 1789 was the sign of dangerous political activity, and pointed to a British need to protect Gothic antiquities and the noble British past for which they stood. Additionally, the uncertainty of travel to the continent during the Napoleonic wars (1803–15) led to a rise in domestic tourism. The inherent beauty of many Gothic structures held an imaginative sway in late-eighteenth-century British culture for their tangible and intangible values, and increasingly they were regarded as symbolising notions of national identity, the historical associations that they stimulated seen as evocative reminders of a vanished chivalric age. Though he was notoriously not averse to taking a mallet to the ancient pile of Tintern Abbey so as to enhance its picturesque potential, William Gilpin's theory of the picturesque considerably enhanced the nascent spirit of conservation in the late eighteenth century. As Chapter 2 of this book has shown, his numerous publications on the picturesque gave rise to picturesque tourism, providing a new impetus to the pleasure to be found in landscape and nature and the pictorial potential of Gothic structures. Ruins, in particular, were brought to the fore as venerable cultural objects and the ideal subjects of amateur painting and sketching; their economic value as a tourist attraction increasingly meant that their decaying fabric was more likely to be preserved than demolished.

The eighteenth-century antiquarian interest in the architectural remains of the Gothic past at once paved the way for the rise of architectural history and set the terms for the nineteenth-century Gothic Revival. The artist and architectural draughtsman Augustus Charles Pugin's illustrations of Gothic antiquities in *Specimens of Gothic Architecture* (1821–3) and *Architectural Antiquities of Great Britain* (1826) created an impulse to use the past as a model for new architectural designs, and his architect son August Welby Northmore Pugin became a leading figure in the Victorian Gothic Revival. As the popularity of a poem such as John Clare's 'Elegy on the Ruins of Pickworth' (1817) attests, Gothic architecture remained firmly embedded in the British psyche in the first few decades of the nineteenth century. As the case study in this book has shown, Kenilworth Castle, Warwickshire, now in the care of English Heritage, became a site of pilgrimage after the publication of Walter Scott's *Kenilworth* (1821); similar fiction-inspired public interest in ruins occurred at Windsor Castle and the Tower of London, both having been the subjects of novels by the popular historical romancer William Harrison Ainsworth. Later in the nineteenth century, the architect-turned-author Thomas Hardy used a ruined Cistercian cloister setting in *Tess of the D'Urbervilles* (1891) as a means of heightening the narrative's emotional resonance at its moment of crisis.

With the terms of modern Gothic-architectural analysis formalised by the publication of Thomas Rickman's *An Attempt to Discriminate the Styles of English Architecture* (1817), ruins became the subject of greater scholarly rigour. The popularisation and commercialisation of the past through cheaply available literature, prints and engravings ensured that the nation's history belonged to everyone: no longer the exclusive preserve of the erudite antiquary, ruins and their conservation became matters of general, public interest. Herein, then, we might identify the origins of the modern 'heritage industry': the notion of preserving national heritage was one that transcended private interest, and by the end of the nineteenth century it was to become a subject of discourse for Parliamentarians and legislators.

Conserving Ancient Monuments

The principle of preserving historic structures has its roots in the European Renaissance, with the rediscovery of the Classical antiquities of Rome. In Britain, by contrast, the impulse to preserve came about largely as a result of the veneration of ecclesiastical Gothic buildings. The restoration of many English cathedrals in the eighteenth and nineteenth centuries, however, was not without its detractors, and interventions by architects were the subject of contentious debates that centred on the church as a site of commemoration, the Classicising tendencies of many modern improvements, and arguments regarding the compromising of the medieval structures' integrity (Sweet 2004: 277–307). The proposed restorations of the cathedrals of Salisbury, Lichfield, Hereford and Durham and of Westminster Abbey by architect James Wyatt, for instance, were much criticised and caused an outcry among many antiquaries of the day. Vehement arguments raged against Wyatt's architectural interventions, many of which were regarded as resulting in loss and damage to the historic fabric and the destruction of the buildings' integrity and authenticity through his conforming to modern ideas of beauty, taste and elegance. Further arguments were provoked about restoration and the place of the Gothic Revival style therein, events which led in 1839 to the formation of the Oxford Society for Promoting the Study of Gothic Architecture. As Prout has argued, the Oxford Society was founded with almost purely antiquarian aims, but it gradually expanded its role to encourage the use of archaeologically correct Gothic (Prout 1989). The Cambridge Camden (later Ecclesiological) Society of 1839 adopted the rallying cry 'God loves Gothic' in its aims to promote 'the study of Gothic Architecture and of Ecclesiastical Antiques' and to promote Gothic Revival style as a national idiom. Aiming to turn it into a more methodical academic study, Edward Freeman's *History of Architecture* (1849) attempted to wrest architectural history from the hands of antiquarian and ecclesiastical research. However, the pivotal role played by John Carter earlier in this philosophical furore should not be underestimated. As Sweet has argued:

> Carter could be said to have generated almost single-handed the concept of national heritage, to have made the connection between buildings and history as a form of public property and to have pioneered the belief in the Gothic as a distinctly English architectural idiom. More plausibly, he could also be said to be the first consistent campaigner in the cause of preservation, and to have

made some of the earliest demands for intervention to protect buildings against the wishes of those who were ostensibly the property owners. (Sweet 2004: 294–5)

His passionate and emotional campaign for the protection of national antiquities, mostly carried out in the pages of *The Gentleman's Magazine* between 1797 and 1817, had made them a subject of patriotic and national importance.

Controversial nineteenth-century Gothic restoration or Revival architects such as Eugène-Emmanuel Viollet-le-Duc in France and George Gilbert Scott in Britain attempted to interpret and rebuild medieval ruins in their original style, often 'enhancing' them with creative modifications and additions. The art critic John Ruskin utterly condemned this practice as 'a destruction out of which no remnants can be gathered: a destruction accompanied with false description of the thing destroyed' (Ruskin 1849: 194). In *The Seven Lamps of Architecture* (1849), Ruskin argued that restoration was tantamount to destruction, and that ancient buildings should be preserved without any attempt made to erase the accumulated history encoded in their decay. This tenet was echoed by William Morris, who was inspired by Ruskin to establish the Society for the Protection of Ancient Buildings (SPAB) in 1877, arguing for the repair rather than the restoration of Gothic piles. As opposed to the moral opprobrium invited by damaging acts of wholesale restoration, recreation and reconstruction, SPAB played a critical role in defining a careful and sensitive approach to architectural restoration and conservation.

Speaking of Castle Acre Priory in 1865, Henry Harrod, Honorary Secretary to the Norfolk and Norwich Archaeological Society, was an early articulate voice in the call for the protection of ruined monuments:

> [...] these noble buildings, raised by the piety and zeal of our forefathers, which our country now contains; and whilst I desire we may never again see such establishments in their ancient strength and vigour and covering the length and breadth of the land, I do trust to see the day when something like an organised system may be entered upon to preserve from further injury these valuable studies for the architect, the antiquary, and the historian. (Harrod 1857: 124)

The debates provoked by these learned societies concerning the correct philosophical approach to the conservation, modification or repair of ancient buildings still pertain to the philosophy and practice of ruin conservation today.

The rescue of Tattershall Castle, Lincolnshire, by Lord Curzon of Kedleston was a turning point in the history of conservation and the subject of much public attention. It became a cause célèbre in 1910–11 when it was sold and its fireplaces removed (Curzon bought and returned them in 1912). Persuasively arguing in favour of taking neglected and vulnerable important historic monuments into the care of the state, Lord Curzon maintained that the educational value of buildings such as Tattershall Castle lay in their ability to bring history to life, thus echoing the claims of the antiquaries and novelists of the nineteenth century. Using history to inspire the popular imagination, he argued that historic monuments 'are part of the heritage of the nation, because every citizen feels an intense interest in them; and they are part of the history of the nation, because they are documents just as valuable as reading the records of the past as is any manuscript or parchment deed to which you can refer' (Thurley 2013: 76). Arguing, like eighteenth-century antiquaries, for the importance of bringing the visual and the textual to bear on the task of conservation, Lord Curzon articulated a principle that still informs interpretation and display strategies at historic monument sites across Britain today.

Protecting Ancient Monuments

The formal legal system for the protection of historic buildings can be traced back to the Ancient Monuments Protection Act of 1882. The Ancient Monuments Protection Act of 1900 invested local authorities with the power to take direct action in the task of protecting ancient monuments, a category that now included medieval buildings. Further minor improvements were introduced in 1910, and the Ancient Monuments Consolidation and Amendment Act was passed in 1913. The key purpose of these successive Acts was to protect and conserve Britain's uninhabited ancient buildings. Legislation now defined its object as any 'monument or part or remains of a monument', claiming that their preservation was 'a matter of public interest by reason of the historic, architectural, traditional, artistic or archaeological interest attaching thereto' (quoted in Ashworth 1971: 349). The listing of inhabited historic buildings was not established until the Town and Country Planning Act of 1944. However, it was with the appointment of Sir Charles Reed Peers, former Secretary to the Society of Antiquaries of London, as Inspector to the Office of Works in 1910 that the care of ancient buildings was fundamentally transformed. Peers heralded a decisive moment in heritage protection, adopting, as he did, a sympathetic approach more akin to the earlier SPAB ethos of the repair rather than the restoration of ancient buildings. Now, interventions were to be made in as subtle and invisible a manner as possible, except in exceptional circumstances where reconstruction was deemed the only viable option to prevent structural collapse.

The Ancient Monuments Consolidation and Amendment Act of 1913 saw the division of the Office of Works's activities into three distinct parts: 'operating the protection system of preservation orders and scheduling; acquiring sites for guardianship and opening them to the public for education and enjoyment; and giving general advice about how best to protect monuments of national importance' (Thurley 2013: 79). Redundant ecclesiastical buildings owned by the Church of England were excluded, but some privately owned churches were taken into guardianship. The Act further extended the powers of the Commissioners of Works to 'prohibit or restrict the construction, alteration or extension of buildings in an area comprising or adjacent to an ancient monument', and for the first time 'the power to protect the setting of ancient monuments' was legally enshrined (Thurley 2013: 175-6). Peers rightly felt proud of what he had achieved in his twenty-three years as Inspector:

> The cumulative effect of a great ruined church and cloister, still retaining a goodly measure of its architectural beauty, and set reverently in a simple setting of grass lawns, can hardly fail of its appeal [...these monuments] may now become objects of pilgrimage to the traveller in Britain [...] and as the years go on, their numbers will increase and still further justify those who just fifty years ago first set legislation for the protection of ancient monuments in the Statute Book. (quoted in Thurley 2013: 147)

Responsibility for ancient monuments was removed from central government control when the National Heritage Act of 1983 established the Historic Buildings and Monuments Commission for England, a body that would later become known as English Heritage. Its remit was to 'secure the preservation of ancient monuments and historic buildings situated in England; to promote the preservation and enhancement of conservation areas situated in England; and to promote the public enjoyment of, and advance their knowledge of, Ancient Monuments and historic buildings situated in England, and their preservation' (quoted in Delafons 1997: 131). The Act was superseded by the British Government's Planning Policy Guidance Notes 15 and 16 (PPG 1990; PPG 1994), followed by the National Planning Policy Framework (NPPF) (2012). Today, English Heritage remains the principal organisation responsible for the care and protection of England's Scheduled Ancient Monuments, while Historic Scotland have responsibility in Scotland and Cadw in Wales.

Conservation Principles

Since the late nineteenth century, the tendency has been to conserve Scheduled Ancient Monuments to a purely technical and intellectual orthodoxy, often with the removal of all vegetation from the structure. This has considerably divested the verdant ruin of the picturesque potential that it held for the spectators, artists, poets and tourists of the eighteenth and nineteenth centuries: as Gustave Flaubert remarked in 1846, 'I love above all the sight of vegetation resting upon old ruins: this embrace of nature, coming swiftly to bury the work of man the moment his hand is no longer there to defend it, fills me with ample joy' (quoted in Roth 1997: 62). Buildings that fell under state protection as Scheduled Ancient Monuments in the late nineteenth and early twentieth centuries, by contrast, could no longer be presented as ivy-clad monuments in a state of decay. Although well intentioned, this had a detrimental effect on the ruins' visual impact and raised significant issues concerning notions of authenticity: as Thurley puts it, 'during the last three decades of the nineteenth century the Office of Works frequently found itself hailed not as the expert saviour of ancient buildings but condemned as the ignorant destroyer of them' (Thurley 2013: 32). The Ministry of Works thus radically altered the picturesque ruin and its setting by systematically clearing the site, often removing any post-medieval accretions, and displaying the monuments amid barren, closely clipped lawns. In the interests of revealing their architectural qualities and archaeological layout, ruins were stripped of many of the qualities that had made them so attractive to earlier tourists. This conflict between the archaeological and artistic approach to ruin presentation, with the corresponding loss of the verdancy and dynamism of nature, meant that the aesthetic, emotional engagement that these ancient ruins had so effectively induced for centuries was now largely absent. That the sterile display of ruins lessened emotional engagement was captured by Rose Macaulay in 1953 with her observation that, 'on the whole our ancestors [...] probably enjoyed themselves more than we, who are faced with the formidable piles of excavated and stratified ruins' (Macaulay 1953: 48). This instructive and non-romantic attitude to ruin presentation accounts for the way in which most of the sites owned by English Heritage, Historic Scotland and Cadw are seen today. Ironically, however, this mode of presentation is, itself, now being considered unsustainable, and the practice of 'soft capping', first trialled at Wigmore Castle, Herefordshire, by English Heritage in 1995, is currently being developed as an innovative conservation technique aimed at better conserving a ruin's romantic appeal. With soft capping, the visual appearance of the ruin remains verdant, although growth is carefully managed so that vegetation does not cause structural instability; interventions are only made to consolidate and repair where essential. Where practicable, Historic Scotland is also developing a similar philosophical approach at several ruined sites in their care. Thus newly developed conservation principles, alongside the four main conservation criteria – reversibility; minimal intervention; conserve as found; and like-for-like repair – may enhance the preservation of ruined structures where there is the imperative to minimise the alteration of its historical fabric, its visual impact and its setting. Together, these do much to preserve the site's *genius loci*, its ambience, its mood and its presiding spirit.

In order to explain and codify the often intangible values that underpin the significance of a site, English Heritage (who, along with the National Trust, has custodianship of many of the most important ruins) has condensed the numerous values of historic sites to produce a set of conservation principles. These have been distilled into an essential shortlist of four: evidential, historical, aesthetic and communal. Evidential value is defined as 'the potential of a place to yield evidence about past human activity'; historical value as 'the ways in which past people, events and aspects of life can be connected through a place to the present'; aesthetic value as 'the ways in which people draw sensory and intellectual stimulation from a place'; and communal value as 'the meanings of a place for the people who relate to it' (Historic England 2008). The National Trust takes a similar approach to English Heritage, referring to 'meanings and values: scientific and technical, aesthetic and spiritual'. These frameworks represent a positive initiative to structure an analysis of key values so that a rationale and policy for proposed works for the protection and conservation of ruins can be formulated (Harney 2014).

The Heritage Industry and Ruin Sites Today

In 1962, visitors to sites in Great Britain cared for by the Ministry of Works reached 7.55 million; by 2012, an estimated 17 million visited the 880 nationwide monuments in the National Heritage Collection managed by English Heritage. The contribution of cultural tourists to the British economy is thus significant and accounts for the largest segment of the tourist industry: some 15 million heritage tourists visit the UK per year, and this, in turn, directly generates £5 billion in GDP and creates no fewer than 134,000 jobs. Most tourists come to Great Britain to see first-hand the nation's distinctive, tangible visual heritage in the care of the National Heritage Collection, National Trust and the Churches Conservation Trust (established in 1969), and it is thus vital that we preserve the value of cultural heritage sites for future generations to enjoy.

The cultural significance and value of ruin sites such as Fountains Abbey and Studley Royal Park in North Yorkshire are recognised in their inscription in 1986 as UNESCO World Heritage sites, and consequently they are visited by hundreds of thousands of visitors each year. The challenge today is to maintain the rich visual iconography and aesthetic quality of these and other such ruin sites while still providing an authentic and engaging visitor experience. Ruins such as the Yorkshire abbeys at Rievaulx, Fountains and Roche were incorporated into landscape parks, and retain much of the evocative romantic character and appeal that they exuded in the eighteenth and early nineteenth centuries. Roche Abbey, South Yorkshire, a Cistercian monastery founded in 1147, still retains early Gothic transepts to their original height, structures that are the finest early examples of Gothic architecture in Britain. Following its dissolution in 1538, Roche Abbey was left as a ruin until it was acquired by the 4th Earl of Scarborough. He commissioned Lancelot 'Capability' Brown to redesign the landscape 'with Poets feeling and with Painter's eye' – a line in the contract from William Mason's *The English Garden* (1772–82) – to enhance his adjoining family seat at Sandbeck Park (Yorkshire Gardens Trust and the New Arcadian Press n.d.). Brown subjected the remains to further ruination by extensive demolition, including the cloister in 1774, leaving only two transepts standing, to give it a more pleasing romantic aspect. Roche Abbey is now in the care of English Heritage, and Sandbeck Park remains in the hands of the Earls of Scarborough.

Much the same applies to Rievaulx Abbey, North Yorkshire. This remarkable ruin became a popular subject for Romantic artists in the eighteenth and nineteenth centuries. The first Cistercian church to be built in England and one of the most important early English-style churches in Britain, Rievaulx was founded in 1132, suppressed under the Dissolution of the Monasteries in 1538 and subsequently granted to the 1st Earl of Rutland, Thomas Manners, who immediately dismantled it with much of the building material being used in other construction projects in the area. In 1687 the estate was sold to Sir Charles Duncombe, whose nephew, Thomas Duncombe, further extended the park along the Rye valley in the 1750s, creating a picturesque setting for the romantic ruin which became a visitor attraction and subject for artists and writers from the 1770s onwards. As W. Monkhouse wrote in 1845, 'Here, in a lovely vale, embosomed amidst steep hills, covered with verdant overhanging woods, the river Rie, from whence the abbey took its name, winds its course through the meadows, and near to it stand the remains of the venerable abbey; which, though presenting a mournful contrast to its former magnificence, is still majestic and enchanting in ruin' (Monkhouse 1845: 8).

Although the abbey ruins are now in the care of English Heritage, with the National Trust managing the estate, this was one of the first sites to be transferred into the guardianship of the Office of Works in 1917. Conserved by Peers, all post-Reformation buildings and fallen masonry were removed from the site in order better to 'read' the original plan, and the landscape adapted to lawn throughout. Albeit with most interventions carefully disguised to give the appearance of authenticity and minimal intervention, the buildings were made structurally more stable by using a variety of largely irreversible conservation techniques, including reconstruction, strengthening through the insertion of modern materials such as steel, and extensive repair work carried out using Portland cement. Current conservation methodologies and practice adhere to revised principles, with soft capping techniques used in some areas to conserve the remains and enhance the visitor experience. Although, along with tile repairs and replacement masonry, evidence of damage and erosion of historic fabric caused by early concrete-based repairs remains clearly visible, these adhere to the SPAB principles of honest repair. While modern signage might diminish the aesthetic experience, it provides necessary interpretation and guidance, and, for the most part, the fine balance between education and the opportunity for imaginative exploration is well handled.

Fountains Abbey, established in 1132 by Archbishop Thurston of York and the largest monastic ruin in the country, was described by John Richard Walbran in the mid-nineteenth century as 'a captivating scene of landscape and architectural beauty, a highly interesting subject of contemplation, and a source of that pensive and pleasing melancholy in which the mind sometimes loves to indulge' (Walbran 1856: 65). The richest Cistercian monastery before the Dissolution, it was voluntarily surrendered to the King in 1539, and by 1540 the abbey had been pillaged, stripped of its lead, glass and timber and left as an empty shell. When Sir Stephen Proctor acquired it in 1597, he used stone from the monastic complex to build Fountains Hall. The Studley Royal Estate, inherited in 1693 by John Aislabie, was separate from Fountains Abbey until 1767. In 1718 John Aislabie began construction of the formal water garden at Studley Royal, and after his death in 1742 his son William purchased the remains of Fountains Abbey in 1767 and, incorporating it into an extended landscape in the picturesque Romantic style, created an important eighteenth-century water garden. The abbey and its landscape remained in family ownership until 1966, when the estate was sold to West Riding County Council. It was acquired by the National Trust in 1983 and is managed in partnership with English Heritage. It is inscribed as a UNESCO World Heritage site today as 'a true masterpiece of human creative genius' (UNESCO).

Fountains Abbey today is an outstanding example of the application of subtle, modern conservation techniques, and, with every endeavour made to camouflage their appearance, the interventions remain discreet. It is a model of minimal intervention insofar as replaced or repaired masonry is indistinguishable from the original and little historic fabric has been removed or replaced. The presentation of the site has been carefully considered to enhance its setting and sense of place or *genius loci,* with vegetation allowed to flourish and bare earth floors throughout the building adding to its naturalistic feel. Apart from strategically placed lighting, signage and interpretation are negligible, allowing the spectator to appreciate the visual integrity of the abbey and its setting in ways that retain its original ambience and imaginative appeal.

Ruin Visiting Today

As the British Government's Policy Planning Guidance Note on 'Planning and the Historic Environment' claims, 'The physical survivals of our past are to be valued for their own sake, as a central part of our cultural heritage and our sense of identity. They are an irreplaceable record which contributes, through formal education and in many other ways, to our understanding of both the present and the past' (PPG 1994: 1 1.1). Ruins today are ubiquitous throughout the British landscape, and collectively represent and exemplify all periods of architectural history and building type. They thus remain as relevant in contemporary society as they did in the eighteenth century. It is true that the conservation of vulnerable ruins requires an approach that is different from that applied to other historic buildings. Because they remain exposed to the elements, they are more prone to an accelerated rate of deterioration; visual and literary presentation is thus as fundamental a consideration today as it was in the eighteenth century. Christopher Woodward has summed up this challenge in the evocative claim that:

> Preservation is not wholly an archaeologist's job: it involves understanding of the ruin as a ruin, and its re-creation of a work of art in its own right [...] A ruin is more than a collection of debris. It is

a place with its own individuality, charged with its own emotion and atmosphere and drama, of grandeur, of nobility, or of charm. These qualities must be preserved as carefully as the broken stones which are their physical embodiment. (Woodward 2001: 212–13)

As it did in earlier periods, it remains the task of literature and visual culture to capture and preserve ruins' spell-binding effects. Although the debates concerning their preservation and conservation were initiated during the eighteenth century, it is testimony to their enduring appeal to our senses and cultural values that we continue to maintain these architectural fragments for the aesthetic pleasure they offer of the unknown, their pathos and their ability to stimulate the imagination through evoking the history and culture of times past.

Further Reading

Briggs, Martin S. 1952. *Goths and Vandals: A Study of the Destruction, Neglect, and Preservation of the Historical Buildings in England* (London: Constable).

Jokilehto, Jukka. 1999. *A History of Architectural Conservation* (Oxford: Butterworth Heinemann).

References

Ashworth, Graham. 1971. 'Contemporary Developments in British Preservation Law and Practice', *Law and Contemporary Problems* 36, no. 3 (Summer 1971): 348–61.

Delafons, John. 1997. *Politics and Preservation: A Policy History of the Built Heritage, 1882–1996* (London: Chapman and Hall).

Denham, John. 1642. *Cooper's Hill. A Poeme* (London: Printed for Thomas Walkley).

Harney, Marion. 2013. *Place-making for the Imagination: Horace Walpole and Strawberry Hill* (Farnham: Ashgate).

Harney, Marion. 2014. *Gardens and Landscapes in Historic Building Conservation* (Chichester: Wiley-Blackwell).

Harrod, Henry. 1857. *Gleanings Among the Castles and Convents of Norfolk* (Norwich: Published by Subscription).

Heely, Joseph. 1777. *Letters on the Beauties of Hagley, Envil, and the Leasowes. With Critical Remarks, and Observations on the Modern Taste in Gardening*, 2 vols (London: Printed for R. Baldwin).

Historic England. 2008. *Conservation Principles, Policies and Guidance*, https://historicengland.org.uk/advice/constructive-conservation/conservation-principles [last accessed 30 May 2017].

Macaulay, Rose. 1953. *Pleasure of Ruins* (New York: Walker and Company).

Monkhouse, W. 1845. *Brief Historical and Descriptive Account of Rievaulx Abbey, in the North Riding of the County of York* (York: R. Pickering).

PPG. 1990. *Planning Policy Guidance Note 16*, November 1990. http://webarchive.nationalarchives.gov.uk/20120919132719/http://www.communities.gov.uk/documents/planningandbuilding/pdf/156777.pdf [last accessed 7 June 2017].

PPG. 1994. *Planning Policy Guidance Note 15*, September 1994. https://www.periodproperty.co.uk/pdf/Planning_Policy_Guidance_15_Sept_1994.pdf [last accessed 30 May 2017].

Prout, David. 1989. '"The Oxford Society for Promoting the Study of Gothic Architecture" and "The Oxford Architectural Society", 1839–60', *Oxoniensia* 54: 379–91.

Roth, Michael (ed.). 1997. *Irresistible Decay: Ruins Reclaimed* (Los Angeles: Getty Research Institute).

Ruskin, John. 1849. *The Seven Lamps of Architecture* (London: Smith, Elder and Co.).

Shakespeare, William. 2008. *The Norton Shakespeare, Based on the Oxford Edition*, 2nd edn, edited by Stephen Greenblatt, Walter Cohen, Jean E. Howard and Katharine Eisaman Maus (New York and London: W. W. Norton & Co.).

Sweet, Rosemary. 2004. *Antiquaries: The Discovery of the Past in Eighteenth-Century Britain* (London: Hambledon & London).

Thurley, Simon. 2013. *Men from the Ministry: How Britain Saved its Heritage* (New Haven: Yale University Press).

UNESCO. *World Heritage List*, Studley Royal Park including the Ruins of Fountains Abbey, http://whc.unesco.org/en/list/372 [last accessed 30 May 2017].

Walbran, John Richard. 1856. *A Guide to Ripon, Harrogate, Fountains Abbey, Bolton Priory, and Several Places of Interest in their Vicinity*, 5th edn (Ripon: W. Harrison).

Walpole, Horace. 1762. *Anecdotes of Painting in England; With Some Account of the Principal Artists; And Incidental Notes on Other Arts; Collected by the Late Mr. George Vertue; and Now Digested and Published from His Original MSS, Vol. I* (Strawberry Hill: Printed by Thomas Farmer).

Walpole, Horace. 1973. *The Yale Edition of Horace Walpole's Correspondence, Vol. Thirty-Five*, edited by W. S. Lewis et al. (New Haven: Yale University Press).

Webster, John. 1986. *The Duchess of Malfi*, edited by Elizabeth M. Brennan (New York: W. W. Norton & Co.).

Williamson, John. 1852. *Glastonbury Abbey: Its History and Ruins* (Wells: Printed and Published by T. Green).

Woodward, Christopher. 2001. *In Ruins* (London: Chatto and Windus).

Yorkshire Gardens Trust and the New Arcadian Press. 'Roche Abbey', http://www.capabilitybrown.org/garden/roche-abbey [last accessed 30 May 2017].

Picture Credits

All images © The British Library Board, except:

Pages 40, 89, 234 British Museum Images; 199 The Clark Institute/Bridgeman Images; 134, 137 Reproduced with the kind permission of Devon Archives and Local Studies Service.

Index

Figures in *italic* refer to pages on which illustration captions appear

A. B., 'Ruins of the Abbey at Aberbrothock' (1775) 106–107
Abbey Dore, Herefordshire 25
Abbotsford, Roxburghshire 195
Aberbrothock (abbey), Angus 106–107
Aberdeen Cathedral 30
Act of Suppression (1536) 16–17
Acts of Union (Britain/Ireland) (1801) 247
Addison, Joseph 85–7
'Adeline' (poet) 236, 237–8
Aikin, Anna Laetitia (later Barbauld) 250
  Eighteen Hundred and Eleven (1812) 264–5
  Miscellaneous Pieces (with J. Aikin, 1773) 169
  'Sir Bertrand' (with J. Aikin, 1773) 143
Aikin, John 83–4
  Miscellaneous Pieces (with A. Aikin, 1773) 169
  'Sir Bertrand' (with A. Aikin, 1773) 143
Akenside, Mark 87
All Hallows, Dublin 27
Alloway Kirk, South Ayrshire 216, 217, 218, 219–21
Ancient Monuments Protection Act (1882) 67, 287
Anderson, James 231
Anderson, William 163
Anon., 'On the Ruins of M__ le Chapel in Hertfordshire' (1759) 109–10
anti-Catholicism 102, 168–9,
171, 185–86
Antiquarian Repertory, The 56, 59, 63
antiquarianism 43, 44–5, 68, 83–4, 159, 278–9, 281, 284
antiquaries 43–44, 66–7, 83, 152, 159
  publications of 46–9, 54–7, 59–62, 281
  'scientific approach' 58–9, 64, 66–7, 74–5, 83, 278
  see also under individual names
archaeology 67
Arthur's O'on, Borders 62
Arthurian legend 80, 81, 204–206, 237
artists 98–9, *98*, 133, *133*, 135, 173; *see also under individual names*
associationism, architectural 84, 86, 87–8, 97, 102, 169
astronomy 77
Athlone church, Co. Westmeath 28
Aubrey, John 77, 276, 279
Augustinian Order 26, 28
Austen, Jane 179, 210

Baalbek 259, 261
Baillie, John 87
Bale, John 13
Bannerman, Anne 211–12
Barbauld, Anna Laetitia *see* Aikin, Anna Laetitia
Barbour, John 163
Berkhamstead Castle, Hertfordshire 107–108
Bartlett, W. H. 204
Basingwerk Abbey, Flintshire 25
Bateman, Dickie 273–4
Bath 77
Bath Abbey, Somerset 279
Bathurst, Lord 90, 280
Battle Abbey, Sussex 22, 23
Bayly, Thomas Haynes 229, 232
Beattie, James 103, 142
  'Retirement' (1758) 144
Beaumaris Castle, Anglesey 270–72
Benedictine Order 15, 17, 24, 73
Bentham, James 59
Bentley, Richard 104
Berkeley Castle, Gloucestershire 36
Berry Pomeroy Castle, Devon 240, 241–2, *240*
Black, Adam and Charles
  Guide through North and South Wales (1864) 270
  Tourist and Road-Book (1847) 153–4, *155*
Blackmore, Sir Richard 205
Blenheim, Oxfordshire, ruins at 278
Bloomfield, Robert 139–40, 148, *148*, 149, 179
Borra, Giovanni Battista 259, 260, *260*, 261
Boswell, James 158
Boughton, Frederica Rouse 154–5
Bouverie, John 259
Bower, John 189, 193, 194, 195–6, 197
Bowles, William Lisle 142, 172
Boxley, Kent (abbey) 13
Boyle Abbey, Co. Roscommon 28
Brand, John 251–2, 254–5
Bray, Eliza 242
Bray, William 64–5
Brayley, Edward *see* Britton, John

INDEX

Bridlington Priory, Yorkshire 25
British history, associating ruins with 90, 95, 108, 109, 126, 145-7, 205-206, 276
Britton, John 66, 237
Beauties of England and Wales (with Brayley, 1801-15) 61-2
Brown, Lancelot 'Capability' 126, 129, 292
Brown, Thomas 205
Brown, William 24
Brunton, Mary 179
Buck, Samuel and Nathaniel 41, 173, 207
Rhuddlan Castle 165, 166
Views of Ruins of Castles and Abbeys... (1726) 51, 52, 53
Buckler, John 20
Buller, John 175
Burges, William 129
Burgess, Thomas 57
Burke, Edmund 87-8, 244, 266
Burns, Robert 215-16
'Tam o'Shanter' (1791) 216-21
Bury St Edmunds church, Suffolk 23
Bury St Edmunds Abbey, Suffolk 18
Bute, 3rd Marquess of 129
Byland Abbey, Yorkshire 24
Byng, John 136-7, 145, 146, 147-8, 149
Tour of South Wales (1787) 151
Byron, Lord 117-18, 121, 122-3
Childe Harold's Pilgrimage (1812) 120-21
Don Juan (1819-24) 112, 121, 122, 123, 221-7
'Elegy on Newstead Abbey' (1807) 117, 119, 121
'Epistle to Augusta' (1818) 121
'Newstead Abbey' (1811) 118, 120
'On Leaving Newstead Abbey' (1803) 117, 118, 119-20

Cadw 289, 290
Caerleon (Roman fortress), Gwent 45
Caernarfon Castle, Gwynedd 40-41, 40, 149
Caerphilly Castle, Caerphilly 138-9

Calvert, Frederick 180
Cambridge Camden Society 285
Camden, William 45, 51, 76, 278
Campbell, Castle, Scotland 138, 141
Capability Brown *see* Brown, Lancelot 'Capability'
Cardiff Castle, Glamorgan 128-30, 128
Carlingford, Co. Louth 28
Carmelite Order 25
Carn Brea Castle, Cornwall 139
Carter, Elizabeth 175
Carter, John 58, 63, 74, 282-3, 285-6
Castle Acre Priory, Norfolk 285
castles 33-36, 56, 57, 58, 59, 254; *see also under individual entries*
Catholics/Catholicism 20, 22, 25-6, 28, 46, 168, 185
in Ireland 28
in Scotland 31, 51-2
see also anti-Catholicism; Counter-Reformation; monasticism/monastic revival
Cathrall, William 207
Catton Jnr, C. 162
Chambers, William 88
Chapman, R. W. 158
Chard, Abbot Thomas 14
Charterhouse, London 23
Charterhouse, Perth 30
Chepstow Castle, Monmouthshire 149
Chertsey Abbey, Surrey 19, 100
Chichester, Sussex 152
Cholmley, Sir Hugh 33-4
Chute, John 282
Cilgerran Castle, Pembrokeshire 143
Cirencester Park, Gloucestershire 89, 53, 90, 280
Cistercian Order 15, 26, 27, 170, 214, 292; *see also under individual entries*
Civil Wars (1642-51) 13-14, 32-6, 41, 45, 95
buildings ruined during 32-6, 46, 73, 97, 233, 254, 277
reflections on (in poetry) 100

Welsh castles, use of 165-6, 268
Clane Friary, Co. Kildare 27
Clare, John 75
Clarke, Edward Daniel 142-3
Tour through the South of England... (1793) 143-4, 146, 147, 149-50
Classicism 86-7, 88, 92, 93-4, 141, 246, 257-8
Claude Glasses 98-9, 176
Clifford, Rosamund 102-103
Clontuskert, Co. Galway (Augustinian friary) 28
Colchester (abbey), Essex 17
Coleridge, John Taylor 141
Coleridge, Samuel Taylor 140, 141
Lyrical Ballads (with Wordsworth, 1798) 177
College Green, Dublin 247, 247, 248-9
Collins, Edward 185
Combe, Thomas 98, 99
conservation 37, 279, 283, 284-7, 288, 290-91, 293, 294-5
and legislation 65-6, 67, 287-9
see also preservationism; restoration
Constable, John 173
consumerism 154, 261
consumption, ruins as places of 132, 135-6, 150, 154, 175
Conwy Castle 233-5
Cooke, J. W. 256
Cooke, Rev. William 103
Cooper's Hill, Egham, Surrey 100-101
Copland, John 193, 253-4
Cotman, John Sell 75, 207
Cottle, Joseph 80
Counter-Reformation 28; *see also* monasticism/monastic revival
Craigmillar Castle, Edinburgh 111
Cranbury Park, Worcestershire 280
Croker, John Wilson 264
Croker, Thomas Crofton 255-6
Cromwell, Thomas 16, 19, 22, 46, 73, 97, 139
Crosby Hall, Bishopsgate 66, 68
Crow Castle *see* Dinas Bran
Crowe, William 142
Croyland Abbey, Lincolnshire

299

72-75, *72*
Cundall, Henry (abbot) 23
Cunningham, John 252-3
Cuttle Mill, Rousham, Oxfordshire 280

Daguerre, Louis-Jacques-Mande 236
Daniel, Samuel
  Complaint of Rosamond (1592) 102
  'Musophilus' (1599) 76-7
Daniel, Walter 170
Darcy, Sir Arthur 18
Dartmoor, Devon 141, 147
Dartmouth Castle, Devon 64
Davies, Sneyd 179
Dayes, E. *178*
de Loutherbourg, Philippe-Jacques 99, *182*
Defoe, Daniel 51
Denbigh Castle, Denbighshire 140, 143
Denham, John 47, 100-101, 277
Dibdin, Charles 144
Dibdin, Thomas 197
Dinas Bran (Crow Castle), Wales *146*, 155
disrepair, ruins falling into 64-5, 66, 149-50, 153, 159
Dissolution of the Monasteries (1536-1540) 13-17, 21-3, 36, 45-6, 49, 79, 102, 139
  destruction/asset stripping 18-21, 27, 254, 277, 279-80, 293
  reflections on (poetry) 100, 167, 172, 184-5
  see also monasticism/monastic revival
Dominican Order 18, 27, 28
Donnington Castle, Berkshire 97
Dover Castle, Kent 36
Drogheda, Co. Dundalk 255
druids 49, 77, 159, 162
Dryburgh Abbey, Scottish Borders 162-4, *162*
Dublin 27
Dudley Castle, West Midlands 142
Dudley, Robert, Earl of Leicester 35
Dugdale, William 34, *35*, 46-7
Dummer, Thomas 174
Dunblane Cathedral, Perthshire 31
Dunbrody Abbey, Co. Wexford 28

Dundee 29
Dunfermline Abbey, Fife 30, 31-2
Dyer, John 103-105, 258-9

Earle, William 165, 166
Edgeworth, Maria 257
Edward I, King of England 233, 270
elegies 106; *see also* poetry; *and under individual authors*
Elgin friary, Moray 32
Elizabeth I, Queen of England 21, 22, 26, 208
England Displayed 56-7
England, medieval 15, 32-3, 36, 45, 59; *see also under individual place names*
English Heritage 289, 290-91, 292, 293, 294
English, John 211
engravings, publications/collections of 41, 51, 53, 54, 62, 68, 281-2, 283, 284; *see also under individual artists*
Ennis Friary, Co. Clare 28
episcopacy, abolition of 30-31
Essex, James 126
Etchingham, Sir Osborne 28
Evans, John 40
executions (of abbots) 17, 79-80

Fairbairn, Margaret 193
Farmer, John 48
Fielding, Henry 205
Fittler, James 188-9
Flamborough parish church, Yorkshire 25
follies *89*, 90, 94, 125, *125*, 168, 179, 274, 280
food and drink, consumption of 135-6, 150
Forde Abbey, Dorset 14
Forsyth, Joseph 49-50
Fountains Abbey, Yorkshire 15, *51*, 279, 291, 293-4
Franciscan Order 16, 19, 27-8
Freeman, Edward 285
French Revolution (1789) 58, 172, 175, 183, 187, 266, 283
Furness Abbey, Lancashire (as was) 17, 61, 112, 131, 132, *213*
ghosts of 212-15

G. J., 'Spontaneous Thoughts...' (1776) 111
Gainsborough, Thomas 179

Gale, Roger 189
Galway, Franciscan church at 28
Gandy, Joseph Michael 237
Gardner, Edmund 179
Gastineau, Henry 207
Gentleman's Magazine, The 59, 63, 66, 109, 283, 285
Geoffrey of Monmouth 76
Gerald of Wales 45
Gerard, Alexander 88
ghosts 86, 103, 166, 210-14, 215, 220, 230-32, 235
  in Romantic literature 211, 222-27, 242; *see also under individual entries*
Gibson, Edmund 278-9
Gilpin, William 54, 64, 94, 98, 139, 254, 283
  Observations on the River Wye... (1782) 95-7, *95*, 181-2
  Observations on the Western Parts of England (1798) 173, 176, 250-51
Girtin, Thomas 75, 188
  Great Hall, Conwy Castle 233, *234*
Glasgow Cathedral 31
Glasgow friary 32
Glasse, J. 107-108
Glastonbury Abbey, Somerset 17, 48, 64, 80, 250-51
Gloucester Greyfriars, Gloucestershire 23
Godstow Abbey, Oxfordshire 102-103
Goldsmith, Oliver 263-4
Goodrich Castle, Hertfordshire 33, *33*, 34, 145, 151
Gothic aesthetic 43, 53, 54, 88, 93-4, 257, 282-3; *see also* Gothic architecture; Gothic Revival
Gothic architecture 49, 54, 61, 88, 93-4, 96, 246, 275, 278, 280-81, 282-3, 284, 292
  and associationist aesthetics 86-7, 88, 102
  use in landscape gardens 53, 280-81
  see also follies; Gothic Revival
Gothic literature 43, 59, 86, 186, 187, 222, 241; *see also under individual author names*
Gothic Revival 129-30, 284, 285
Gough, Richard 50-51, 58, 63,

73, 74, 282
Bibliotheca Topographica Britannica 74-5
Grace, Pilgrimage of (1536) 17
Grand Tour, the 50, 100; *see also* tourism
Graveyard School 103-104
Gray, Thomas 140, 142, 173-4, 179, 214
  The Bard (1757) 205
  Elegy Written in a Country Church Yard (1751) *104*, 105, 140
  'Paths of Glory lead but to the Grave' (1751) 105
Greece, ancient, ruins/monuments of 50
Grenville, Lord 138-9, 145
Grey, Lord Deputy 27
Grose, Francis
  Antiquities of England and Wales (1772-6/c. 1784) 55-56, 59, 61, 179, 186
  Antiquities of Ireland (1791-5) 56
  Antiquities of Scotland (1789-91/1797) 56, 162, 163, 189, 217, 239
  Pevensey Castle 55
guidebooks 135, 145, 150-54, 159, 173, 189, 191, 193; *see also under individual entries*
guides/guiding (tourism) 148-9, 159, 194, 196

Hagley Hall, Worcestershire 90, *91*, 125, 262, 280-81
Hailes Abbey, Gloucestershire 21, 25, 279
Haistwell, Edward 54
Halesowen Abbey, Worcestershire 279-80
Halley, Edmond 77
Hamilton, Gavin 261
Hamley, Edward 172
Hardwicke, Lord Chancellor 125-6
Hardy, Thomas 284
Harewood Castle, Yorkshire 142
Harlech Castle, Gwynedd 207-208, *207*
Harood, Henry 285
Harraden, J. B. 133, *133*, 173
Hartley, David 87
Hawkesworth, Colonel Joseph 34-5
Hearne, Thomas 59, *60*, 61, *213*, 282
Heath, Charles 151-3

Descriptive Account of Tintern Abbey (1793) 152-3, 181
Excursion down the Wye (1826) 149, 150-52
Heely, Joseph 281
Heman, Felicia 163
Henry II, King of England 80, 81, 102, 103
Henry VIII, King of England and Ireland 13, 15-16, 24, 46, 47, 73, 172, 184
Herbert, William 72
heritage industry 284, 291, 293
Historic Scotland 289, 290
Hitchins, J. 245
Hodge, William 108
Hogg, Thomas 204
Holm Cultram, Cumberland, monastic church at 22
Home, Henry, Lord Kames 93, 257
Howitt, William 238
Hume, David 87
Hurd, Richard 57
Hutcheson, Francis 87
Hutchinson, William 189
Hyatt, Sophia 122

Ince, Henry 239
Incholm Abbey 32
industry/industrial activity 180-82, *181*, 183-4, 234
Ingulphus 73, 74
Inverness friary, Invernessshire 32
Iona, Argyll and Bute 158, 159-60, *159*
Ireland 26, 27-8, 255
  ruins in 37, 255-7
  see also under individual place names
Irving, Washington
  Abbotsford/Melrose abbey visit 195-6, 197
  Newstead Abbey visit 117-18, 122
ivy *see* vegetation

Jacobite Rebellion (1745) 90, 95
Jedburgh Abbey, Roxburghshire 29
Jerningham, Edward 179
  Elegy... (1765) 168-9, 252
Jervaulx Abbey, Yorkshire 18
Jesus College, Cambridge 15
Jewry Wall, Leicester 67

Johnson, Samuel 41
  Lives of the Most Eminent English Poets (1779-81) 100-101
  Tour to the Hebrides (1785) 158

Keate, George 171-2, 253
Kenilworth Castle, Warwickshire 33, 34-5, *35*, 131, 142, 283
King Alfred's Hall, Cirencester *89*, 90
King, Edward 59
King's College, Aberdeen 29, 30
Kirkstall Abbey, Yorkshire 19, 20, 24, 64
  Swete's visit to 137-8, *137*, 139
Knight, Richard Payne 94, 282

Lake, J. W. 116
landscape 73, 94, 95-6, 99, 132, 145, 274, 279
  and art 96-7, 145, 251, 275
  and poetry 100, 101
  see also landscape gardens
landscape gardens 43, 53, 84, 88-92, 93, 94, 97, 99, 257, 280; *see also* follies
Langhorne, John 106
Leadbeater, Mary 267
Leasowes, The and Priory, Worcestershire *92*, 93, 168, 280
Leland, John 23, 80, 205
Lewes Priory, Sussex 19
Lewis, George Robert *273*
Lewis, Matthew
  The Castle Spectre (1798) 235
  The Monk (1796) 210
libraries 23-24, 25
Lichfield Cathedral 32
Lincoln, Bishops' Palace 32-33
Lincolnshire Rising 17
Lindores Abbey, Fife 29
literature/novels 73, 174, 284; *see also* Gothic literature; *and under individual author names*
Llanthony Abbey, Monmouthshire 64
Llwyd, Richard 271
Locke, John 84-5, 87-8
Longfellow, Henry

Wadsworth 101
Lovell, Viscount Francis 230-31
Ludlow Castle, Shropshire 108
Lyttelton, Charles 53, 281
Lyttleton, Thomas 91, 262-3

Mabinogion, Macsen Wledig romance 41
Malkin, Charlotte 137, 138, 141
Malmesbury, Wiltshire, ruins at 22, 49, *60*, 62, 279
Manners, Thomas, Earl of Rutland 18, 292
Margam Abbey, Glamorgan 149-50
Mary, Queen of England 20, 22, 25-6
Mason, William 93-4
Maton, William George 205-206, 241
Maturin, Charles Robert
  Milesian Chief (1812) 257
  Women (1818) 248-9
Maynooth College, Co. Kildare 27
McLellan, Henry Blake 193
Meaux Abbey, Yorkshire 19
medievalism 25, 26, 29-33, 36, 41, 45, 57, 58, 63-4, 68
melancholy, ruins inciting feelings of 56, 57, 91, 93, 103-106, 108-109, 138, 172, 257, 260, 275; *see also* memento mori
Melrose Abbey, Roxburghshire 29-30, 162, 176, 188-89, 198-99, *199*, 253, 254, 264
  guidebooks 189, 193, 194
  tourist experience at 189, 193-5, 197-8, 199-200
memento mori, ruins as 89-90, 109-11, 138
Miller, Sanderson 53, 90, 125, 126, 262, 280-81
Milles, Jeremiah 53
Milton, John 101-102, 103, 142
Minsden Chapel, Hertfordshire 107, 109
Minster Lovell Hall, Oxfordshire 229-30, *229*
Mitford, Mary Russell 170
monastic buildings 13, 21, 22, 26, 46, 47-9, 169
  asset stripping 17-21, 23-5, 27
  conversion of 15, 21-3, 27-8, 32, 279
  see also recycling/salvage (building materials)
monasticism/monastic revival 14-15, 20, 22, 25-6, 168
Monk Bretton Priory, Yorkshire 24
Montague, Edward 240-41
moonlight, viewing ruins by 4, 133, 152, 173, 190, 191, 193, 194, 196, 197-8, 199-200, *199*
Moore Abbey, Co. Kildare 28
Moore, James 12, *229*
Moore, Thomas 194
Morgan, Lady (previously Owenson, Sydney) 249-50
Morris, William 285
Murray, John 154
music 139-40, 146

Nash, John 282
National Trust 291, 292, 293-4
Neath Abbey, Glamorgan 58
Netley Abbey, Hampshire 23, 99, 133, *133*, 170-76, *173*, 280
Newstead Abbey, Nottinghamshire 116-23, *116*, 123, 222, 279
Newton, Richard 205

O'Keefe, Adelaide 248
Owain Glyn Dŵr, uprising of 208
Owenson, Sydney *see* Morgan, Lady

Palladianism 87, 96
Palmyra 259-60, 261
Parliament House, Dublin 247, *247*, 249, 250
Pearce, William 174-5, 176
Peele Castle, Lancashire 112
Peers, Sir Charles Reed 288
Pennant, Thomas
  Tour in Scotland (1774/1776) 30, 159, 188
  Tour in Wales (1778-83) 207
Penny Magazine 68
Pershore church, Worcestershire 22
Petty-Fitzmaurice, Lord Henry, Marquess of Lansdowne 246
Pevensey Castle, Sussex 55
Pichot, Amédée 193
picturesque theory/movement 43, 54, 55, 57, 64-5, 66, 84, 94, 180, 282
  and architecture 94-5, 96-7, 183, 254
  and art 83, 96, 98-9, *98*
  and landscape 91, 95-6
  and literature 83, 183
  and tourism 98-9, *98*, 132, 133-5, 170, 178-9, 282
  pilgrimage, sites of 13, 27, 123
  see also under individual place names
Pinkerton, John 111
Plas yn y Pentre, Valle Crucis Abbey, Denbighshire 23
poetry 40, 57, 76, 80, 100, 112, 140-43, 145, 178
  ruin 100-103, 111-12, 117, 142, 170, 186, 251-2, 259, 260
  topographical 77-8, 100-101, 103, 106-12, 142;
  see also Graveyard School; *and under individual names*
politics 243, 247
Pontefract Castle, Yorkshire 35-6, 109, 139
Pope, Alexander
  'Eloisa to Abelard' (1717) 102, 103, 142
  An Epistle to... Richard Earl of Burlington (1731) 92-3
Portinari, Giovanni 19
preservationism 52-3, 59, 62-63, 65-6, 67, 282, 283, 284-6, 294-5
Price, Uvedale 58, 94-5, 282
Prince, Rev. John 240
print trade 54, 63, 68; *see also* engravings, publications/collections of
Protestant Reformation (1560) 13, 29-32, 36, 46, 51, 73, 102, 168-9, 184, 210, 226, 253
Protestants/Protestantism 13, 28, 29-32, 102
  and anti-Catholic sentiment 102, 168, 185-6
  see also Protestant Reformation
publishing industry 54, 67-8; *see also* antiquaries; print trade
Pugin, August Welby Northmore 284
Pugin, Augustus Charles 284

R. S. 'An Evening Walk' (1760) 110-11
Radcliffe, Ann 212-14
Radway Grange, Edgehill, Warwickshire 90, 125, 280
Raglan Castle, Monmouthshire 97, 149, 150-51

INDEX

railway guides 68
Rawlinson, Richard 48, 80
Reading Abbey, Berkshire 17, 21
recycling/salvage (building materials) 17, 25, 27, 32, 36, 62, 74, 279–80
Reeve, Clara 230–32
Reformation *see* Protestant Reformation
Repton, Humphrey 282
restoration 66, 67, 234, 285
Restoration (1660) 46
Rhuddlan Castle, Denbighshire 165–6, *165*
Ribbans, Frederick Bolingbroke 185–6
Rickman, Thomas 59, 284
Rievaulx Abbey, Yorkshire 18, 53, 291, 292–3
Roberts, T. S. *247*
Robertson, Archibald 31
Roche Abbey, Yorkshire 20–21, *20*, 23, 24, 25, 136–7, 291, 292
  Swete's journal notes on 134–5, *134*, 149
Romanticism 112, 142, 177–8, 226
Rome, ancient 45, 50, 67, 129, 258–9, 285
Rosslyn Chapel, Midlothian 141, 236–9, *238*
Rowlandson, Thomas *98*
Rufford Abbey, Nottingham 25
ruins, visiting 89–90, 109–11, 138, 172, 175, 177, 189, 191, 283, 290
  and contemplative behaviour 137–38, 160, 170
  damage caused by 176
  eating and drinking at 135–36, 175
  as literary inspiration 144, 159, 178, 275–6
  and music 139–40, 146
  poetry recitals 141, 142–3
  sketching/recording experiences 131, 132, 133–5, *133*, 137, 139–40, 173, 275
Ruskin, John 285

Sandbeck Park, Yorkshire 292
Sandby, Paul *128*, 207
Scarborough Castle, Yorkshire 33–4
Scone Palace, Perthshire 32
Scotland 29, 31, 37, 51–2

destruction of churches/ monasteries 29–30, 46, 162–3
medieval architecture 29, 30–31
and tourism 56, 137, 138, 141, 150, 159
see also Protestant Reformation; *and under individual place names*
Scott, Walter 163, 194, 195, 198
  Border Antiquities (1814) 194–5
  Ivanhoe 73
  Kenilworth (1821) 284
  Lay of the Last Minstrel (1805) 112, 176, 188, 189–93, *190*, 194–5, 198, 199, 200, 236, 238–9, 264
  Minstrelsy of the Scottish Border (1802–3) 195
  tomb of (Dryburgh Abbey) 162, 163, 164
Seller, Abednego 260
Shakespeare, William 101, 142, 144, 214, 223, 277
Shaw, Stebbing 182
Shenstone, William *92*, 93, 168, 280
  'The Ruin'd Abbey' (1743) 167–8, 169–70
  'Unconnected Thoughts on Gardening' 91–2
Shirebrook, Michael 20–21
Shobdon estate, Herefordshire 273–4, *273*
Shotover, Oxfordshire 280
Simond, Louis 175
singing *see* music
Skinner, John 147, 152
Slezer, John 51, 239
Smith, John 77
Society for the Protection of Ancient Buildings (SPAB) 285
Society of Antiquaries of London 44, 64, 65, 278–9, 281
soft capping 290, 293
Southey, Robert 140, 177
souvenirs 176; *see also* tourism
Speed, John 80
St Albans church, Hertfordshire 22
St Andrews Cathedral 30, *30*, 31, 253
St Clair, Sir William 236, 237–8
St Leger, Anthony 27
St Mary's Abbey, York 24

St Mary's church, Chester 25
St Oran's burial ground, Iona *158*, 159
St Radegund nunnery, Cambridge 15
Stephens, Edward 90
Stonehenge, Wiltshire 76–8
Stow, John 80
Stowe, Buckinghamshire 53, 280
Stowe, Harriet Beecher 162, 163, 188, 197–8, 200
Strata Florida Abbey, Ceredigion 18
'Strawberry Committee' 282
Strawberry Hill, Twickenham 119, 273, 282
Studley Royal Park, Yorkshire 291
Stukeley, William 49, 50, 62, 63, 73, 280
  Itinerarium curiosum (1776) 50, *50*, 51, 74
  Stonehenge (1740) 76, *77*
sublime, the 54, 84, 87–8, 94
supernatural 85, 144, 149, 212, 214, 216, 219, 235; *see also* ghosts
Suppression bill (Ireland, 1536) 26–7
Sweetheart Abbey, Dumfries and Galloway 31, *31*
Swete, John 64, 139, 141, 147
  Yorkshire tour (1790) 134–5, *134*, 137–8, *137*, 139, 149
Swift, Jonathan 255
Switzer, Stephen 88–9, 90, 109

Tattershall Castle, Lincolnshire 287
Taylor, John 40
Taylor, Walter 172, 174
Tennyson, Alfred 187–8, 205
Tewkesbury church, Gloucestershire 22
Thelwall, John 179, 266
Throckmorton, Elizabeth 24
Tintagel Castle, Cornwall 204, *204*, 205
Tintern Abbey, Monmouthshire 4, 54, 63, *95*, 99, 112, 149, 153, *178*, 179, 180, *182*, 279
  ghost stories in environs of 211
  guidebooks on 152–53, 181–82
  industry at 180–82, *181*
  inhabitants of 148, 181–82

303

and tourism 133-34, 135-36, 137-8, 139-40, 147, 150, 179
writing about 179-80, 183-5; *see also under individual authors*
Titchfield Abbey, Hampshire 22
Tonna, Charlotte Elizabeth 257
Topographer 57
topographical literature 53, 84, 170, 266; *see also under individual authors' names*
tourism 43, 53, 56, 61, 62, 68, 143, 147-50, 234, 242, 281
and commercialisation 154, 155, 176
in search of the picturesque 98-9, *98*, 131-2, 170, 172, 178-9, 193-4, 282
and service industry 131, 132, 148, 150, 154
see also ruins, visiting; tourist industry
tourist industry 131-2, 150-51, 154, 164, 200, 283, 291; *see also* guidebooks; heritage industry; souvenirs
Towneley family 24-25
travel 53, 68, 172, 234, 281, 283; *see also* tourism
travel writing 151, 189, 193; *see also* guidebooks
Tretower Castle, Powys 148, *148*
Trinity College, Edinburgh, church of 29
Turner, J. M. W. 62, 99, 179, 233, 270-71
Caernarvon Castle 40, 41
Harlech Castle 207
Melrose Abbey 198-9, *199*

UNESCO World Heritage sites 291, 294

Valle Crucis Abbey, Denbighshire 23, 136, 147-8, 149, 155

Valor Ecclesiasticus 16
Van Lerberghe, Peter *4*, 133-4
Vanburgh, Sir John 278
Varley, John 207
vegetation 64, 96-97, 107, 173, 289, 294
Vertue, George 281
Volney, Constantin-François 250, 265-6

Wales
castles 40-41, 138-9, 149, 165-6, 207-208, 268, 270
literature of 41
ruins in 37, 97, 145-6
and tourism 136, 140, 145-6
see also under individual place names
Walmsley, Thomas 240
Walpole, Horace 53, 54, 119, 171, 261-2, 273, 280-81, 282
Anecdote of Painting (1762) 93, 282
Castle of Otranto (1764) 186
'Detached Thoughts' 93
Walsingham Priory Church, Norfolk *12*, 13
Waltham, monastic church at, Essex 48
Warner, Richard 64, 139, 147
Netley Abbey (1795) 174
Tour through the Northern Counties of England... (1802) 142
Walk through Wales (1798) 179, 184
Warton, Thomas 61, 103
'Grave of King Arthur' (1777) 81-82
Observations on the Fairy Queen of Spenser (1762) 59
Waterford, Franciscan friary 27-28
Webster, John 101, 243, 277
West, Thomas 214
Westminster, Palace of, London (1834) 245-6, *245*
Whalley Abbey, Lancashire 24-5

Whately, Thomas 89-90, 179
White, James 233
Whiting, Richard 79-80
Wigmore Castle, Herefordshire 290
Williams, William Frederick 128
Williamson, John 276
Willis, Browne 47, 52, 73
Wimpole, Cambridgeshire 90
Gothic folly 125, *125*, 126-7
Winchelsea Castle, Sussex 111
Wishart, George, execution of 253-4
Woburn (abbey), Bedfordshire 17
Wollstonecraft, Mary 244
Wood, John 77
Wood, Robert 259, 260, *260*, 261
Woods, James 259
Wordsworth, Dorothy 179, 215-16
Wordsworth, William 112, 215-16
'At Furness Abbey' (1844) 215
Guilt and Sorrow (1842) 78
Lyrical Ballads (with Coleridge, 1798) 177, 215
'The Ruined Cottage' (1797) 266-7
'Tintern Abbey' (1798) 112, 177-80, 182-3
Worsborough Hall, Yorkshire 24
Wricklemarsh House, Kent 266
Wright, Thomas 67
Wyatt, James 285
Wye Valley 95-7, *95*, 150, 151

York, medieval walls of 63-4

Ziegenhirt, Sophia 187